D1260983

BRIDGE, CHURCH AND PALACE IN OLD LONDON

by the same author

THE TOWER

The Great Fire of London, 1666. The City from the east at about 8 p.m., Tuesday, 4th September.

Bridge, Church and Palace

in Old London

JOHN E. N. HEARSEY

John Murray
FIFTY ALBEMARLE STREET LONDON

Printed in Great Britain
by William Clowes and Sons Limited
London and Beccles

TO
MISS CICELY STANHOPE
WITH AFFECTION

Contents

Illustrations

Acknowledgements

I should like to express my thanks to the staff of the Hove Public Library, especially to J. Dove, Esq., Librarian and Curator, and Miss L. Green, Reference Room, for assistance in obtaining books, both from their own and other libraries.

To the following Trustees and Directors I should like to offer my thanks for permission to use reproductions of paintings and prints as illustrations: the Dean and Chapter of Westminster; the British Museum; the Society of Antiquaries; the London Museum; the Ashmolean Museum at Oxford; the Westminster Public Library; the Ministry of Works, and also to Geoffrey Harmsworth, Esq.

Lastly, my thanks to all those who have helped bring the book itself into being.

J. E. N. H.

Introduction

Only in the mind's eye is it possible to look over the Thames to Old London Bridge with its scores of precariously balanced houses, stand in the magnificently furnished galleries of Old Whitehall Palace or gaze up at the smoke-begrimed walls of Old St Paul's Cathedral. Fire and outlived usefulness have between them reduced the three to the printed page.

> And like the baseless fabric of this vision
> The cloud capp'd towers, the gorgeous palaces,
> The solemn temples, the great globe itself,
> Yea, all which it inherit, shall dissolve,
> and like this insubstantial pageant faded,
> Leave not a rack behind.

But in this context the last line is not strictly true: a handful of greatness still remains, to underline what is irrevocably lost. Alcoves, iron railings and two sculptured coats of arms from Old London Bridge; the Banqueting House at Whitehall—magnificent, but only a fragment of the vast palace, and at Old St Paul's a few fragments of carved stonework, fire-ruined effigies and in the churchyard of the present cathedral the foundations of the Medieval Chapter House.

With the exception of the Banqueting House, which is the United Services Museum, these few relics are insufficient to bring the past to life. A Westminster Abbey or a Hampton Court are needed before history becomes almost tangible; and when the buildings themselves have vanished the sense of reality, of the immediacy of their story, is to a large extent also lost. And yet the story of Old St Paul's is only a little less rich than that of the Abbey. If Westminster was the royal church, Old St Paul's was the commoner's. Old Whitehall Palace had an infinitely more varied and interesting history than its near neighbour across the park, the Palace of St James. As for Old

London Bridge—if not unique, its place among the histories of the world's bridges is unrivalled.

Throughout nearly the whole of its existence Old London Bridge resembled a microcosm of the City itself. Shops, square, taverns, wardens to guide its affairs, and even its own stocks for miscreants. Here, some thirty feet above the river, a whole cross-section of life was played out. The 'prentice only too ready for a fight, the tradesman and his household living above the family business, merchants who made the bridge their private address, pedestrians threading their way among the congestion of carts and horsemen in the incredibly narrow street, and from time to time the unfortunate individual who fell to his death in the mill-race surging through the narrow pile-protected arches below. Birth, marriage, death: all have their part in the story of the bridge, perhaps the most robustly alive of all London's vanished buildings.

If Old London Bridge reflected the life of the City, Old St Paul's can be taken to represent the place of the Church in that teeming City. In its nave the barons met under the leadership of Simon de Montfort, bent on regaining the rights wrung from a reluctant monarchy at Runnymede; right through the Middle Ages came the files of pilgrims to the tomb of St Erkenwald. So holy was the area that even the dust collecting about his glittering bejewelled shrine was considered to have curative properties. State occasions of rejoicing and thanksgiving: the vast interior hung with tapestries, to make a rich setting for the magnificently dressed congregation come to attend the marriage of Katharine of Aragon and Prince Arthur: Elizabeth I come to give thanks for the defeat of the Armada—high overhead the long pennants taken from the Spanish galleons hung out on the central tower. Or there was the horse Marocco who climbed to the very top of that tower, to look out over a city crowded with parish churches rising out of a choppy sea of steep-roofed houses; their towers and spires jostling the skyline with the inconsequential variety that only the Middle Ages could produce.

Only in the mind's eye can Old Whitehall Palace be visited: once it rivalled Hampton Court, and both were the work of

Cardinal Wolsey. Like a peacock in its pride he displayed himself at York Place, as he knew it. Then, after it became a royal palace, it saw the secret marriage of Henry VIII to Anne Boleyn, and fourteen years later was the scene of his death. There, at a window of the Holbein Gateway, Mary Tudor literally sat-out the turmoil and panic of Wyatt's Rebellion when an attempt was made to storm the palace. In more peaceful times Elizabeth I entertained foreign ambassadors within its walls; and in the Great Hall and the wooden-built Banqueting House James I poured out thousands on the most lavish masques ever seen in this country. There, as his life moved towards its unprecedented climax, Charles I achieved a nobility not even his enemies could deny. Then the strangest page of all: Cromwell, the destroyer of kings, emulating royalty and finding it all very much to his liking. The Restoration, and Charles II surrounded by his dogs and his mistresses—and from the back stairs his brother James II was to flee during England's bloodless revolution. To succeed him came his daughter Mary, whose first action after her arrival from Holland was to turn down the beds and look in the cupboards. Such events, whether important or trivial, all have their part in the history of the Old Palace of Whitehall—as much as the building of the Great Hall or the painting of the Banqueting House ceiling by Rubens.

Today the bridge, the cathedral and the palace have no reality other than their history, and to rediscover a little of that vanished greatness is the aim of this book, a triptych in which something of the different backgrounds of those connected with the three great buildings—all long since destroyed—can also perhaps be glimpsed. I hope so.

J.E.N.H.

Old London Bridge

(The City)

1

' . . . some others got over a little way upstream, after which they assailed the barbarians from several sides at once.' And in that brief reference to a minor military operation during the conquest of Britain, recorded by the Roman historian Dio Cassius, London Bridge enters the pages of history. But it is only a glimpse: even when Londinium was a flourishing city no one found it necessary to refer to the bridge spanning the Thames. The only evidence of its existence between the first and fifth centuries A.D. is internal: the remains of the iron-tipped wooden piles driven into the river bed, and coins, covering the whole period of the Roman occupation, dredged up during the last century and a quarter along the site of this first bridge.

Then with the departure of the Romans comes the long night of the Dark Ages. Only when the tenth century has nearly run its course does the bridge suddenly and dramatically re-emerge into the light of day. There, during the time Athelwold was Bishop of Winchester (d. 984), a woman was put to death by drowning for witchcraft. Her son, equally guilty, took to his heels and though declared an outlaw escaped with his life. The cause of all the trouble was a wax effigy of the bishop which they had jabbed through with pins of iron. 'They took then that woman', recorded the *Codex Diplomaticus*, 'and drowned her at London Bridge, and her son escaped and was outlawed and the land was forfeited to the King. . . .'

Next comes an oblique reference to the bridge in a law passed in 979 during the reign of the unready Ethelred, one of the Saxon kings buried in Old St Paul's (p. 80). For fishing boats coming to the bridge, close to Billingsgate, which even then was associated with fish, the toll was 1d., while ½d. was levied on smaller vessels.

Then, as attacks on London by Danish pirates became more frequent, the bridge really finds its place in history, and remains there. Towards the close of Ethelred's incompetent reign the Danes held both the City and Southwark: then called Suthverki. But in 1014, with the help of Olaf of Norway, Ethelred made an all-out attempt to become king in his own capital. Up the Thames from Greenwich sailed the combined fleets of the two kings, bent on destroying the wooden bridge and by so doing dividing the Danish forces.

Samuel Laing's translation of the *Olaf Sagas* includes a remarkably detailed description of what happened that day over nine centuries ago. 'Between the Castle and Suthverki there was a bridge, so broad that two waggons could pass each other upon it. On the bridge were raised barricades, both towers and wooden parapets in the direction of the river, which were nearly breast high; and under the bridge were piles driven into the bottom of the river.'

The advantage lay with the Danes, high up on the bridge, who could put down a murderous barrage of spears into the open ships below. Eventually Olaf—the brains of the expedition—evolved a plan. His men constructed great rafts protected with thatched roofs taken bodily from nearby cottages, and filled with soldiers these little floating forts were rowed towards the bridge.

'But King Olaf, and the Northmen's fleet with him, rowed quite under the bridge, laid their cables around the piles that supported it, and then rowed off with all the ships as hard as they could go down the stream. The piles were thus shaken in the bottom, and were loosened under the bridge. Now as the armed troops stood thick upon the bridge, and there were likewise many heaps of stones and other weapons upon it being loosened and broken, the bridge gave way; and a great part of the men upon it fell into the river, and all the others fled, some into the Castle, some into Southwark. Thereafter Southwark was stormed and taken. Now when the people in the Castle saw that the River Thames was mastered and that they could not hinder the passage of ships up into the country, they became afraid, surrendered the tower and took Ethelred to be their king.'

For the first time in its recorded history London Bridge was broken down, but the Danes were no longer masters in the City. Ottar Svarte, the Norse poet, and chronicler, recorded the event:

'London Bridge is broken down,
Gold is won and bright renown.
Shields resounding
War Horns Sounding,
Hildur shouting in the din!
Arrows singing,
Mailcoats ringing—
Odin makes our Olaf win!'

Obviously a good stiff fight was the breath of life to Ottar Svarte. The poem continues:

'King Ethelred has found a friend:
Brave Olaf will his throne defend—
In bloody fight—
Maintain his right
Win back his land
With blood red hand,
And Edmund's son upon his throne replace—
Edmund, the star of every royal race!'

But all was in vain. Two years later Ethelred was dead, and now it was Canute attacking London Bridge. The *Anglo-Saxon Chronicle* tells that to get his ship past, Canute dug a canal through the marshy ground at the Southwark end, and so bypassed the obstacle.

At the time of his invasion Canute was very much a pagan, but in 1023, reverent and penitent, he himself lifted the coffin of St Alphege—martyred at Greenwich in 1012 by the Danes during a drunken feast—and placed it on a boat close to London Bridge. Temporary burial had been given to the old archbishop in Old St Paul's, but now he was going to Canterbury. Evidently the authorities expected trouble. Instead of using the bridge, the Thames was crossed by boat, while before that, as the procession made its way through the City, the inhabitants were drawn towards the land gates where Canute's followers were engineering disturbances. As the cortège set out along the road to Canterbury, Canute and the then Archbishop of Canterbury waited at the end of the bridge, itself heavily guarded, until they were well on their way.

14th October 1066 saw Harold, the last Saxon king, killed in battle, and a few days later William the Conqueror looked across the Thames, far broader then than now, to the walled city of London. He made no attempt to force the bridge, but after burning Southwark turned his hard face towards the west and made for Berkhampstead. It was not until Christmas Day that he was crowned in his newly subjugated capital. (William went through Kent, Surrey, Hants, Berks, Beds, etc., before entering London.)

Before long London's skyline underwent a symbolic change at the hands of its new ruler. To the east of the bridge there arose the ninety-foot-high keep of the White Tower (1078), while to the west the huge Old St Paul's reared up to the sky—Phoenix-like, renewed by its second fire—from the ashes of the old Saxon cathedral destroyed along with so much of the City itself in the conflagration of 1087.

Such was the strength of a south-easterly gale in November 1091, that not only was the bridge swept away, but the unfinished White Tower 'sore shaken by tempest', St Mary le Bow unroofed and over six hundred houses demolished. But if the Thames overflowed its banks during that particular storm, on 10th October 1114 for twenty-four hours the tide never came in. Wrote John Stow in his *Survey of London* ' . . . between the Tower of London and the Bridge, and under the Bridge, not only with horse, but also a great number of men, women and children did wade over on foot.' Such a phenomenon must have caused many to fall to their prayers, fearing the worst in the way of divine wrath—but it was not until the war between Stephen and his domineering cousin Matilda that England's afflictions really began.

Not only was the wooden bridge a constant source of worry, but also of expense to the Londoners. In 1131 a certain Geoffrey was paid £25 for rebuilding two arches, but five years later the whole structure went up in flames, and in 1136 whatever was still standing was replaced with a bridge of elm.

2

All through the very early years, with the exception of Olaf and Ethelred's attack, the illuminating description that brings the scene to instant life is missing. But Fitzstephen (died 1190) at least throws a shaft of light on London life at its most relaxed. 'In Easter holidays they fight battles on the water, a shield is hung upon a pole, fixed in the midst of the stream, a boat is prepared without oars, to be carried by violence of the water, and in the forepart thereof standeth a young man, ready to give charge upon the shield with his lance; if so he breaketh his lance, he runneth strongly against the shield, down he falleth into the water, for the boat is violently forced with the tide; but on each side of the shield ride two boats, furnished with young men, which recover him that falleth as soon as they may. Upon the bridge, wharfs, and houses, by the river's side, stand great numbers to see and laugh thereat.'

This bridge of elm was the work of Peter of Colechurch: later to be responsible for its celebrated stone successor. Peter was chaplain of St Mary Colechurch—hence his name—a church and parish that vanished after the fire of 1666. According to Stow, writing at the end of Elizabeth's reign, St Mary contained nothing of interest: but by a singular coincidence two archbishops, both of whom became saints after their murder—though the second was not recognized by the Church—were christened there. The first was Thomas à Becket, martyred in his cathedral in 1170, while the second was Edmund Scrope, Archbishop of York, beheaded for suspected treason at the beginning of Henry IV's reign.

'Thus much for the old timber bridge, maintained partly by the proper lands thereof, partly by the liberality of divers persons, and partly by taxations in divers shires, have I proved for the space of two hundred and fifteen years before the bridge of stone was built.' So, in the stately language of his day, Stow closes his account of the bridge's early history.

Now at last, in 1176, a bridge worthy of London's other stone buildings was begun by Peter of Colechurch, who also held the office of Bridge Master. England, it seems, had no equivalent of the Frères Pontifs, a religious guild which held the virtual monopoly of bridge-building in France and Italy.

That any bridge built without their assistance had a curse upon it was a piece of superstition they most certainly did not discourage. But in England, if there was a religious guild of bridge-builders, it lacked the power of its European counterpart.

The undertaking to span the Thames with a bridge of stone was without doubt the biggest feat of engineering in England since Hadrian laid his wall across Northumbria, and Peter was not to live to see its completion. The site he chose was a few yards west of the existing wooden structure, which would therefore be able to remain undisturbed until the last stone of its successor was safely in position.

Nine hundred and ten feet ten inches in length, the new London Bridge was amongst the longest in medieval Europe, rivalling the Pont d'Avignon, which exists today as only a magnificent fragment. In common with most bridges of its day, London Bridge was narrow; only twenty feet wide. So many illustrations tend to exaggerate its height and width that it is difficult to realize that with the addition of the houses on either side, the actual roadway was only twelve feet wide. So the most important artery connecting the North, the Midlands, and London itself with the South-east was no wider than a country lane—and perpetually congested. Two carts could only just pass, and right down to the mid-eighteenth century there are accounts of unwary pedestrians being caught between their wheels. Another thing, the bridge was not absolutely level: it rose to a point near the centre where the roadway was thirty-one feet eight inches above low water, but was considerably lower at either end.

The piers supporting the nineteen stone arches and one wooden drawbridge were irregularly spaced. This may have been due to the fact that a few feet either way the river bed was more satisfactory for the foundations, or quite simply—the medieval mind was never overburdened with questions of symmetry. At least from late Tudor times onwards the twenty openings had their individual names. From the north, the City end, they were:

(1) London Shore (or First Wheel Lock)
(2) Second Wheel Lock
(3) Third or Borough Wheel Lock
(4) Fourth or Index Wheel Lock
(5) Shore Lock or Fifth Wheel Lock
(6) King's Lock
(7) Little or Queen's Lock
(8) St Mary's Lock
(9) Chapel Lock
(10) Long Entry or Narrow Passage Lock
(11) Gut Lock
(12) Pedlar's Lock
(13) Nonsuch Lock
(14) Draw Lock
(15) Roger Lock
(16) Fifth Lock
(17) Fourth Lock
(18) Rock Lock
(19) Second Lock
(20) Shore Lock (Southwark Bank)

The wheels referred to were fifteenth- and sixteenth-century mill wheels: at the north end for pumping up water and at the south for grinding corn. The width of the arches varied as much as 19 feet, from the 34-foot span of Rock Lock to the 15 feet 9 inches of Long Entry. Within each arch itself the width was inclined to vary: In the case of Long Entry, by as much as 6 feet 3 inches. On the east side it measured 15 feet 9 inches, but on the west the opening was 21 feet 1 inch wide. All these measurements are taken from the table drawn up in 1799 by the architect George Dance the Younger.

With a width of some thirty-four feet, St Mary's Lock—reasonably near the middle—may well have been the one most used by watermen, though at the outset of its career London Bridge was infinitely easier to navigate than in later centuries, owing to the continual additions made to the piles, called starlings, which protected the piers.

Only in a metaphorical sense was London Bridge built upon

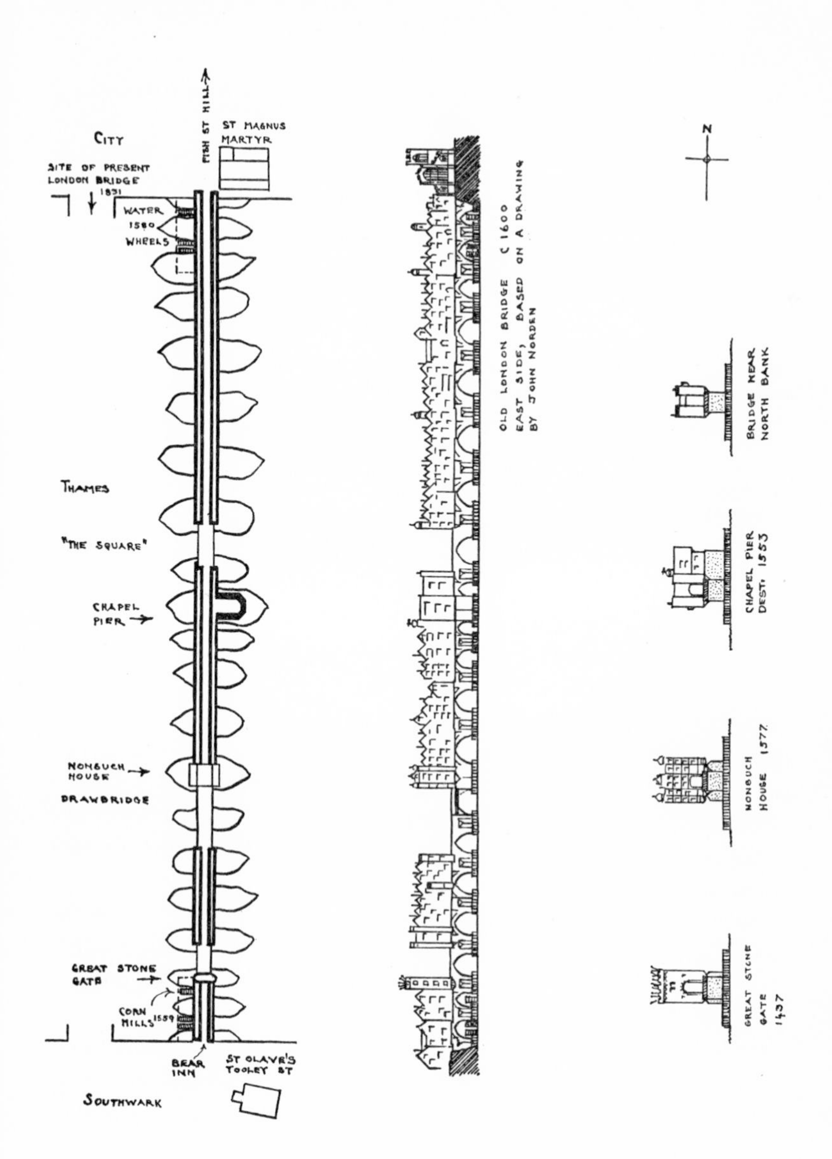
CITY
SITE OF PRESENT LONDON BRIDGE 1831
FISH ST HILL
ST MAGNUS MARTYR
WATER 1580 WHEELS
THAMES
"THE SQUARE"
CHAPEL PIER
NONSUCH HOUSE
DRAWBRIDGE
GREAT STONE GATE
CORN MILLS 1589
BEAR INN
ST OLAVE'S TOOLEY ST
SOUTHWARK
N
OLD LONDON BRIDGE C 1600
EAST SIDE, BASED ON A DRAWING
BY JOHN NORDEN
BRIDGE NEAR NORTH BANK
CHAPEL PIER DEST. 1553
NONSUCH HOUSE 1577
GREAT STONE GATE 1437

woolpacks: Henry II imposed a tax on wool to help defray the cost. The foundations were more prosaic, though from the start they gave trouble. Around where the pier would stand, three rings of piles, six or seven feet in length, were driven in; the area enclosed filled with rubble which was covered over with massive oak planking twenty-one inches thick. (All this came to light during the bridge's demolition in 1831–2.) On these platforms of rubble and oak the piers were raised, and since the Thames is tidal, there is little cause for surprise that they were frequently undermined by the current. With the addition of more and ever more piles the starling grew to such a size that the flow of the river was seriously impeded; stopping boats for two hours at every flood, while the difference in the height of the water on either side could be as much as five feet. Indeed, so big had these starlings grown by the end of the Middle Ages that Old London Bridge had the appearance of standing on snow-shoes.

The focal point of the bridge, both structurally and to the eye, was the ninth pier from the northern end. Far bigger than the rest, it served as the substructure for a two-storeyed chapel which projected well beyond the line of the bridge on the east side. The upper part opened off the roadway, while the lower was reached by a newel staircase at its south-west corner.

As in the Tower of London, much of the material used for the bridge was Kentish Ragstone, easily transported from the Medway up the Thames, while stone from the Merstham quarries in Surrey was also used.

In 1205 the old architect-priest Peter of Colechurch died, four years before the completion of his masterpiece. As a stone structure it was not quite continuous: the seventh arch from the southern end was omitted. In its place was an opening twenty-eight feet seven inches wide, spanned by a wooden drawbridge which had its winding mechanism in a tower (probably of wood) on the north side of the gap. Astride the Southwark entrance stood another gate, this time of stone, making a double defence to this particular entry into London. The whole bridge in fact formed a part of the City itself.

'Bridge Ward Within', wrote Stow, 'so called of London

Bridge, which bridge is the principal part of that ward, and beginneth at the stuples [i.e. staples: posts and chains marking the boundary] on the south end by Southwark, runneth along the bridge, and north up Bridge Street, commonly called of the Fish Market, New Fish Street, from Fish Street hill, up Grass Street, to the north corner of Grass Church.'

For at least twenty-six years London Bridge had been part of Peter of Colechurch's life, and when he died they buried him in the undercroft of the little chapel, dedicated to St Thomas à Becket, above the river. And there he remained to the very end, at one with the bridge he had created.

In 1201 there had been some talk of finding a successor—evidently old age was already taking its toll of Peter, and the French bridge-builder Isambard de Saintes was mentioned as a likely candidate. Nothing came of the idea. King John, then at the outset of his infamous reign, took a personal interest in London Bridge, and suggested the rents and profits from houses to be built along its length should go towards its upkeep. This is the first mention of the houses: the most celebrated and distinctive feature of Old London Bridge.

With some truth it could be said the bridge was plagued, if not cursed, by fire and by water. Below, the insinuating current was always at work trying to undermine the piers, while above fire was frequently breaking out among the timber houses. Only three or four years after its completion came the first disaster. The chronicles are vague whether it was 1212 or 1213. But they do agree on 11th July, when a fire broke out in Southwark. Wrote Stow ' . . . an exceeding great multitude of people passing the bridge, either to extinguish and quench it, or else to gaze at and behold it, suddenly the north part, by blowing of the south wind, was also set on fire, and the people which were even now passing the bridge, perceiving the same, would have returned, but were stopped by the fire; and it came to pass, that as they stayed or protracted time, the other end of the bridge, namely, the south end, was fired, so that the people thronging themselves between two fires, did nothing else but expect present death; then came there to aid them many ships and vessels, into which the multitude so inadvisedly rushed, that the ships being drowned, they all perished. It was said, that through fire and shipwreck there were destroyed about three thousand persons, whose bodies were found in part, or half burnt, besides those that were wholly burnt to ashes, and could not be found.'

News of a disaster never loses in the retelling: perhaps three hundred casualties would be nearer the mark, but what is certain is that Peter of Colechurch's upper chapel was ruined, and had to be rebuilt. The damage could hardly have been made good before Louis, the French dauphin, came riding by. The distracted English had invited him over to take the place of the deposed, but far from defeated John, and in June 1216 he entered the City in some style, going first to Old St Paul's to hear Mass (p. 90). But with the death of John and the collapse of hostilities the barons could count themselves lucky when he quietly returned home of his own accord.

The new king, Henry III, was only a child, and, at least as far as London Bridge was concerned, the next four decades slip by without incident. High up over the river the shopkeepers and housewives go about their daily business, while carts lumber past the chapel door: inside are two priests and four clerks repeating their offices, while from time to time travellers turn aside into its quiet interior to pray for the success of their journey and their safekeeping from all the hazards of the road, or else to give thanks for its safe and prosperous conclusion. It is very much the wayfarers' and sailors' chapel, and surely if Thomas à Becket (to whom it was dedicated) had not been the pre-eminent saint in England, St Nicholas or St Christopher might have received the dedication.

Excitement there was, of a very mild kind, in 1240, when 'a monster of prodigious size', which turned out to be a whale, swam under the bridge and as far upstream as Mortlake. There men and boys, in a swarm of small boats, hounded it to death. Just how different was the state of the Thames from its present condition can be gathered from the fact that salmon were swimming in it during the thirteenth century. If the whale came to a sad end from shooting the bridge, so did swans going in the opposite direction. Any appearing opposite the Tower automatically became the property of the Constable of the fortress, and in due course appeared on his table.

Like so many monarchs and governments both before and after his day, Henry III had difficulty in paying for his wars. Even the bridge did not escape his net: on 20th May 1249 the Lord Mayor of London opened a roll bearing the royal seal and started to read: 'We command that without delay, you. . . .' The rest can be imagined. The revenues that by rights should have gone towards the upkeep of the bridge were henceforth to be diverted into the royal coffers. Among those who suffered genuine hardship as a result were the Brethren of the Bridge, the body of men responsible for its maintenance. With no income they could do nothing; nor could their salaries be paid, and they were reduced to penury. So much so that on his next visit to England from France, Henry III felt it was necessary to do something: he shifted the responsibility for their welfare on to the Church. To the archbishops he wrote ' . . . when the aforesaid Brethren, or their Messengers, shall come to you, for your alms for their support, or for that of the aforesaid Bridge, ye shall courteously receive them, and cause them to be so received in all your churches, Towns and Courts: and that ye will bestow upon them of your goods, according to your charity and the sight of our precept, the alms which they desire. So that in reward thereof ye may be worthy of the blessings of mercy, and our special thanks shall be due unto you.' That done, Henry returned to making a mockery of Magna Carta, and to his wars with France. But as with his father, King John, there was to be a day of reckoning. For Henry it came with the Battle of Lewes in 1264 when he was captured by Simon de Montfort. After that the earl marched north towards London, but on reaching Southwark he found the Lord Mayor had raised the drawbridge, closed the gates and thrown the keys into the river. Now it looked as though, for the first time, London Bridge would have its defences put to the test. But no storming took place.

If the Lord Mayor and aldermen supported the King, almost to a man the Londoners were on the side of de Montfort and the barons. They swept on to the bridge from the City end, burst open the gates and lowered the drawbridge. Soon London was in the hands of de Montfort, and before long a new lord mayor had been 'elected'.

But all that was changed by the earl's death, stabbed in the back at the Battle of Evesham in 1265. Once again Henry III was a king and not a prisoner, with Cardinal Otho mediating between him and the barons. While the Earl of Gloucester, the new leader of the malcontents, conferred with the Cardinal, the barons remained in Southwark, and all went well until some of their followers started looting. Up went the drawbridge as the City prepared for the worst, but it was too late. Enough of Gloucester's men were already in London to be able to call the tune. Soon they controlled not only the bridge, but also the land gates. Eventually the quarrel was patched up. Henry graciously forgave the City, but not before the unlawfully elected Lord Mayor had been imprisoned in Windsor Castle, where he quietly and mysteriously disappeared from sight.

In 1264 the custody of London Bridge was transferred to the Master and Brethren of St Katharine's Hospital, who were instructed to comply with any reasonable requests from their still hamstrung namesakes, the Master and Brethren of the Bridge. Also, in that year the City began the custom of electing two wardens to watch over its affairs and interests.

All this time the revenues were still going into the royal purse, but not to finance the war in France, and the man in the street—or rather, on the bridge—knew exactly where they were going: to help support the Queen's sponging relatives. The Queen's grasping, avaricious habits had made her detested, and on 13th July 1263 the Londoners found a practical way to show their feelings. That day Queen Eleanor decided to go by barge to Windsor from the Palace in the Tower. On the bridge the mob was waiting, noisy and well armed with missiles. The royal barge approached and prepared to shoot the bridge. Then the resentful, revenue-cheated bridge-dwellers and others let fly with eggs, stones, mud, filth, and abuse. The barge veered off, and then made back to Tower Wharf. The first round had gone to the Londoners.

The King bided his time, and then in 1269 revenged himself

in the neatest possible way. For six years Eleanor was to have the revenues for her personal use—no pretence about using them for the war now—and that as everyone knew meant squandering the money on her relatives.

Within a year of becoming nominal guardian of the bridge Queen Eleanor received a strong warning about its condition, and rather than risk being responsible for its upkeep, she resigned. That lasted for a fortnight. Then, deciding the risk was worth while, she reasserted her right to the revenues. Even her husband's death in 1272 did not put an end to the abuse, and it remained her property until 1281. Had it not then reverted to its rightful owner, the City of London, without doubt part or the whole of the structure would have collapsed through lack of funds to carry out urgent repairs.

But more than rent-money from the houses was needed to put the bridge into order again after the years of neglect, and in 1283 Edward I took sufficient time from hammering the Scots, Welsh, and French to inform the Lord Mayor he was to supervise the levying of tolls to make good damage done 'about the year 1282, through a great frost and deep snow, [when] five arches of London Bridge were born down and carried away.' Any man crossing in either direction was now obliged to pay ¼d., pack horses ½d., and horsemen 1d. Additional funds were raised from the rents charged for fish and meat stalls in the Stocks Market in the heart of the City. So named from the stocks for the punishment of the turbulent and dishonest that stood there, the market vanished in 1739 with the building of the Mansion House.

At about this time the Bridge House begins to emerge from obscurity. In describing London Bridge in the thirteenth century Stow wrote ' . . . and many charitable men gave lands, tenements, or sums of money, towards maintainance thereof, all which was sometime noted and in a table fair written for posterity remaining in the Chapel, until the same Chapel was turned into a dwelling house at the dissolution, and then removed to the Bridge House.' Whether the early House stood upon the bridge itself, possibly next to the chapel, is not known, but in later years it was situated some hundred and fifty yards to the east of Old London Bridge on the Southwark bank.

2

And now, year by year, the bridge comes alive; slowly emerging from brief references in the Patent Rolls and in the pages of the chronicles. Now it is a reality, with a very real part to play in the lives of those whose existence was spent along its length, or made use of by others going about their daily business.

Sooner or later, as might be expected, the question of the tolls flared into a quarrel. On 7th March 1299 John le Leche, a miller, was stopped at the south end by John le Wayer, the customs officer, and informed that the corn merchant for whom he worked had not paid the duty owing on the last four loads of wheat. Le Leche declared only ½d. was outstanding, lost his temper and pulled the tax gatherer's hat down over his face. Le Wayer hit out blindly at the miller. Then both drew their knives. No doubt the crowd sided with the miller, hoping the tax gatherer would be on the receiving end of some shrewd blows, but at the sight of steel the time had come to part them. Justice was rough and ready, and like as not inaccurate. The crowd did not want to find themselves involved in a brawl concerning one of the King's men, so the fight came to an inconclusive end. But by now the horse was nowhere to be found. Wisely, it had ambled off to its stable, while everyone was too preoccupied to notice.

All the time people were being drowned: falling off the bridge, boats being overturned in the mill-race below, killed in the collapse or burning of houses, or run down in the narrow, congested street. One Gilbert Clope was unwise enough to go to sleep leaning against the parapet in one of the openings, overbalanced, fell into the Thames and was drowned before a boat could bring him to Tower Wharf. That was in May 1278. In July 1301 a schoolboy, Richard le Mazon, stopped to play on the bridge whilst on his way back to school after his midday meal. A beam tempted him. Up, out and over the river he climbed, and hung there by his hands. Only for a moment; then back to safety and on his way to school. But his arms were not strong enough to support his weight, and unnoticed by the passing crowds Richard lost his grip, fell and was drowned. He was eight years old.

Death came to the bridge in a most stark form in 1305, and stayed for three hundred and fifty years. That year, at the beginning of a new century, saw the head of William Wallace, the Scots patriot, placed on a pole set above the drawbridge gate: to be joined within twelve months by that of Sir Simon Fraser. Both were tried and executed for treason. Presumably their treachery to the English lay in not agreeing to Edward I's claim to the Scottish throne. In particular Wallace's trial was an injustice worthy of Tudor times. But to the Londoners, whose ears were full of the atrocities committed by the Scots in England—though the authorities were rather more reticent about English atrocities committed in Scotland—he was a rival in wickedness to Herod and Nero. So the City dwellers gladly paid their ¼d. toll, and took their wives and children across the bridge to look at Wallace's head, high above the southern end.

From 1315 onwards the Londoners were able to enjoy such simple medieval pleasures free of charge. In that year the tolls were abolished.

Strangely enough for a reign so distraught as was Edward II's (1307–27), the bridge had no part of any consequence to play in his quarrels with either the nobles or his wife, Isabella of France. But with the accession of his son, Edward III, there began the Hundred Years War. Who could say? London itself might be attacked by French ships, so the City defences were put in order. Temporary breast-work was erected along the quays, while great wooden catapults for firing iron bolts stood ready on the bridge itself. That was not all: piles were driven into the river bed, leaving a narrow channel up which only one ship at a time could approach the bridge. Those underwater obstacles must have been very similar to the type encountered on the beaches of Normandy during the invasion of 1944.

But in June 1340 Edward III set sail from Ipswich with a fleet of some three hundred vessels, bound for the Flanders coast and Sluys. Thereafter, for the Londoners, the war became something to talk about and wonder at, safe in the knowledge that an attack by French ships was a very remote possibility. Now it only touched their lives at first hand when great prisoners, such as the very King of France himself, were brought in triumph to London.

John of France became 'the noble prey' of the Black Prince at Poitiers (1356), who brought him with all honour to the palace-prison that was the Tower of London. So on 24th May 1357 London Bridge witnessed the most colourful and exciting event in its history to date. Already it was nearly one hundred and fifty years old. The Lord Mayor, the aldermen and about a thousand of the more important citizens crossed over to await the coming of the King and the Black Prince to Southwark. Meanwhile the inhabitants of the bridge itself hung out tapestries, carpets and the like from their windows overlooking the narrow street, turning it into a riot of colour. According to Froissart, that was not all: ' . . . by exposing in their shops, windows, and balconies, such an amazing quantity of bows, arrows, shields, helmets, croslets, breast and neck pieces, coats of mail, gauntlets, vambraces, or armour for the arms, swords, spears, battle axes, harness for horses, and other armour offensive and defensive, that the like had not been seen in the memory of man.'

Capgrave, the monk-chronicler of King's Lynn, recorded that although the royal party arrived at the bridge in the morning, it was afternoon before they reached their destination, so great was the crush of excited and awed Londoners who had made a very special holiday of the occasion. King John rode a richly caparisoned white horse, while at his side the Black Prince was mounted on a smaller black horse.

Galling though the restraint must have been, King John was allowed a certain amount of freedom, including visits into the City (p. 103). Other prisoners of war who in all probability clattered over the drawbridge on their way to the Tower included the Counts of Tankerville and Eu, and possibly those famous six burghers of Calais.

By the mid-fourteenth century London Bridge had quite established its identity: while forming a strong addition to the City's defences it was also a village in itself. The northern half lay within the parish of St Magnus Martyr, while the southern end was served by St Olave's (Olaf), Tooley Street, also within a few yards of the bridge. Halfway along this village street stood its own chapel, that of St Thomas à Becket. In addition to its own shops the bridge had a tavern at each end.

At the City end stood the Three Neats' (Calves') Tongues, and within the staples on the Southwark bridgefoot was the Bear Inn; built inappropriately enough by one Thomas Drinkwater. With silver-handled mugs and cloths to put over the broached casks, Drinkwater's establishment was obviously no rowdy low-class beer house.

Fights were commonplace in that less inhibited age, and a woman was the cause of a quarrel ending in death, which took place within a few yards of the chapel, in the open street, on 18th May 1339. Apparently a certain Elena Sharp had quarrelled with Roger de Ingleby, and later—on that particular evening, after the bells had just stopped tolling for Vespers as the record puts it—this woman, together with her brother William and two other men, all set on him and knifed him to death. The brother and sister fled, as did one of the other men; but the fourth of the party, Roger le Brewer by name, was arrested and sent to Newgate Gaol. Presumably he was hanged; but that was one detail the historian did not bother to record. Perhaps it was a foregone conclusion.

Eleven years later there was another fight which found its way into the records. In 1350 Thomas de Kingstone, a clerk, and one Edmund were settling an argument in the 'High Street of London Bridge', just as a prosperous-looking citizen came along. He intervened. The two men forgot their own fight and turned on the new enemy, beating and abusing him. But they had picked the wrong man for a quarrel. He was John Lovekyn, until lately Lord Mayor of London. Both brawlers pleaded not guilty at their trial, but once again the records are exasperatingly silent as to the sentences passed.

Although the Wardens of Bridge House received a considerable income from rents and bequests: as diverse as a widow's mite—in this case a wedding ring—one Johanna Bythewaye's twelve pence and occasional property in the City;

in 1356 they found it necessary to impose a toll on all carts to help pay for the damage done to the road surface by their iron-shod wheels.

The shops in the High Street on London Bridge were enough to fill the needs of a quite large town: one hundred and thirty-eight of them in fact. How they were disposed along the nine-hundred-foot length of the bridge we can see from a list drawn up by the wardens in 1358.

'Between the Staples of the Bridge and the Stone Gate on the East Side.

Ten Shops.

In the aforesaid gate is a certain house which is delivered to John Bedell for keeping the gate.

Sum of £11.9.4d

On the West Side

Ten shops and a mansion in the Stone Gate.

Sum of £8.2.4d

Between the Stone Gate and the Drawbridge on the East Side.

Seven Shops (3 with hautpas)

Sum of £6.8.0d

On the West Side.

Seven Shops (3 with hautpas)

Sum of £8.0.0d

Between the Drawbridge and the Chapel on the East Side.

Seventeen Shops (5 with hautpas)

Sum of £14.6.8.d

On the West Side

Twenty Shops (4 with hautpas)

Sum of £16.2.8d

Between the Chapel and the Staples of the Bridge towards London on the East Side.

Thirty Five Shops (9 with hautpas)

Sum of £50.0.0d

On the West Side. A new shop next the counter.

Thirty Two Shops (10 with hautpas)

Sum of £43.16.4d'

Old London Bridge and the City from the south-east in the mid-16th century, by Anthony van den Wyngaerde.

Old London Bridge, about 1635, by Hollar.

Evidently the better shops were situated between the Chapel and the City end of the bridge. There the rents were slightly higher than towards the Southwark bank. An hautpas was an additional storey built out over the street, connecting the houses on either side. Since at this time there were eighteen bridging the roadway, the perspective view of the High Street must have been tunnel-like, broken at irregular intervals by pools of light alternating with areas of near darkness. As well as providing additional rooms for the houses, these hautpas must have functioned like tie-beams, bracing together the whole somewhat ramshackle superstructure, and so checking any tendency to topple outwards into the river. In Anthony van den Wyngaerde's drawing of 1550 what looks like three huge tie-beams can be seen at the Southwark end of the bridge, just beyond the Great Stone Gate, while to the north of the Chapel the roofs appear to be continuous across the street. No doubt the number of hautpas increased with the passing of the centuries. In 1358 there were thirty-four, and by the time Wyngaerde made his detailed drawing the number may well have been doubled.

Just how constricted were the houses can be gathered from the fact that from back to front they could not have been more than twelve feet deep (those built over the pier abutments did project a little, but not so very much). Of that twelve feet, only four rested on the stonework of the bridge, the rest overhung the river, supported on massive wooden struts. Nor can the average width of each house have been much more than twelve feet. A door, a window or perhaps a large hatch through which customers were served, and a breakneck staircase to the room above.

Curiously enough no mention is made during the whole time the bridge was inhabited of a water supply to the houses. Both John Norden's engraving and an anonymous drawing in the Pepysian collection of Magdalene College, Cambridge (both *c.* 1600), show buckets being lowered into the river from upper windows, but no water appears to have been laid on. As early as 1400 a beneficent grocer paid for the piping of fresh water to Newgate and Ludgate Prisons, and in the next year 'sweet water' was piped from Tyburn Brook to Cornhill: but even

Stow, who wrote so fully of London's water supply in his *Survey*, makes no mention of the bridge. Certainly all the water needed for household purposes was waiting at the end of a rope and bucket, but every drop of pure water for drinking and cooking must have been carried from one of the pumps or conduits in Bridge Ward Within. But at that time, and for centuries to come, the water carriers were a familiar part of the London scene.

Comparatively little water was used for drinking: all classes preferring large quantities of the not-so-weak beer, which perhaps was as well. By the end of Elizabeth I's reign the Thames had become sufficiently polluted for foreign visitors to comment on the smell clinging to garments washed in the river.

In one respect at least, that of sanitation, London Bridge was far ahead of the City. While his landlocked neighbour lived almost literally over an open sewer, he had the advantage of running water. Significantly enough, there were practically no deaths on the bridge during the Great Plague of 1665. But in 1349 came that earlier and far more terrible scourge, the Black Death. Many must have sickened and died in the stuffy little rooms overlooking the Thames, but they went unrecorded, and it is only at Old St Paul's that there is a brief glimpse of the grotesque horror which followed in the wake of the Plague (p. 101).

On two further occasions the inhabitants of the bridge were to see King John II of France pass by. In 1360 when he returned on parole to France, and again in 1364 when he voluntarily returned to England after his son had escaped from the English at Calais (p. 104). But within a few months of his return he died in the Savoy Palace, and now it was his funeral procession that headed out of the City, bearing his coffin on the first part of its journey back to Paris.

These were peaceful days for the bridge-dwellers: history had nothing to record. But since the Black Death, when nearly half England's population died, labour was hard to come by, and in the countryside tempers were rising at the taxes and already outdated feudal laws binding man to master. The explosion came in 1381 when Hales, treasurer to the boy-king Richard II, imposed his Poll Tax on all those over the age of fifteen. Almost before he realized, Wat Tyler of Dartford in Kent, found himself the leader of the rebels in south-east England.

'When Adam delved and Eve span,
Who then was the gentleman?'

chanted the peasants as they marched to meet up with John Ball and his followers converging on London from East Anglia. In Southwark the Kentish rebels divided their time between breaking open the Marshalsea and King's Bench Prisons, the Bishop of Winchester's Palace and wrecking the Bankside Stews. The latter was done to spite William Walworth, the Lord Mayor of London, who owned these brothels. On his orders the drawbridge had been raised and secured with a great chain. But unfortunately for many in the City, the defence of London Bridge was entrusted to a most inept alderman, Walter Sybyle. When a reinforcement of armed Londoners arrived on the bridge, volunteering for its defence, he sent them off again, saying their help was not needed. But when the time came, on the morning of Friday, 13th June 1381, he capitulated without a fight. Wat Tyler presented himself at the end of the bridge and threatened to burn down the houses on the first six arches. Almost at once the drawbridge was lowered. The mob streamed across into the City where a number of the inhabitants welcomed them openly.

As they passed the chapel the priests inside were 'earnest in procession and prayers for peace', but soon John of Gaunt's great palace, the Savoy, was a smoking ruin. Then attention was focused on the Tower where the King, Hales, the Archbishop of Canterbury, and many of the court had fled for safety. The next day, in fear and trepidation, Richard II rode out to meet a number of the rebels at Mile End. No sooner had he left than others of their number pushed in through the still-open gates of the Tower, searching for their arch-enemies Hales and Simon of Sudbury. Both men were literally dragged from the altar in the Chapel of St John to instant execution on Tower Hill. After nailing the archbishop's hood to his skull the mob paraded through the City and down to the bridge with their horrible trophies, which were soon raised high over the draw-bridge gate. Eventually the archbishop's head was returned to his birth-place in Suffolk, where it is still preserved in an iron box in the vestry of Sudbury St Gregory.

All that day London was in the grip of the mob; now in a killing mood. Lawyers, tax gatherers, officials of any kind, Flemish settlers—both men and women—all were killed without compunction. But on Sunday, when William Walworth rode out between the King's party and the rebels and killed Wat Tyler, all the fire went out of the mob. By now there were about ten heads on the bridge: soon they were removed and in their place grinned those of Wat Tyler himself and Jack Straw, another of the rebel leaders. To the present day the inn called Jack Straw's Castle in Hampstead still keeps his memory half alive.

As the unstable King grew older his reign fluctuated between frantic gaiety and setbacks brought about by the more dissatisfied of his nobles. A joust held on the bridge on 23rd April 1390, for the honour of England and Scotland, represents the brighter side of the picture. The contestants were the English Ambassador to Scotland, Lord Wells, and a Scottish knight, Sir David de Lindsay. As might be expected neither had been able to agree that the other man's countrymen were the braver in battle. Although this discussion took place north of the Border, Lord Wells chose London Bridge as the site on which to settle this burning question of honour. Already the bridge was something akin to a wonder of the medieval world, and national pride may well have had something to do with the Ambassador's odd choice of locale.

Relations being what they were, a safe-conduct was issued for Sir David's journey south. 'The king to all and singular, our Sheriffs, Mayors, Bailiffs, Ministers, and faithful subjects, within and without our liberties, to whom these present letters shall come, Greeting. Know ye, that because our beloved and faithful John de Wells, for the perfecting of a certain Passage of Arms within our Kingdom of England, against David de Lindeseye, of Scotland, Knight, as he appears to have been calumniated by the said David, with his followers and servants coming into our Kingdom aforesaid, for the cause aforesaid, and graciously to provide for their remaining here, and returning hence again, to their own country.'

The day came, the bridge was prepared, Richard II and his court took up the places of honour, while the bridge-dwellers and citizens jostled for what few vantage points there may have been. Since the High Street was only twelve feet wide the actual jousting must have taken place in one of the open places, probably adjoining the Chapel. There there was a space approximately thirty-five feet long by twenty feet wide, which in fact later became known as The Square. Even so, this tilt-yard was small enough.

Mounted, the two upholders of their countries' honour, charged past the shop fronts, and met with a great clash and splintering of lances. According to the chronicler Holinshed, de Lindsay remained as firm as a rock, whereupon the English began to make audible remarks to the effect he must be locked in his saddle. Even de Lindsay heard them. He leapt from the saddle in full armour, and then remounted unaided. Now his critics were silent.

A second course was run, with no advantage to either side, but at the third Lord Wells was unseated and fell heavily, injuring himself severely. At once de Lindsay was off his horse, and supporting him in his arms until a doctor arrived. To the London crowd, so quick in slander, de Lindsay was now the hero of the hour; and his daily visits to Lord Wells during the latter's recovery further endeared him. His unofficial actions probably did more for Anglo-Scottish relations than any official treaties and oaths of undying friendship and brotherly love.

Richard's next visit to the bridge resulted, oddly enough, from some doubtful financial dealings in the City. In 1392 he attempted to pawn a valuable jewel, but the merchants regretfully declared it was beyond their resources to help. Whereupon a Lombard came to the King's rescue. All might have gone well if Richard had not discovered that a number of merchants originally approached, who had declined to help, had provided the Lombard with the necessary financial backing.

At the best of times Richard was a petulant young man. Now he ordered the arrest and imprisonment of the Mayor and sheriffs. A warden and new sheriffs were elected, and the unfortunate City fined £100,000, an enormous sum for those days. More than once in the past Anne of Bohemia, his queen, made up in some degree for his lack of stability and common sense, and now she and Bishop Braybrook between them brought him round to a reasonable state of mind. To show his quarrel was at an end Richard agreed to ride from Southwark, through the City to Westminster. Accompanied by the Bishop and a host of choristers, the royal couple came to London Bridge, where the leading citizens were waiting to present two white horses, decked out with cloth of gold and little jingling bells on the harness. Perhaps the Queen rode side-saddle. She should surely have done so, seeing that it was she who introduced it into England from her native Bohemia. Then the whole cavalcade crossed the bridge to receive an emotional welcome from a City that metaphorically speaking had crossed its fingers. All went well, and in due course Richard was graciously pleased to remit the fine and free the rightful Lord Mayor and sheriffs.

Anne of Bohemia died in 1394, and within a year Richard II married again. Once more the crowds pressed down to the bridge, to see the King and his bride from France arrive in London. If any of them commented that he was old enough to be her father, they were justified. Isabelle of France was just eight years old. 13th November 1395 should have been a holiday, but for some it was a fatal day. So great was the throng 'that on London Bridge nine persons were crowded to death, of whom the Prior of Tiptree, a place in Essex, was one, and a matron on Cornhill was another'.

That inauspicious entry into London was the last occasion on which Richard in all his glory—and in his time he must have spent thousands on fashions—would be seen at the bridge. The rift between himself, his uncle Thomas of Woodstock and Henry Bolingbroke continued to grow. Both were banished, Thomas to the castle at Calais and Henry right into France itself. Four knights had hurried to Canterbury over two centuries before to carry out a king's wish, if not his word; and now four more knights, Sir Bernard Brocas, Lord Marclais, Lord Stelle, and John Derby, crossed the Channel in the reverse direction. Soon Thomas of Woodstock was dead, smothered between two feather mattresses.

Retribution for the knights was not long in coming: after the death of John of Gaunt—Henry Bolingbroke's father—the son returned to England, and soon Richard was his prisoner, mewed up in the Tower, along with the other four. After being tried in their absence in the Guildhall as the murderers of Thomas of Woodstock, the Lord Mayor and leading citizens (now the loyal and devoted supporters of Henry Bolingbroke) came straight to the Tower, and as Froissart recorded: 'Without saying a word, these four were dragged from the Tower, through the streets to Cheapside, and, on a fishmonger's stall their heads struck off, which were placed over the gate on London Bridge.'

That scene, among the shoppers and stalls piled high with the goods of everyday life, catches up in an instant all the sudden savagery and horror lying just below the surface of life in the Middle Ages. Which was the true picture: the fishmonger selling his wares to the careful housewife, or the running blood of a few minutes later? Both perhaps.

With something approaching relief one can remember this was also the age of the garden-loving Chaucer. As the earth quickened to life beneath the showers of April, he and his future companions in travel crossed London Bridge to collect at the Tabard Inn. Singly they would have ridden down Fish Street Hill, for only at the inn would they discover who else was in the party. The little prioress with her so-English French accent and brooch bearing the words 'Amor Vincit Omnia'. The knight who was always a perfect gentleman, and the miller who was not. The over-married, over-bejewelled Wife of Bath, and all other such pilgrims who rode if they were lucky, or walked if they were not, over the bridge—stopping halfway to pray and make an offering that all would go well on their journey to Canterbury: begun at the Chapel of St Thomas and ending at his shrine in the cathedral. Then on their return, another pause at the chapel, and a thank-offering for a pilgrimage free from mishap.

The chapel was prosperous: so much so, that between 1384 and 1396 Henry Yevele rebuilt it in the current Perpendicular style. At a salary of £10 per annum he had in 1365 been elected one of the Wardens of the Bridge—and who better to watch over its safety than England's leading architect? Yevele remained in office until 1395, and as the new century began he died, and was buried in St Magnus Martyr. The bridge's creator, Peter of Colechurch, lay halfway along its length, and now like a guardian hound at the foot of a recumbent effigy, Henry Yevele lay close by at the north end.

The new chapel he designed followed the disposition of the old. Below was the undercroft, reached either by a newel staircase leading down from street level—or more rarely used, from a door opening on to the starling. By this side entrance sailors could enter without having to go up on to the bridge. Outside, the upper chapel was capped with battlements and a pointed roof surmounted by a little pinnacle. The windows—nearly as large below as above—were filled with stained glass, most of it heraldic. Now it was served by four priests, but only one clerk. The 15d. paid to the latter, very roughly equals £1 8s. 0d. of present money. Nearly every cathedral, church and chapel had its sacred relics in the Middle Ages (p. 126), and St Thomas's Chapel was no exception. 'Divers relics of the saints; with two silver phials, which are shut up in a certain chest with an iron lock. . . . Also a cross, in which is set a portion of the Cross of Christ; and a vessel of crystal; with a silver foot, and a ring with a tooth of St Richard (of Chichester), as it is said; together with divers relics in it, which always stand upon the altar of St Thomas, for pilgrims to resort thereto.' Obviously these were the great days of the Bridge Chapel.

By rebellion Henry IV came to the throne, and before long he himself was rebelled against. A falling-out among nobles took place when the King and the Earl of Northumberland could not agree over the division of ransom money paid by a number of Scottish knights as the price of their freedom. The earl, together with his son, the famous Harry Hotspur, rose in open rebellion. Harry fell in battle at Shrewsbury in 1403, and not only was his head sent to London Bridge for display on the bridge, but one of his quarters as well: to bring home to any other would-be traitors the fate they could expect.

The earl was pardoned on payment of a huge fine, but he bore no love for Henry IV, and again he rebelled. In 1408 the skull of the son was joined by the head of the father.

Traitors appeared all through Henry's reign, and in due course their heads went to the bridge. William Fyssher, a parchment maker in the City, executed in 1413, was only one. His crime was that of harbouring Sir John Oldcastle after the latter's escape from the Tower where he lay charged with treason and Lollardry; while another was Benedict Wolman who in 1416 planned to introduce a pretender into England who claimed to be Richard II.

But with the Battle of Agincourt the scene lightens once again: a month after Henry V's victory in October 1415, the Lord Mayor, aldermen and guilds and citizens—between ten and twenty thousand of them—together with the clergy, all crossed the bridge to meet Henry at Blackheath. As the procession moved back again, the King in their midst, their ranks were further swollen at St Thomas à Waterings by yet more clergy and choristers.

From end to end the bridge was decorated in honour of the occasion. By the staples at the Southwark end stood a huge giant armed with a spear and an axe, and his equally enormous wife. A little further on the drawbridge was decorated with more of these carnival-like figures: a lion armed with a lance and opposite a hart with the royal arms emblazoned on a shield about its neck. Over the gateway itself hung a silken banner of St George. As was usual the guilds, who footed the bill for the decoration and pageants inseparable from such occasions, had not stinted themselves. When Henry V approached the drawbridge three queens, wearing bejewelled crowns, came out with their white-clad attendants, two groups of seven young girls, and welcomed him in song:

> 'Sovereign Lord, Welcome to your City.
> Welcome our joy, and our heart's pleasance,

Welcome our gladness, Welcome our suffiance
Welcome, Welcome, right Welcome, must ye be;
Singing to fore thy royal majesty,
We say of heart, without variance,
Sovereign Lord, Welcome, Welcome, our joy.'

Since it was not until 1421 that Henry V brought his newly married wife, Katharine de Valois, to London, and another great welcome at the bridge, it looks—with regret—as though the scene in *Henry V* where she brushes up her English on the eve of Agincourt is only an endearing addition by Shakespeare. Without doubt the guilds produced many attractive pageants and decorations; but if the Londoners had not had enough of them, the chroniclers had. 'I will pass over the great and curious ordenance provided by the citizens . . .' wrote Hall. 'Marvel though it is to write, but more marvel it was to see', echoed another, 'which for tediousness I overpass'. And with that lazy but most convenient consideration for the reader's staying powers, they dip their quills in the ink and pass on to other events.

After only six months Henry V loved and left his Katharine, to return to the wars in France. Soon Katharine, the daughter of a mad king, became the mother of another, the future Henry VI. But now, when Henry V was at the height of his fame he died at Vincennes—in August 1422. But at least he was spared the fate of Charles XII, who in the eighteenth century made a Swedish lake of the Baltic, and then lived long enough to see his empire crumble. Within thirty years of Henry's death the English were out of the greater part of France.

His homecoming to London was a spectacle of sombre magnificence excelling even the six-week journey from Brussels to Dijon in 1404 of Philip the Bold. First his coffin was taken in state to Notre Dame, Paris: from there down the Seine to Rouen, through Abbeville to Calais. At Dover the Archbishop of Canterbury waited to escort it to his cathedral. From there the cortège passed through Rochester and approached London. Throughout the journey from France the accompanying priests recited the Office of the Dead without ceasing, and as the procession neared Southwark it was joined by no less than fifteen bishops.

Both in England and in France the peasants abandoned their reaping to run to the roadside and gaze up at the wax effigy lying upon the coffin. Now as it passed slowly along London Bridge it was almost within touching distance of the inhabitants. Perfect in every detail, the robed, crowned, and bejewelled effigy stared up at the canopy borne over it by peers of the realm, as it lay on a bed of gold brocade placed over the coffin.

The bridge, like the streets of the City, was newly swept and gravelled: the houses hung with black, and in the doorways stood the occupiers, lighted tapers in their hands, as five hundred men-at-arms, in black harness, their arms reversed and even their horses trapped out in black, passed by. There followed another three hundred carrying lighted torches. In the enclosed space the bridge must have reverberated with the tramp of feet and the chanting of priests, ever increasing in volume. Then came the chariot itself, drawn by six horses bearing the arms of France, England and France quartered, St George, King Arthur, St Edward, and the arms of Normandy. Soon it was gone, on up Fish Street Hill into a city of mourning, towards Old St Paul's, leaving at the bridge a page unrivalled in its history for darkly glowing magnificence.

3

The early years of Henry VI's reign saw several changes to the architecture of London Bridge, notably at the southern end. In 1426 the old timber drawbridge gateway, standing on the seventh pier, was demolished and 'John Reynwell, Mayor of London, laid one of the first corner stones in the foundation of this work, the other three were laid by the sheriffs and bridge masters, upon every of the four stones was engraven in fair Roman letters the name "IHESUS" '.

The 'New Stone Gate', to distinguish it from the Great Stone Gate near the Southwark bank, was shaped like a squat tower with four turrets that rose no higher than the battlements. Above the main archway on its southern face was a gallery commanding the drawbridge below. This drawbridge was intended not only for defence, but also to allow ships to pass through to reach Queenhithe Dock, a few hundred yards upstream on the north bank of the river. The fee for raising was sixpence; approximately 14s. at present rates. In 1465 a foreign captain paid one of the householders 12d. to replace windows knocked in when his vessel came too close to the bridge. In recent years there was a curious parallel when on two separate occasions gusts of wind blew a Spanish liner against the present bridge. Then it was the ship and not the bridge that was damaged.

Like its predecessor the New Stone Gate received the gruesome decoration of skulls on poles; a number of which must have been saved when the wooden gateway was demolished, and then put in place on the new structure.

Two years later, in 1428, London Bridge just failed to claim what would have been its most notable victim. In the November dusk the Duke of Norfolk's barge was wrecked against one of the starlings. He and several of his party managed to jump on to the starling just before the boat heeled over, and were hauled to safety on the bridge itself. But his other companions and the boatmen seem to have been swept through in the mill-race. Whether they were drowned or not the contemporary chronicler did not make clear.

As far back as 1425 ominous cracks began to appear at the southern end of the bridge: so much so that carts with metal-rimmed wheels were forbidden to cross. Instead of rebuilding the drawbridge tower when they did, the Bridge Wardens would have been wiser to concentrate on consolidating the foundations of the Great Stone Gate. But that was not to be, and on 14th January 1437 the whole structure toppled backwards into the river, breaking down two arches and completely cutting off Southwark from the City. With the passing of time people came to regard the all-but-submerged masonry, left where it fell, as a natural hazard and called the archway Rock Lock. With a width of thirty-four feet it was the widest of all London Bridge's twenty arches. Did the inhabitants have a few minutes' warning of what was to happen? A number of the houses were completely wrecked, but no one was killed or injured.

Many prominent citizens subscribed to the rebuilding of the gateway: when finished it consisted of a large archway, surmounted by the city arms flanked on either side by statues in niches. Bastions built out on corbles over the pier abutments flanked the gateway, and the whole scheme was capped by fairly steeply pitched roofs; the tallest in the centre. At some later date, before 1550, the roofs and bastions were removed, leaving a nearly square gateway, surmounted by battlements.

As if a strong strain of insanity was not enough, Henry VI also suffered the affliction of scheming, ambitious relatives. So, as might be expected in such troubled times, traitor's head after traitor's head was placed on the bridge. Among them was that of Roger Bolingbroke, a priest who became involved in what was perhaps the scandal of the century.

Eleanor Cobham, Duchess of Gloucester, who hoped one day to see her husband on the throne, procured Bolingbroke's services to make a wax image of the King which they then melted away, hoping his life would also come to an end. But the whole story came out, to the embarrassment of her husband, the Great Duke Humphrey (p. 104). Bolingbroke, Southwell (a Canon of St Stephen's, Westminster), Margaret Jourdain (a witch), and the Duchess were all arrested. The witch was burnt, Southwell died in the Tower before the sharp edge of the law could overtake him, and for three days Eleanor Cobham walked in penance through the streets of the City before being banished, while on 25th July 1441 Bolingbroke was exposed as a necromancer at Paul's Cross (p. 113). Then on 18th November, a few days before Eleanor Cobham's public humiliation, he was both tried and executed, and his head placed above the New Stone Gate. A warning to both traitors and would-be dealers in the occult.

The ceremonial arrival of Henry VI's bride, Margaret of Anjou, at the bridge on 18th May 1445 seems like a falsely bright and cheerful prologue intended to heighten the bitter and protracted savagery of the years to come. The interminable Wars of the Roses. After meeting the royal couple at Blackheath, the Lord Mayor and the violet-clad City fathers all rode together to London Bridge where two pageants awaited them.

The first, enacted before the Great Stone Gate, represented Peace and Plenty: later that couple were to be most conspicuous by their absence—but all that lay in the future. The second pageant, at the drawbridge, depicted Noah's Ark coming to rest after the flood. That was more appropriate. England was in for a deluge, of blood.

John Lydgate, the monk-poet (p. 112), provided verses suitable for the occasion:

> 'So trust thee your people, with assurance
> Through your grace, and high benignity—
> 'Twixt the Realms two, England and France,
> Peace shall approach, rest and unity:
> Mars set aside with all his cruelty,
> Which too long hath troubled the Realms twain:
> Bidding your comfort, in this adversity,
> Most Christian Princess or Lady Sovereign.'

The bridge was decorated, but the thought arises; were the traitors' heads removed? The outlook of the Middle Ages being what it was, the answer is probably an emphatic no.

During the summer of 1450 events were like a repetition of 1381; the Peasants' Revolt. Although Henry VI was now a man of twenty-eight, he did not show the courage of the fourteen-year-old Richard II who rode out to face the rebels in person. Despite the entreaties of the City, which even threw in the bribe of offering to pay all his household expenses for six months if only he would stay in their midst, he rode off to the distant safety of Kenilworth.

By then the armed mob, under the leadership of Jack Cade, had marched up from Kent and camped in Southwark while they took stock of the situation. Then Cade threatened to fire the bridge unless the gates were opened and the drawbridge lowered. Again a fifteenth-century Quisling did as an earlier one had done in 1381. This time the man's name is known. Thomas Godfrey, a spur maker. Cade and his followers crossed the bridge, taking care to cut the ropes that wound up the drawbridge; so leaving the way open for retreat, should that be necessary. Once in the City, Cade made his way to the

London Stone by St Swithin's Church, and striking it with his sword proclaimed himself master of London.

Again history repeated itself: on 4th July Lord Saye, the Lord Treasurer, was dragged from the Tower and beheaded in Cheapside. When the mob tired of parading the streets with his head they took it, together with the head of Sir James Romer, Sheriff of Kent, and placed them on the bridge. Each night the rebels returned to Southwark, across the now defenceless bridge; feeling themselves safer there than in the enclosed City. Jack Cade, who passed himself off as Mortimer, an illegitimate son of the Earl of March, lodged at the White Hart, while his followers stayed where they pleased, and no doubt sampled the pleasures of Bankside.

Now the Londoners, at first moderately well disposed towards the rebels, were in fear of their lives and for their property. After dining with Griste, a prosperous citizen, Cade 'like an unkind guest, robbed him of all that there was there to be found worth the carriage'.

By the evening of Sunday, 5th July, Lord Scales, the Constable of the Tower, was in a position to counter-attack. After the rebels had as usual withdrawn into Southwark as darkness fell, a company of men-at-arms under the command of Matthew Gough, a tough old veteran of the French wars, prepared to move on to the bridge. Without a sound they crossed, past the silent shops and houses, and between ten and midnight killed the rebel guard posted at the southern end. But there were others to carry the news back to Cade at the White Hart. Like a swarm of hornets the rebels streamed towards the bridge, and in the dark of that summer night the fight began. No quarter was given, and none asked. Inch by inch Gough and his men were driven back; to the drawbridge itself. If they were fighting like soldiers, the rebels were fighting with just that extra urgency of men with everything to gain if they won, and certain death if they lost.

Now the fire flickered up as regardless of the inhabitants, Cade's men burnt the houses along the stretch they had just won back. The chronicler Hall wrote: 'Great ruth it was, to behold the miserable state, for some desiring to eschew the fire lept on his enemies weapon, and so died: fearful women with children in their arms, amazed, and appalled, lept for fear into the river: others doubting how to save themselves between fire, water and sword, were in their houses suffocated and smouldered.'

Somewhere in the small hours the men-at-arms were driven back as far as St Magnus Martyr at the north end of the bridge. Then their fortune turned and the rebels found themselves driven right back to the Southwark end. All this in the lurid, uncertain light of the houses burning between the Great Stone Gate and the New Stone Gateway.

By dawn Matthew Gough was dead, but neither side had the advantage. At 8 a.m. a truce was called. Cade agreed not to advance into the City, and the Londoners agreed not to cross into Southwark. On the promise of a pardon Cade and his men returned quietly to Kent, only to be pounced on within a few days when it was annulled. Cade had the good fortune to be killed fighting, and so escaped the agony of a traitor's death, but after identification as the 'Captain of Kent' by the innkeeper's wife at the White Hart, his head, along with those of many followers, was set up on top of the New Stone Gate, overlooking the ruins of those houses burnt not long before during the bitterest fighting in all Old London Bridge's history.

The memory of those events must still have been fresh in the mind of many living on the bridge when twenty-one years later, in 1471, Warwick the Kingmaker and Thomas Falconbridge attempted to restore the demented Henry VI to his throne. For the past nine years he had been imprisoned in the Tower, but now Warwick, discontented with his reward from the usurping Edward IV, planned a *coup d'état*. He took Henry from the Tower while Falconbridge, an illegitimate son of the first Lord Falconbridge, 'having assembled a riotous company of shipmen and others in Essex and Kent, came to London with a great many ships, near to the Tower; whereupon the Mayor and Aldermen, by consent of a Common Council, fortified all along the Thames side, from Baynard's Castle to the Tower, with armed men, guns, and other instruments of war, to resist the invasion of the mariners, whereby the Thames side was

The Great Frost, December 1676.

The east end of Old St Paul's as it was in 1641, from an etching by J. Harris

The west end of Old St Paul's in 1641. (Finden, after Hollar)

safely preserved and kept by the Aldermen and other citizens that assembled thither in great numbers.'

This time the bridge was well defended, the drawbridge raised and loopholes cut in it for three small cannon. As a protection against fire, great strips of canvas, soaked in vinegar, were hung against the drawbridge, while the troops stationed in the New Stone Gateway were equipped with buckets of water.

On Sunday morning, 11th May, the attack came. Falconbridge's fleet anchored in what is now the Pool, and troops landed on both sides of the river. Some made for the Tower, others for the Southwark end of the bridge. The Great Gate, rebuilt as recently as 1437, was burnt, along with thirteen houses (elsewhere in his *Survey of London* John Stow gives the number as seventeen). But this time the bridge did not fall, and after the killing or capture of his companions in and around the City, Falconbridge called off the venture. The drawbridge rattled down, out raced the armed citizens, and the enemy's retreat turned into a rout. Falconbridge escaped, for the time being. But by the middle of September his head was on top of the gate, turned towards Kent from where he had come originally with such high hopes. As for Henry VI, he had been murdered in the Wakefield Tower (p. 117).

Even now the misfortunes of the bridge in the fifteenth century were not at an end. 'In the year 1481 a house called The Common Siege on London Bridge fell into the Thames, through the fall whereof five men were drowned.'

Evidently the lessees of Queenhithe, upstream of the bridge, either lacked sufficient pull with the authorities, or were not dependent on large ships berthing at their dock, for by 1500 it was all but impossible to raise the drawbridge. In fact only with great difficulty could it be raised to let Henry VII's barges pass upstream from Greenwich. The trouble was not so much the wooden bridge, as the New Stone Gateway itself. Although only seventy-five years old, the strain of raising the drawbridge might risk another disaster similar to the collapse of the Great Stone Gate in 1437. Its useful days were over, and when for the last time it saw action, during Wyatt's rebellion of 1554, the authorities had to smash it down to halt the rebels.

4

From the time the houses were burnt in Falconbridge's attack until the defacing of the Chapel in Edward VI's reign, little or no alterations took place. With the help of two illustrations, one painted about 1485 and the other by A. van den Wyngaerde, already referred to, we can reconstruct nearly the whole length of the east side of the bridge at this comparatively early date. On his marriage to Princess Elizabeth (Edward IV's daughter), the new king, Henry VII, gave her an illuminated copy of the poems of Charles d'Orléans, written while he was a prisoner in the Tower. Among the illustrations was one combining several scenes during those long years of captivity after Agincourt, while much of the background is filled by the northern half of Old London Bridge. Tantalizingly it stops just beyond the chapel, but we can see the houses, mostly in three storeys, supported over the river on massive struts. The last few piers before the north bank are masked by the elaborate gables of the Customs House at Billingsgate. Not only is this the earliest representation of London Bridge, but also of the Tower itself.

Next in date and importance comes the Wyngaerde panorama of London which included the bridge. It is a bird's-eye view, from somewhere over Southwark, which shows the southern end in considerable detail; while owing to the perspective the northern end is only sketched in. After the chapel comes a jumble of roofs, and then the New Stone Gateway of 1426, complete with its crop of heads, the drawbridge with handrails on either side; more houses—here we can see just how narrow they are: an open space over Rock Lock, and the Great Stone Gate itself: then still more houses stretching to the Southwark bank.

When Henry VIII was suing for a divorce on the grounds that Katharine of Aragon's first marriage to his sickly elder brother, Prince Arthur, had been consummated, thereby making his own invalid, she bitterly declared that the first union had been made in blood. The blood belonged to Edward IV's nephew, the unfortunate Earl of Warwick (no connection with the Kingmaker), who spent sixteen of his twenty-five years in prison, simply because his very existence was a threat to the newly arrived house of Tudor. So long as he lived Ferdinand and Isabella would not agree to their daughter Katharine marrying Prince Arthur. An *agent provocateur* went to work in the Tower between Warwick and another prisoner, the Pretender Perkin Warbeck, and before long both were dead, judicially murdered by words and ideas put into their heads by Henry VII's agent.

On this ruthless foundation Katharine of Aragon's first marriage was built, though when the fifteen-year-old girl came to London she doubtless knew nothing of the whole discreditable affair. She reached London from Plymouth on 12th November 1501, and a pageant of girls representing St Ursula and St Catharine waited at the bridge to greet her.

The High Street, as in the City, was swept and gravelled, stands and crush barriers (rayles) set up all along the route from Grace Church Street, near the north end of the bridge, to the cathedral (p. 120), and with largess typical of the age the inhabitants had the choice of getting a little drunk on either the red or the white wine flowing in the conduits.

The sight, as the procession came off the bridge and clattered up the hill past St Magnus Martyr, must have been a brave one: '. . . the costly apparel', wrote Hall, 'both of goldsmiths work and embroidery, the rich jewels, the massy chains, the stirring horses, the beautiful barbes and glittering trappers, both with bells and spangles of gold . . . also the rich apparel of the princess, the strange fashions of the Spanish nation, the beauty of the English Ladies, the goodly demeanour of the young damsels, the amorous countenance of the lusty bachelors.'

Little could the dark-haired princess have realized that some thirty years later she would be the unwitting cause of head after head being sent to the bridge.

Life, death, life. The processions alternated. Eight years after Katharine's arrival, Henry VII returned on 9th May 1509 to London after his death at Richmond Palace. Preceding the coffin were one hundred and four black-clad citizens and members of the London guilds, the latter carrying lighted torches. In silence they passed on to the cathedral on Ludgate

Hill, and expectantly all England turned to see how he compared with his eighteen-year-old son. Withdrawn, outwardly unemotional and miserly: Henry VIII shared none of these traits so characteristic of his father. Indeed the history of Old London Bridge during his reign is like a distillation of the history of the whole country. One day glittering, beflagged barges are shooting beneath the arches, while the next the head of some churchman, statesman, or nobleman who has not knuckled under to the royal whim or policy, is placed above.

Now Wolsey is Archbishop of York, just starting to enlarge York Place (p. 175) in accordance with his grandiose ideas. For him the See of York is only one step along the road to the triple crown, and in 1515 he moved further towards that goal when his cardinal's hat, newly arrived from Rome, was carried in great state across London Bridge. A weakness Wolsey shared with many of his fellow men was a dislike of shooting the bridge. In fact he flatly refused to do so. Whenever his journeys took him downstream to Greenwich (p. 163) he chose to land at The Three Cranes on Vintry Wharf where his little white mule would be waiting to carry him along Thames Street, past the end of the feared bridge, where he rejoined his barge after it had shot the mill-race running between the starlings. So even a man like Wolsey had his share of private fears and weaknesses. Another was spiders: at Hampton Court one of the type still known as cardinal spider nearly succeeded in frightening him to death.

Three years after the arrival of the cardinal's hat, Campeggio —one day to be bedevilled by Henry's divorce—rode over the bridge, while the clergy from all the City churches lined the route from St George's, Southwark, right along the way into the City itself. In the High Street, enclosed and tunnel-like, the air must have been heavy with incense. As the Cardinal passed by, bent on obtaining a subsidy from the English clergy, the priests censed him; swinging their incense burners to and fro.

Almost the only people to benefit from the alliance with Charles V, of the Holy Roman Empire, were a number of prisoners in the Marshalsea and King's Bench Prisons in

Southwark. When in 1522 he arrived at St George's Bar, where Henry and the official welcoming party was waiting, the Emperor indulged in one of those prearranged little royal gestures that on the face give the impression of being spontaneous. Could the prisoners be released? he asked. And since most were only held for debt, a large number were set free. As might be expected, Charles V did not embarrass Henry with a similar request at the Tower. Then, after the speeches of welcome, the procession moved on to the bridge where, at a cost of £64, great carnival figures had been set up. On either side of the drawbridge stood Sampson and Hercules, holding between them a large scroll bearing the Emperor's titles. Further on was Jason, with the Golden Fleece, 'and', wrote the chronicler Gregory, 'on the one side of him stood a fiery dragon, and on the other side stood two bulls which beasts continually cast out fire'. Beyond was a tower in which stood a girl representing that murderous queen and mother, Medea.

Indirectly, prisons fared on more than one occasion as a result of the state visit. For the occasion Bridewell Palace was built in a matter of weeks on the banks of that noisome little river, the Fleet. One can only hope it was cleared out in honour of the occasion. In later years the place became a place of correction for scolds, bawds, and similar kindred spirits.

Now Old London Bridge enjoyed a period of peace. The New Stone Gateway showed no further signs of collapse, and apart from a fire in 1504 when six houses adjoining St Magnus Martyr were burnt, there were no sudden alarms. Not only did the shopkeepers live over their businesses, but a number of prosperous merchants whose interests were in the City itself chose to live there, out over the river. What was lost in space had its compensations in the fresher atmosphere. Instead of his neighbours' roofs his view, if he lived on the east side, embraced the Tower, the Pool with all its shipping and sparsely built-up Bermondsey: to the west the City stretched round in a curve to where Westminster appeared to rise above the fields and trees of the south bank; so much does the Thames wind.

But soon enough the darker side of Henry's reign became increasingly obvious to any who glanced up while crossing the bridge. The refusal to accept the Act of Supremacy, which declared Henry and not the Pope Head of the Church in England, was a sure way of ensuring death on Tower Hill or at Tyburn. One of the first heads to go to London Bridge in this prolonged bloodbath was that of a woman, Elizabeth Barton, the self-styled Maid of Kent.

Her career started with religious utterances made during an epileptic fit. The notoriety was to her liking, and aided and abetted by Edmund Bocking, an unscrupulous monk, she achieved a nationwide fame as a prophetess and mouthpiece of divine wisdom. But like all such people, she eventually over-stepped the mark by announcing if Henry divorced Katharine of Aragon to marry Anne Boleyn, within a month he would die a 'villain's death'. Henry married his Anne Boleyn and continued to flourish, while Elizabeth Barton and Edmund Bocking died the 'villain's death' at Tyburn.

The worst feature in the shabby little adventuress's career was that in her downfall Sir Thomas More was implicated. He had questioned her about some of her utterances. That, coupled with his refusal to accept the Act of Supremacy, was enough for Henry. On 6th July 1535 he was executed and his head set up on the bridge in the place occupied by that of Bishop Fisher: himself a victim of a fortnight earlier. Like More, Fisher had refused to accept the Act of Supremacy, and all unwittingly his end was precipitated by the Pope, who on hearing of his imprisonment in the Tower, dispatched a cardinal's hat. When Henry heard it was on its way he savagely remarked that by the time it arrived Fisher would have no head on which to put it. This was a very different sovereign to the man who in the twenties of the century was in the habit of inviting himself to York Place (p. 163), to amuse himself with dancing, feasting, and beautiful women.

The reason for callously throwing Fisher's head in the river was a story spreading around London: '. . . after it had stood up the space of fourteen days, upon the bridge, could not perceived to waste nor consume . . . but grew daily fresher and fresher, so that in his life time he never looked so well. The people coming daily to see this strange sight, the passage over the bridge was so stopped with their going and coming, that almost neither Cart nor horse could pass.'

In due course Sir Thomas More's head was obtained, possibly by a little judicious bribery, by his beloved daughter Margaret Roper, and when she died it was buried with her in the vault beneath St Dunstan's, Canterbury.

And still they came to the bridge: the heads of the Abbots of Bridlington, Jervaulx and Fountains; all from Yorkshire; and knights such as Sir Thomas Percy and Sir Francis Bigott. The last two for their part in the Pilgrimage of Grace.

Even the chapel did not escape the upheavals of the times. Three and a half centuries before Thomas à Becket defied another Henry, and became England's greatest saint. Now, once and for all, Henry VIII was determined to stamp out his memory. At Canterbury the unbelievably rich shrine was destroyed, and a decree passed ordering the rededication of all places of worship which bore his name; together with the defacing of all paintings in which he appeared. As a result St Thomas's Chapel on the bridge became the Chapel of Our Lady, and at a cost of two shillings the offending paintings were either destroyed or painted out. In all England only a very few representations of Becket were overlooked, but a fresco does still survive in Hadleigh Parish Church near Southend.

Just three weeks after the execution of Anne Boleyn, Henry came upstream from Greenwich bound for Whitehall Palace with his third queen, Jane Seymour. As the guns at the Tower boomed out in welcome the procession of barges approached. 'And so', wrote Charles Wriothesley in his *Chronicle of England*, 'the King passed through London Bridge, with his trumpets blowing before him, and shawms, sackbuts and dromeslaws [drummers] playing also in barges going before him, which was a goodly sight to behold.'

In this year of blood and pageantry a story had its beginning on the bridge, which if true in all its details, must count as the big romantic story in its history. Among those living there was William Hewet, a well-to-do cloth-worker who had young Edward Osborne as an apprentice. Then one day in 1536 came the beginning of the chain of events. Hewet's young daughter, about six years old, was playing by an open window overlooking the river, when she fell out. A horrified maidservant could do nothing, but Osborn dived in after the child, and brought her to safety. The years passed: William Hewet waxed ever more prosperous; received a knighthood and became a Sheriff of London, while Anne became a desirable bride, particularly to those of the aristocracy who felt their title was a fair exchange for her dowry. However, her father had long since decided that if Edward Osborn really got on in life, he should have the opportunity of marrying the girl. He did make good in true Dick Whittington fashion, and Anne did accept him. In due course he became Lord Mayor, died full of honour in 1591 and was buried in that church not rebuilt after the Great Fire which had such an extraordinary name: St Dionys Backchurch. One slight flaw in the story concerns the dates. If Anne was married in 1561 when aged about eighteen, she would have been born nine years after the episode of Osborn rescuing her as a baby from the river. In that case 1546 seems a more reasonable date: then she would have been three years old.

Another spectacle, another head. Both events were related. In February 1540 a procession of barges shot the bridge in rapid succession as Henry came from the palace at Greenwich to Whitehall. With him was his fourth wife. But they were not together. He travelled in one barge, and alone in another following astern sat Anne of Cleves: out of sight but most definitely not out of mind. Thomas Cromwell, the Lord Chancellor, had failed as a matchmaker, and—felt the mortified King—had duped him with the plainest royal bride in the European marriage-market. Another divorce, another execution. The latter on 28th July 1540 when Thomas Cromwell's head was sent to join the others mouldering over the New Stone Gateway.

Eight months later Henry was coming up the river on his way from Greenwich to Whitehall with his fifth queen; Catharine Howard. Eighteen months later the heads of Francis Derham and Thomas Culpepper, two of the cheerful little adulteress's lovers, gazed over Southwark, while Catharine herself lay in the Chapel of St Peter ad Vincula in the Tower.

But in January 1547 Henry VIII died at Whitehall Palace (p. 181); which in the light of the foregoing events was perhaps as well for Catharine Parr, his sixth wife.

During Henry's reign a new ward was created: Bridge Ward Without. It was carved out of that part of Southwark adjoining the bridge, and the 'Without' referred to the fact that although outside the walls, it none the less formed one of the City Wards.

One day in the previous year was black for the watermen who plied between the north and south banks, as well as for the Doll Tearsheets and Winchester Geese of the Bankside Stews. Then Henry VIII, of all men, ordered the Cardinal's Hat, the Cross Keys, the Boar's Head and similar red-light establishments to close down. The Bear Garden and Paris Garden were allowed to remain, but at least until the Stews quietly opened up again, there must have been a considerable loss in trade to the watermen. By and large any gallant out for an evening's pleasure in Southwark preferred to cross the Thames by the privacy of a boat rather than show himself to the knowing leers of the loungers on London Bridge. This must have been particularly true where any of the well-known young bloods of the Court were concerned.

Perhaps the oddest things to shoot London Bridge in the sixteenth century were two whales, killed at Woolwich in 1552 and towed by barge to Whitehall Palace so the boy-king Edward VI could see them when he returned from a progress; the last he was to make. Though it was late in the evening of 10th October when he reached the palace, sufficient of the schoolboy still remained in him to insist on seeing the whales then and there, instead of waiting until the following morning (p. 183).

In the next year Stow records the drowning beneath the bridge of two Tower gunners: Gilbert Pott and John Owen by name, who lost their lives when a wherry overturned. But for two victims who found some slight immortality in the pages of the chronicles of contemporary historians, each year there must have been scores or even hundreds whose personal disaster passed either unnoticed or at least unrecorded.

Now the feeling was that the little bridge chapel was a thing of the past, and after its fate hung in the balance for three years from the time of a demolition order 'to cause the chapel upon the same bridge to be defaced, and to be translated into a dwelling house . . .', it was no more. In 1553 the upper chapel was replaced by a shop and house for a grocer, who used what remained of the undercroft as a cellar for his wares. Now the chapel had gone, and with it went the most beautiful single feature of Old London Bridge.

The death of Edward VI and the accession of his sister Mary Tudor meant a violent swing away from Protestantism to Roman Catholicism. For many of her subjects, their discontent reached a head when her proposed marriage to Philip of Spain became known. Once again Kent became a centre for rebellion when Thomas Wyatt, George and Thomas, sons of Lord Cobham, and the Earl of Suffolk (Lady Jane Grey's father)—among many others—planned a rising meant to save the Queen from herself and England from Spain, by stopping the marriage.

As Wyatt with ten thousand supporters marched on London from the south-east, the Duke of Norfolk set out with an opposing army. No battle took place. The duke and many of his soldiers sided with Wyatt, while those who wished to remain loyal to the Queen were allowed to return to London. Only a short while after setting out, they tramped back over the bridge, deprived of their arms, their jackets turned inside out and thoroughly humiliated. For a while it looked as though Wyatt would have it all his own way. The Queen's commanders were dithering, and any really decisive action on his part would bring the waverers straight into his camp.

By Saturday, 3rd February 1554 Wyatt and his men had reached the foot of Old London Bridge. The outer gates were shut, and since the drawbridge could not be raised, it had been broken down, cutting off the City from Southwark. Behind the gap the bridge itself was thick with the Queen's troops. Wyatt, no strategist at the best of times, was baffled; unsure whether to attack, wait and see, or march upstream to Kingston, where the next bridge was situated. He chose to wait, and according to Holinshed (though Stow does not mention the incident), that night clambered on to the top of the Great Stone

Gate through a hole made in the wall of an adjoining house. Colour is lent to this part of the story by van den Wyngaerde's drawing of *c.* 1550, which shows a house, its roof built on to that of the gateway.

From the top of the Great Stone Gate Wyatt and his party made their way down to the lodge, where they found the porter asleep, and his wife and a few companions sitting by the fire. If they kept quiet, Wyatt assured them, they would come to no harm. While several of his followers stayed to guard them, Wyatt and the rest tiptoed along the bridge as far as the breach in the drawbridge. On the other side, beneath the arch of the New Stone Gateway, a number of the Queen's supporters were discussing their plan of defence by the uncertain light of torches. High above in the darkness, the skulls of traitors rattled in the fitful gusts of wind and rain. A warning lost to the rebels. 'It troubled Wyatt and all his company very sore, to see that London did so stiffly stand and hold out against them: for in the assistance which they looked to have in that city, all their hope of prosperous speed consisted.'

The party returned the way they had come. Now Wyatt was more uncertain than ever what he should do. Having raised a full-scale rebellion, he had no idea how to manage it. All the next day he remained inactive, but that night, 4th February, several of his men precipitated the inevitable crisis by shooting dead one waterman and injuring another. This happened near the stairs leading to the Bishop of Winchester's Palace, upstream of the bridge. The dead man was employed at the Tower, and although seriously injured, his companion managed to shoot the bridge, and return to the fortress to tell the Lieutenant what had happened. By first light next morning the battlements of the Tower overlooking the river were bristling with cannon, all aimed at Southwark and the rebels. At this a deputation came to Wyatt: 'Sir, we are all like to be utterly undone, and destroyed for your sake, our houses shall by-and-by be thrown down upon our heads, to the utter spoil of this borough, with the shot of the Tower, all ready bent and charged towards us, for the love of God therefore take pity upon us.'

Before all was over Wyatt would have enough blood on his

conscience, including that of Lady Jane Grey, executed to prevent her becoming the centre of another such rebellion, but he had no wish to ruin Southwark in his cause. 'I pray you my friends be content a while, and I will soon ease you of this mischief, for God forbid that you, or the least here, should be killed, or hurt, in my behalf.'

Off they moved at 6 a.m. the next morning, bound for Kingston bridge and an entry into London from the north-west. Twenty-four hours later all was lost, leaving only the law to take its inevitable course. Just how unsuccessful the rebellion was, to say nothing of all the lives thrown away upon it, was brought home at the bridge when, on 19th August, Philip of Spain passed the welcoming pageant figures of Corineus and Gogmagog as he entered a suspicious and apprehensive London for the first time (p. 129). But a few months earlier, during the aftermath of the rebellion, the bridge had played a dramatic if unsuccessful part in Princess Elizabeth's desperate attempt to stave off being sent to the Tower from Whitehall Palace (p. 187).

Amid all the sufferings of the last part of Mary Tudor's reign, the bridge was remarkably peaceful. No noteworthy trophies of Tudor despotism or religious persecution were added to the collection above the New Stone Gateway, and the inhabitants continued their daily round unharmed by fire or flood.

During the sixteenth century, and for many years to come, medicine was still in its infancy. The brew concocted by the Weird Sisters was by no means merely the depraved conceit of a poet, but a probability, as several unfortunate East Europeans employed at the Tower found to their cost. On a number of occasions during the reigns of Henry VIII and Edward VI (and as early as Edward IV for that matter) the coinage had been debased. At the beginning of Elizabeth I's reign her ministers decided to make a fresh start. All the old currency was called in and melted down in the Tower Mint in order to extract the base metals; but the fumes given off in the process affected the workmen, who were advised by a learned fool to drink from cups made from the skulls of men. There, over the river, was a plentiful supply. After permission had been sought from the Council, a number were removed from the New Stone Gateway, and made into drinking cups: 'Whereof they drank and found some relief although the most of them died.' Which is as unpleasant a story as any to be found in the history of medicine.

The macabre, however, was only a small ingredient in the life of Old London Bridge. More normal, and more cheerful, were wedding festivities held at the Bridge House in July 1562 which lasted for two days after one Mr Nicolls was married in St Olave's church. Since the parish included half the bridge, no doubt either he or his wife were among its inhabitants. The occasion was most social; graced by the Lord Mayor and aldermen, and on both nights supper was followed by masques. Though compared with the lavish entertainments at Whitehall (p. 197), they were modest, and judging by the description of that given on the second night, somewhat tasteless: 'The next masque consisted of Friars, and the third of Nuns. And after they danced by Times: and lastly, the Friars and the Nuns danced together.'

Once again the appearance of the bridge was to change. Although another two hundred years of life lay ahead for the superstructure, the erection of Nonsuch House and the block between the drawbridge and the Great Stone Gate were the last buildings that could really be considered as embellishments. By 1577 the New Stone Gateway at last showed definite signs of disintegrating; as it had threatened to do for the greater part of its existence, and it was demolished down to the level of the roadway. In its place an ornate timber framed house, made sectionally in Holland and shipped piecemeal to London, was raised.

The name Nonsuch, which it shared with a royal country house at Cheam, meant literally No-other-such-house. The uniqueness in this case being based on the claim that only wooden pegs, and no nails, were used in its construction. The towering bishop's throne in Exeter Cathedral was reputed to be similarly constructed, but there iron pins came to light when it was dismantled and taken to a place of safety during the Second World War.

Four storeys high, with large windows, pilasters and balustrades of Renaissance design, the south front was capped by an elaborate—typically Dutch—gable, like the stern of a galleon, while at each corner was a turret surmounted by a cupola and a weathervane. The whole house was painted, and if the cupolas were copper and therefore with a patina of green, the effect must have been as charming as it was unlikely.

Demolition of the New Stone Gateway meant a new place must be found for the poles bearing the heads of bygone traitors. At no time did the authorities miss the chance of reminding the man in the street what to expect if he let his allegiance wander, so they were removed to the top of the Great Stone Gate overlooking the Southwark bridge-foot. There they remained, a row of punctuation marks on London's skyline, until their final removal some time in the 1680s.

Since the rush of water beneath the bridge resembled a mill-race, that was the use to which it should be put. Such was the opinion of the Common Council of the City of London in 1559 when it ordered the setting up of three mill-wheels on the west side of the Surrey Shore and Borough Wheel Locks adjoining the south bank. Once these mills, powered by the rise and fall of the tide, were common, particularly along the east coast estuaries, but today only one, at Woodbridge, is still in working order. The others have been converted to more up-to-date methods, or simply allowed to fall derelict.

That was in 1559 that the corn mills were set up: in 1580 the ingenious Dutchman Peter Maurice, in the service of Sir Christopher Hatton, harnessed the river at the north end. After demonstrating the power of his new pumping apparatus by sending a jet of water right over the tower of St Magnus Martyr, perhaps sixty or seventy feet high, the authorities allowed him to undertake to pump water up the hill into the adjoining parts of the City: 'into divers men's houses in Thames Street, New Fish Street, and Grass Street, into the north west corner of Leadenhall, the highest ground in the City, where the waste of the main pipe rising into this standard [at the crossroads on Cornhill], provided at the charge of the City, with four spouts did at every tide run, according to covenant, four ways, plentifully serving to the commodity of the inhabitants near adjoining in their houses, and also cleansed the channels of the street towards Bishopsgate, Aldgate, the Bridge and the Stock Market.' The water was for household purposes; for drinking there were the conduits of 'sweet water' set up at convenient points throughout the City. As for the water carriers, they raised a great fuss, declaring they would be ruined by Maurice's invention, and made an unsuccessful attempt to stop the scheme. In fact so successful was the whole project that another wheel was added under the second arch from the north end. For this the Dutchman and his heirs were granted a lease of no less than five hundred years, at an annual rental of ten shillings.

Tourism may seem very much a product, not to say an industry, of the twentieth century, but as early as Tudor times travellers were coming to Britain not only on business but quite simply to see the sights. One such visitor was Paul Hentzner, tutor to a German nobleman, who made a quite thorough tour through England in 1598. Among the places he visited were Old St Paul's (p. 138), Westminster Abbey, the Tower and Whitehall Palace (p. 193). But first he and his companions rode over Old London Bridge after landing at Rye. Evidently Hentzner had a copy of Stow's *Survey of London* in his luggage, though by its size hardly in his pocket, and drew upon this Tudor Baedeker when he came to write his fascinating *Journey into England*.

For once, in the measurements of Old London Bridge, Stow was less than accurate, and Hentzner not unnaturally repeats the mistakes. 'On the South, is a bridge of stone 800 feet in length, of woodwork; it is supported upon 20 pillars of square stone, 60 feet high, and 30 feet broad, joined by arches of about 20 feet diameter. The whole is covered on each side with houses, so disposed, as to have the appearance of a continuous street, not at all of a bridge.' Then Hentzner continues with a personal observation: 'Upon this is built a tower on whose top the heads of such as have been executed for high treason, are placed on iron spikes: we counted above thirty.'

Most travellers stopped in their tracks on first glimpsing

the barbarous display—and started counting. Jacob Rathberg, a visitor in 1592, counted 'about 34', while ten years later the Duke of Stettin made it a round thirty. This aspect of Old London Bridge, it would seem, was the least subject to change.

Hentzner also mentions Maurice's water-wheels, and repeats Stow's mistake about his nationality: 'I shall say nothing of the Hall belonging to the Hans[a] Society; or the conveyance of water to all parts of the town by subterranean pipes; nor the beautiful conduits and cisterns for the reception of it, nor the rising water out of the Thames by a wheel invented a few years since by a German.'

The noise of these wheels, turning to grind corn at the southern end and to pump up water at the north, must have been maddening to anyone new to the bridge; but for the true inhabitant familiarity bred indifference. When the houses were finally demolished in the mid-eighteenth century one old man found he could not sleep in his new quarters for lack of noise. Just how noisy those wheels were, can be gathered from a casual reference that would have been understood by all play-goers watching a performance of Beaumont and Fletcher's *The Woman's Prize*. Remarks one of the characters, 'The noise of London Bridge is nothing to her'.

5

Now the years pass almost as swiftly as the river itself; though less turbulently. But in 1605–6 came the Gunpowder Plot and the sending to the bridge of Father Garnet's head after his execution in Paul's Churchyard (p. 140). After that the pages are blank until 1625 when Charles I and his French queen, Henrietta Maria, came from Gravesend. In drenching rain and a thunderstorm, the royal barge shot Old London Bridge as they made their way upstream to Somerset House, and later to Whitehall Palace where began the cat-and-dog existence of the early years of their married life (p. 210).

Eight years later the merchants and shopkeepers were jolted out of their placid routine when fire suddenly swept away half the houses on the north end of the bridge. John Briggs, a needlemaker whose house nearly adjoined St Magnus

Martyr, possessed a servant girl who was either very lazy, very stupid, or both. On the night of 11th February 1633—bitterly cold, and below the windows the Thames was starting to freeze over—she left a tub full of hot ashes under the stairs, and went off to bed. Not long after, about ten o'clock, fire swept through the house, and Briggs, his wife and child escaped only just in time. Within minutes the houses on the east side of the bridge were burning, and before long those opposite had ignited, making a crackling inferno of half the High Street.

By providence that part of the bridge adjoining the one-time chapel had never been built upon. In fact it was called The Square, and this gap of some thirty feet saved the remaining houses. Three fire engines brought up to tackle the blaze from the City end broke down, while since the tide was out there was practically no pressure in the pipes. In desperation the fire-fighters breached the conduits in Fish Street, and as the water flowed out, swept it down the hill towards the bridge. But these measures were futile against such a fire. Those approaching from the Southwark end were better equipped. The brewers brought out their drays which were loaded with anything capable of holding water. These were then driven on to the bridge, right up to The Square, to within a few feet of the blaze.

According to Nehremiah Wallington, a turner living in the City, many lives were lost, but he did not state how many. Although the worst was over by midday following, he has to write: 'Yet the timber, and the wood, and the coals in the cellars, could not be quenched all that week, till the Tuesday following, in the afternoon, the 19th February, for I was there myself, and had a live coal of fire in my hand, and burnt my finger with it. Notwithstanding there were as many night and day as could labour one by another, to carry away timber, and bricks, and tiles, and rubbish cast down into the lighters. So that on Wednesday the Bridge was cleared that passengers might go over.'

Although the flames must have reached to the walls of St Magnus Martyr, it was not damaged, and in her will a certain Susanna Chambers left twenty shillings, so that each year a sermon could be preached on the anniversary of the fire. In his

Anecdotes of Painting Walpole relates: 'The father [Harley] of the Lord Treasurer Oxford passing over London Bridge, was caught in a shower; and stepping into a goldsmith's shop for shelter, he found there a picture by Holbein—who had lived in that house—and his family. He offered the goldsmith £100 for it, who consented to let him have it, but desired first to show it to some persons. Immediately after, happened the fire of London, and the picture was destroyed.'

But when the story is examined closely there seems little doubt but that it is a picturesque fabrication. The painter is also supposed to have lived in the Holbein Gate over the road at Whitehall Palace (p. 174). Therefore if both accounts were true, Holbein would have spent one half of his life in London over a road, and half over a river. Anyway, it is known he did not live in the great gate at Whitehall. And Walpole speaks of the fire of London, presumably that of 1666, but in that case the painting would have been destroyed in the earlier disaster of 1633. A third point: presuming the reference was to the fire of 1666; Harley went into a goldsmith's shop to avoid rain. For days before the Great Fire the wind was blowing from the east, and all London was as dry as tinder through lack of rain. Finally; Nehremiah Wallington's account of the 1633 disaster includes a list of the names and trades of those whose shops and houses were destroyed. No goldsmith was numbered among them.

Even if the list demolishes Walpole's anecdote, it tells something of great interest; what was sold in nearly half the shops on the bridge. Eleven haberdashers (including two specializing in hats), six hosiers, one shoemaker, three sellers of silks, one milliner, two glovers, two mercers, one distiller of 'strong waters', one girdler, one linen draper, two woollen drapers, one seller of salt, two grocers, one needleworker, and one scrivener. Presumably the shops on the southern end of the bridge were much the same, so a fair idea can be gathered of this High Street, some three hundred yards in length.

Such was the variety of shops, that the inhabitants could satisfy almost all their daily needs without having to set foot in either Southwark or the City.

Rebuilding was slow, and by 1651 houses covered only the first two arches from the north end. Beyond that was a gap until The Square and the one-time chapel was reached. But this part of the bridge was not entirely open: on either side were hoardings ten feet high with six recesses or refuges for pedestrians, three on either side.

But before the rebuilding, such as it was, the bridge claimed its most notable victim; Mrs Kirke, a lady of the bedchamber to Henrietta Maria. A number of the court, including Mrs Kirke, were in the queen's barge when it overturned after hitting a log as it shot the bridge. Fortunately for her Henrietta Maria was not among the passengers. The entry for 6th July 1641 in Lord Cork's diary recorded the incident. 'This day Mrs Kirke was drowned coming through London Bridge; the Earl of Denbigh, and his daughter, my dear, dear daughter in law, the Lady Kynalmeaky through God's great providence and mercy being also cast away in the Thames were miraculously preserved; for which great delivery God make me and her ever thankful. Sir Fredrick Cornwallis his lady was saved.'

Mrs Kirke, painted by Van Dyck, was related to the Killigrew family, who occupied apartments at Whitehall Palace during Charles II's reign. Ann Killigrew, something of a poetess, recorded her aunt's death in couplets à la Dryden.

> 'When, angry Heav'n extinguish'd her fair light,
> It seem'd to say, Nought's precious in my sight;
> And I in Waves this paragon have drown'd,
> The nation next, the king I will confound.'

Her poems were not published until 1686, and the reference to Charles I would seem a case of hindsight. Presumably it was not written until after his execution in 1649.

August 1647 saw General Fairfax's troops dragging up guns and setting them in position against the closed gates of Old London Bridge, but no violence was needed. On 6th August the City opened its gates as he approached from the north-west, and next day his troops marched out again, over the bridge, on their way to Croydon. Within a year the Civil War flared up into its tragic last act, and for the last time in its recorded history, the gates on the bridge were closed against the threat of a hostile army—in this case the Royalists—who as it so happened never reached the capital. Now, on a cold January day Charles I went to his death outside Whitehall Palace, but on the bridge life went on as before. The shopkeepers and their customers discussed the unprecedented events, and while they may have thought killing the king an extreme measure, for the most part their sympathies lay with Parliament and its sober and holy outlook on life.

With the exception of the few houses, already mentioned, that were rebuilt at the north end of the bridge, nothing of interest happened during those eleven years before the Restoration. Then on 29th May 1660 all was excitement as the inhabitants—who by now had had more than enough of sobriety and piety—awaited the entry of Charles II into London.

The Lord Mayor, the aldermen and leading citizens met the King at St George's Fields, and after refreshments served in a tent set up near the southern end of the bridge, the procession formed up for the great moment. At the head went three hundred gentlemen in cloth of silver, and three hundred soldiers in velvet: then more and yet more troops; two trumpeters; the Sheriff's men; representatives of the City Companies and their men, the latter carrying streamers, trumpets and drums. Next came the Life Guards, the City Marshal, the two City of London sheriffs, aldermen, the Mace, the Lord Mayor resplendent in his new knighthood and carrying the Sword of London unsheathed before the King—a great privilege that—then the brilliant opportunist General Monck; the Duke of York (later James II) and the unmemorable Duke of Gloucester.

As might be expected royal vengeance was not long in catching up with the Regicides; those who signed Charles I's death warrant. On 20th October 1660 Pepys wrote '. . . a bloody week this and the last have been, there being ten hanged, drawn and quartered.' But with the execution of Thomas Venner and a number of the Fifth Monarchy Men, all members of that fanatical religious sect, the use of the Great Stone Gate for the display of heads was nearly a thing of the past.

Pepys's *Diary* contains many references to the bridge, and to those he knew who had the courage to admit they could not, or would not, face shooting it in a frail little boat.

25th March 1661. 'Come Mr Salisbury to see me, and showed me a face or two of his painting, and indeed I perceive that he will be a great master. I took him to Whitehall with me by water, but could not by any means be moved to go through the bridge; and we were fain to go round by the Old Swan.'

In another entry, 15th June 1664, the bridge appears as the one blot on an otherwise perfect outing. After what must have been an excellent lunch at Pepys's house in the City, he, his wife, Mr Creed from the Tangier Office and the three young daughters of Lord Sandwich (Pepys's kinsman and patron), the party set out on an excursion: ' . . . and about five o'clock by water down to Greenwich; and up to the top of the hill, and there played upon the ground at cards. And so to the Cherry Garden and then by water singing finely to the Bridge, and there landed; and so took boat again (after walking round the north end) and to Somerset House, and by this time, the tide being against us, it was past ten of the clock; and such a troublesome passage in regard to my Lady Paulina's fearfulness, that in all my life I never did see any poor wretch in that condition.'

Pepys did not share such qualms: on more than one occasion he climbed up on to the starlings around one of the piers, walked under the bridge, and then when the watermen had brought his boat through, re-entered it. For all that his wife was French (a tavern on Fish Street Hill overlooking the bridge had been the scene of their wedding breakfast during the Commonwealth) Pepys bore little love for her compatriots, and on 8th August 1662 he recorded with just a touch of malice this story: ' . . . it being rough, he (Mr Falconer) told me the passage of a Frenchman through London Bridge, where, when he saw the great fall, he begun to cross himself, and say his prayers in the greatest fear in the world, and soon as he was over, he swore, "Morbleu! C'est le plus grand plaisir du monde", being the most like a French humour in the world.'

Nor are references to going over the bridge absent. In the entry for 26th October 1664 he sheds light on the deplorable condition of the roadway, and also mentions a traffic hold-up: an everyday occurrence. That particular day he had attended the launching at Woolwich of the *Royal Catharine*, and watched the interesting spectacle of the Duchess of Buckingham being seasick in a small boat. 'Dark when we come to London, and a stop of coaches in Southwark. Into the Bear, at the Bridge foot, to Sir William Batten. Presently the stop is removed, and there going out to find my coach, I could not find it: so I was fain to go through the dark and dirt over the bridge, and fell in a hole broke on the bridge, but, the constable standing there to keep people from it, I was catched up, otherwise I had broke my leg: for which mercy the Lord be praised!' Presumably the hole was in the wooden part where once the drawbridge had been.

A few months later, when feeling very under the weather, Pepys visited the Bear and drank sherry. During a time of deadly peril the diarist's good angel kept him from harm: the Great Plague. The Court and all the well-to-do had fled for safety into the country (p. 240), while in the City the poor and the small shopkeepers who could not leave their homes and businesses, died in their thousands. Pepys sent his household into the country, and only when the Navy Office was removed out of London did he himself leave. Those who lived on the bridge, perhaps the healthiest place, were luckier than most in the stricken City. According to a statement made by one Thomas Soaper, an apothecary on the bridge, only two of the inhabitants died during the summer of 1665. If so it is remarkable.

Again, when London was hit by its second disaster, fire, the bridge was fortunate by comparison. Faryners, the King's baker—where it all began—was only a few yards from St Magnus Martyr. By breakfast time on Sunday, 2nd September 1666, three hundred houses, the church, all Fish Street and the few houses rebuilt on the northern end of the bridge, were all ablaze.

Pepys made his way to the Tower, '. . . and there I did see

the houses at that end of the bridge all on fire, and an infinite great fire on this and the other side of the bridge; which among other people, did trouble me for poor little Mitchell and our Sarah on the bridge'. At one time 'our Sarah' had been a maid in his household; not to say one of his numerous infidelities. 'So I down to the waterside, and there got a boat, and through bridge, and there saw a lamentable fire. Poor Mitchell's house, as far as the Old Swan, already burned that way, and the fire running further, that, in a very little time, it got as far as the Steele-yard, while I was there. Everybody endeavouring to remove their goods, and flinging into the river, or bringing them into lighters that lay off; poor people staying in their houses as long as till the very fire touched them, and then running into boats, or clambering from one pair of stairs, by waterside, to another. And among other things, the poor pigeons, I perceive, were loth to leave their houses, but hovered about the windows and balconies, till they burned their wings, and fell down. Having stayed, and in an hour's time seen the fire rage every way; and nobody, to my sight, endeavouring to quench it, but to remove their goods, and leave all to the fire. . . . I to Whitehall (p. 241).'

Because of the gap left by the earlier fire of 1633, the remainder of the Tudor superstructure of the bridge survived at a time when nearly all medieval London was like a vast funeral pyre, with the great cathedral at its centre (p. 153).

Dryden did not forget the bridge and its relics when writing his *Annus Mirabilis*:

> 'The ghosts of traitors from the bridge descend,
> With bold frantic spectres to rejoice;
> About the fire into a dance they blend,
> And sing their Sabbath notes with feeble voice.'

But though the houses were to survive for almost another century, there were those even then who wished to see them swept away: Wren and Evelyn among them. Before the ashes of the old city were cold Wren presented himself at Whitehall Palace (10th September), with his plan for a magnificent and spacious successor.

(1) To let the Royal Exchange on its existing site stand free.

(2) Give to St Paul's the significance which the metropolitan cathedral required.

(3) Improve the bad communications with London Bridge.

(4) Clear the river bank from the Temple to the Tower and construct thereon a broad public quay.'

Needless to say none of this ever came about.

Although what was burnt at the north end of the bridge was not great, the falling debris was sufficient to block the twelve-foot-wide street completely; so cutting off help from Southwark. If Southwark was to escape with only two houses and a stable fired by flying embers carried across the river, its turn came in a fire that raged around the bridge foot on 26th May 1676. Among the buildings destroyed was the White Hart, where Jack Cade put up during his rising of 1450, Chaucer's Tabard Inn and the predecessor of the present George, London's sole remaining galleried inn.

But to return just once again to the mid-1660s and Samuel Pepys. 24th February 1667: 'Going through bridge by water, my waterman told me how the mistress of the Bear Tavern, at the bridge foot, did lately fling herself into the Thames, and drowned herself, which did trouble me the more, when they tell me it was she that did live at the White Horse tavern in Lumbard Street, which was a most beautiful woman, as most I have seen. It seems she hath had long melancholy upon her, and hath endeavoured to make away with herself often.'

By 1671 houses once again occupied both sides of the bridge, from the new St Magnus Martyr, designed by Wren, to The Square, just short of the Chapel House. But instead of being built half on, half off the bridge, the new houses almost entirely overhung the river. This meant that for half its length the roadway was nearly twenty feet wide; a great improvement. Now the superstructure extended downwards, below the road level, allowing the houses additional cellar space. This growth hid the tops of the pointed arches, giving a stunted, not to say top-heavy appearance which, from an aesthetic point of view, compared unfavourably with the older Tudor portion which still remained much as it had been in the time of Elizabeth I.

Little by little Old London Bridge was ceasing to be a fashionable address for well-to-do merchants, who now preferred to live right outside the City and its confines. Only eight were listed as living on the bridge in *A Collection of the names of the Merchants living in and about London*, printed in 1677. Another change that took place about this time was an end to the placing of heads on the Great Stone Gate. The last may have belonged to William Stayley, executed as a result of the monstrous Popish Plot, in November 1682. 'A Prospect of London', engraved about that year by Robert Morden, shows some eighteen skulls, many of which must have been there twenty years and more.

On a number of occasions in the past, the Thames had been completely frozen over; notably in 1565 when people treated it as a road, and before that in 1282 when melting ice destroyed five arches of the bridge. But in 1684 the Londoners seized the opportunity to enliven the bitter and lengthy winter by holding a Frost Fair. For six weeks, from the beginning of January the river between the Temple Stairs and the bridge resembled a fairground, complete with all the attractions of the day. That meant a bull ring, a puppet show, racing with horses and carriages, skating—a sport made popular in England by those Royalists who spent their exile in Holland—ale houses, ox-roasting and printing presses. How one shares with Pepys his regret that in 1669 defective eyesight forced him to give up his diary. His account of the Frost Fair would have been infinitely worth having. He possessed that blessed gift of humanity which Evelyn, with his fastidious, almost over-cultured mind, lacked. But Evelyn it must be. Although he censures the 'tippling and other lewd places', he tells something of the printing presses. 'The people and the ladies took a fancy to have their names printed, and the day and year set down when printed on the Thames: this humour took so universally, that it is estimated the printer gained £5 a day for printing one line only, at sixpence a name, besides what he got by ballards etc:'

Before long Charles II and all the Court came to sample the pleasures of the fair, and were not above having their names printed by 'G. Croom, on the ICE on the River Thames, January 31st. 1684.'

Printers on the ice may have been a novelty, but by this date the printing of books on Old London Bridge was a commonplace. Bookseller's shops were fairly numerous: with signs like the Sun and Bible, the Angel or the Seven Stars. Nearly all shops still had signs as well as the owner's name and what he sold. The Roe-buck and the Hand of Beads indicated a leather-seller and a necklace maker respectively. Others had about them the ring of a tavern sign. But in reality the Sceptre and Heart made and sold surgical instruments, while the Blue Boar specialized in toys and hardwear.

Among other trades carried on in the hundred years between 1650 and 1750 were a brushmaker, cork seller, breeches maker, map seller, rope maker, stationer, and instrument maker.

All the while as the centuries passed, the bridge continued to take its toll of human life. Hundreds must have died by accident in the boiling, eddying waters, but on 14th April 1689 John Temple, son of a diplomat, evidently felt himself a failure, incapable of managing his recent appointment as Secretary of War—together with the treachery of a friend who had gone over to the exiled James II in Ireland—and emulated the hostess of the Bear Inn by deliberately drowning himself. After loading his pockets with stones he hired a boat, and as it shot the bridge, jumped overboard, leaving a pathetic note: 'My folly in undertaking what I could not perform, whereby some misfortunes have befallen the king's service, is the cause of my putting myself to this sudden end. I wish him (William III) success in all his undertakings, and a better servant.'

And with that the seventeenth century, which saw such radical alterations to the northern half of the bridge, came to a close without further incident.

6

'London Bridge is broken down,
Gold is won, and bright renown;'

so wrote Ottar Svarte after the wrecking of the wooden bridge in 1014.

'London Bridge is broken down,
Dance o'er it with my lady lee,
London Bridge is broken down,
With a gay lady;'

sang a girl in Charles II's reign, though her version of the rhyme was not written down until 1753, towards the end of her long life. Another version refers to a 'fair lady', but how old was the song by the seventeenth century? Was there a direct link with Svarte's poem of 1014? Nothing is certain, but in each case the first line is the same, and in fairness to Old London Bridge the falls occurred comparatively early in its history. On only two occasions, in 1282 and 1437, was the actual stonework breached: fire was responsible for the other disasters. The real anxiety lay in the unceasing struggle to keep the piers stable, with the resultant growth to enormous size, of the starlings as more and yet more piles were driven in. Old London Bridge certainly fared better with only two breaches than its celebrated rival at Avignon. There in 1430 nearly half that bridge was broken down; carried away by the fierce current of the Rhône, and never rebuilt.

To return to the rhyme: sometimes 'lady lee' is given as 'lady Lea'. The origin of the name is obscure, but both versions seem equally authentic. The 'lady lee' version, the one reputed to be current in Charles II's time, was reprinted in the *Gentleman's Magazine* in 1823, while 'lady Lea' appeared as early as 1760 in a book amusingly called *Gammer Gurton's Garland: or the Nursery Parnassus. Gammer Gurton's Needle* is the title of one of the earliest English stage comedies.

Cutting out the innumerable repetitions, the *Nursery Parnassus* version runs:

'London Bridge is broken down
Dance o'er my lady lea:
London Bridge is broken down
With a gay lady.
How shall we build it up again?

Build it up with silver and gold.
Silver and gold will be stole away,
Build it up with iron and steel:
Iron and steel will bend and bow,
Build it up with wood and clay,
Wood and clay will wash away,
Build it up with stone so strong,
Dance o'er my lady lea.
Huzza! t'will last for ages long,
With a gay lady.'

The Charles II version (for want of a better name) varies the order of the suggested building materials, and includes additional inane—or should it be picturesque—ideas.

'Silver and gold will be stolen away:
Then we must set a man to watch,
Suppose the man should fall asleep;
Then we must put a pipe in his mouth:
Suppose the pipe should fall and break;
Then we must set a dog to watch.
Suppose the dog should run away;
Then we must chain him to a post.'

Could it be that 'lady lea' or 'lee' was not a person at all, but the River Lea. In the fourteenth century the wardens of London Bridge were also responsible for two of the bridges over that little river. Does 'Dance o'er (London Bridge) my lady lea' refer to some obscure connection between the two structures? Possibly concerning building materials—like 'robbing Peter to pay Paul' (p. 127).

By the early part of the eighteenth century fire and alterations had completely obliterated the characteristic appearance dating from Tudor times. For the most part the picturesque assortment of gables had given way to uniform roofs topped by balustrades, and—an unusual and pleasant innovation—roof gardens. Now Nonsuch House, the pride of the bridge in Elizabeth I's reign, had come down in the world. The cupolas had disappeared and no doubt it sadly needed a coat of paint.

'Behold the Liquid Thames now frozen o're,
That lately ships of mighty Burthen bore.
The Watermen for want of Rowing boats,
Make use of Booths to get their pence and Groats.
Here you may print your Name,
tho' cannot write,
'Cause numb'd with Cold;
'tis done with great delight.
Then lay it by, that Ages yet to come,
May see what Things upon the Ice were done.'

It would seem that through the ages Old London Bridge had inspired enough verse, some bad and some indifferent, to fill a slim volume. In this particular case another Frost Fair was being commemorated, and the rhymster was nearer the mark than he could ever have realized in the last two lines. This particular card was laid by, and the now arrived 'Ages yet to come' can see 'what things upon the Ice were done'. It is on view in the London Museum.

The winter of 1715–16 was bitter, and this time the fair seems to have been held nearer the bridge than on the earlier occasion in 1684. The souvenir card with the verse just quoted has at the top a cartouche containing the purchaser's name, one Mrs Mary Malkinson, and underneath: 'Printed on the Ice, at the Maidenhead at Old Swan Stairs, Jan. 2. 1715–16.'

The Old Swan Stairs, taking their name from a nearby tavern, was the upstream landing place for those unwilling to shoot the bridge, and for this very special event a press had been brought from a printing house in Bow Church yard. The illustration is of little interest from an architectural point of view, but the happenings in the foreground give a fair idea of the pleasures to be found on the ice. Near the bridge a circle of spectators watch a game of ninepins, while another looks on at 'Cripple Atkins roasting an Ox'. Everywhere are booths, primitive canvas tents with a sign hanging from the ridge pole. At the sign of the Rat in a Cage a shoulder of mutton is roasting, while in other booths the visitor could find music, a goldsmith, taverns—one selling only gin—and a gingerbread stall. An important figure is 'Will Ellis, the Poet, and his wife Bess, Rhyming on the hard Frost'.

Now it is the timbers of the drawbridge that in 1722 are giving trouble, and for a short while the bridge was closed to traffic while they were replaced. In Malcolm's *Anecdotes of London Manners* he relates how the shopkeepers brought out tables and chairs into the High Street, and caroused away an afternoon; so in later years they could boast how they sat and drank punch in the middle of London Bridge. And by that date the bridge must have been the most congested area in all London, in spite of three men employed to keep the traffic on the move and also see it kept to its own, the left side of the road.

In 1698 a careless servant had destroyed Whitehall Palace by fire, and in 1725 another started a blaze at the Southwark end of the bridge which destroyed not only the houses over the first two arches, but so severely calcined the Great Stone Gate that a complete rebuilding was necessary. Two octagonal turrets arose in its place, surmounted by ball-shaped finials, between them a round-headed archway with a room above. The arms of George II were placed on the southern side, and above a clock surmounting the battlements completed the not very inspiring design.

Slowly but surely Old London Bridge was on the decline, both architecturally and socially. Prosperous merchants no longer lived there, and many of the houses were let as cheap lodgings. What had once been a wonder of the medieval world was fast becoming a pontine slum. Towards the end of the century the historian Pennant looked back to his youth and wrote: 'I well remember the street on London Bridge, narrow, darksome, and dangerous to passengers from the multitude of carriages: frequent arches and strong timber crossed the street, from the tops of the houses, to keep them together, and from falling into the river. Nothing but use could preserve the rest of the inmates, who soon grew deaf to the noise of falling waters, the clamours of the watermen, of the frequent shrieks of the drowning wretches.'

The loss of life which gave rise to the saying that London

Bridge was built for wise men to go over and fools to go under was horrifying. But since the casualties came in ones, twos or threes, they never really made news in the accepted sense. By the mid-eighteenth century watermen and others were being drowned or killed in one way or another at the rate of fifty a year. In the hundred years between 1650 and 1750, 5,000 lives could well have been lost. If that figure is reduced by half in each of the preceding centuries to take into account the smaller population, the figures are: 1550–1650 2,500; 1450–1550 1,250; 1350–1450 675; 1250–1350 337; and in the years back to 1176 another 250 lives, at least, could be added to take into account the undoubtedly heavy loss of life during the building of the bridge. That makes a total of no less than 10,013 lives lost during six centuries, and the story of the bridge is not yet at an end.

Nor were the only casualties beneath the bridge. In 1752 a young man died from injuries after being caught between two carts going in opposite directions, while six years later a woman and her child were killed in a similar accident.

The pace of the traffic may have been slow, but then as now, a pedestrian needed all his wits about him if he wished to stay alive. This continual loss of life provided ammunition for those in favour of the bridge's replacement who considered the authorities dilatory in taking action. *The Quarterly Review* delivered a slap at the city fathers: 'Had an alderman or a turtle been lost there', wrote the editor, 'the nuisance would have been long removed.'

There was no denying it: the sad fact was London Bridge was fast becoming out of date: a bottleneck above and a death-trap below. Even in decline it was still an astonishing structure, heavier in outline than in former times, when its roofs were enlivened with little cupolas and glittering weathervanes. Now twenty years of life remained for the houses.

In 1740 the inhabitants living on the west side of the bridge looked out on yet another Frost Fair. This time the ice broke up unexpectedly early, and the booths still standing on the floes piled in confusion against the piers and starlings of the bridge, but before they could find their way through and down to the sea, the ice froze again and their owners were able to retrieve their property.

During those last years of decline, a number of artists could be numbered among the tenants. The earliest of the group was the Channel Islander, Peter Monamy, who about 1685 was apprenticed to a sign painter on the bridge. From these humble beginnings Peter graduated to seascapes, and after 1730 was himself painted by Hogarth—exhibiting one of his seascapes to his patron, Mr Walker. The second artist was yet another of French origin: John Laguerre, son of the Louis Laguerre who among other commissions had added frescoes in that part of Hampton Court Palace built by William of Orange.

Evidently John lacked his father's not over-distinguished talents: before long he threw down his brushes, took to acting and in 1748 died a pauper. The third was Dominick Serres, a Frenchman who ran away to sea and was brought a prisoner of war to the Marshalsea Prison in 1758 during the Seven Years War. On his release he set up shop on the bridge; exhibiting for sale his seascapes. At the longest Serres can only have been there a matter of months before demolition forced him to move to an undeniably better address: Piccadilly. The year before his death (1793) he became Marine Painter to George III, and Librarian to the Royal Academy. But the most famous of the artists was William Hogarth (1697–1764), though the foundation for adding his name to those of the bridge-dwellers seems almost as shaky as some of the foundations of the bridge itself. Apparently he lived on the first floor on the east side of the bridge near the Southwark end; in the rooms later occupied by Laguerre, which shook as the tide raced beneath. Also to an artist, the continual clatter of the mill-wheels must surely have been destructive to any real concentration. Hogarth painted the bridge, or at least a glimpse of it, as seen through an open window in 'The Death of the Countess', part of the 'Marriage à la Mode' series, painted about 1744.

It fell to the architect George Dance the Elder to design the last houses built on the bridge. And extremely ugly they were too. Evidently the houses and shops built after the fire of 1633 were already dilapidated by 1745, the year of their replacement. If the outer faces were bald and uninteresting, the inner fronts had the advantage of a colonnade at street level, behind which was a footway for pedestrians. These colonnades were reminiscent of those surrounding the square at Covent Garden, so they too were christened the Piazzas.

What was perhaps the worst traffic jam in the whole history of the bridge, was caused on 27th April 1749 by Mr Handel and his music for the royal fireworks! The rehearsal in Vauxhall Gardens on the south bank was public, and afterwards, the huge crowd returning to the City completely blocked the bridge for three hours. Those who attended the rehearsal had the best of it. At the actual performance in Green Park, to celebrate the peace of Aix-la-Chapelle, the fireworks set all alight, including the music stands.

Now, halfway through the eighteenth century, a number of the older houses on the east side towards Southwark had sagged as much as eighteen inches, and were tilting outwards over the river. Again Dance was called in, this time to survey the whole bridge and decide on its future. All the houses and gateways were to be demolished, the width of the road increased to at least forty-two feet, and the two arches nearest the centre thrown together, giving a span of over fifty feet.

On 25th June 1756 an Act came into force allowing the Common Council of the City to buy and demolish the houses, and impose a toll to help defray the cost of alteration, estimated at £160,000. For those days the charge was high. Coaches drawn by six horses, paid 2s.; 4 horses 1s. 6d.; less than that 1s.; while horses, mules, and asses being used as pack animals were charged at 1d. each, and pedestrians at ½d., though on Sundays this went up to 1d. Not only the road traffic, but the boats passing beneath were charged. Up to 5 tons, 2d.; up to 10 tons, 3d.; up to 25 tons, 6d.; over that, 1s.

The first step in the transformation was the erection of a temporary bridge along the west side: to carry the traffic during the actual demolition and widening. But then there was a setback. Late on the night of 11th April 1760, the wooden bridge burst into flames. The circumstances seem curious—too curious for it to have been an accident, but although a reward of £200 was offered, the nearest the authorities came to solving the mystery was a statement by one Mrs John Dennys. In this she declared that shortly before the fire broke out she saw lanterns, three of them, moving about near the chapel pier. Within minutes the timbers burst into flames. Could it have been bridge-dwellers, disgruntled at having to leave, revenging themselves on the authorities in this spiteful way? Whatever the cause, the temporary bridge was completely destroyed, but strangely enough none of the remaining houses on the old structure went up in the fire. When a new wooden bridge was completed in October of the same year it was guarded at first by five armed watermen in a boat, and later by two watchmen who patrolled up and down on a gallery built just below the roadway.

Soon the houses were crumbling beneath the picks of the demolition workers, and this was when two separate hoards of gold and silver coins of Elizabeth I's reign were discovered. Only the upper part of the chapel was demolished, leaving about half the undercroft below the level of the roadway intact for another seventy years. During the breaking up of Peter of Colechurch and Henry Yevele's work, the font came to light. By some miracle it had survived the defacing in Edward VI's reign, but unfortunately its re-emergence into the light of day was all too brief. Apart from one reference in the *London Chronicle* of 14th August 1760, it has vanished into the obscurity from whence it came. The loss is the greater as evidently it was one of those imported during the twelfth century from an *atelier* in Tournai which specialized in these black marble fonts and incised grave slabs. Today there are four in Hampshire, two in Lincolnshire and one in Suffolk.

Soon Nonsuch House and the Southwark Gate belonged to the past, though the royal coat of arms from the latter was saved. Originally set up in 1728, when George II was on the throne, they are carved 'George III 1760'. It seems what happened was this: the owner of the nearby King's Arms bought them in 1760, the year of George III's coronation, and had the new cypher and date added before it was set in place on the front of his own tavern. Now, with the demolition of the King's

Arms itself, the carving from Old London Bridge must once again find a new home. Some of the building materials from the houses on the bridge were re-used on new sites. A number of the pillars which supported Dance's colonnade went to decorate the front of Garrick's new villa at Hampton on Thames, while the iron railings from The Square went to the churchyard of St Botolph's, Aldgate, where they are to this day.

By 1762 the last shop was closed, the last tenant, one John Evans, had moved elsewhere and all was levelled. Among those shops above the Thames, now gone for ever, the Blue Boar in particular must have been fascinating. There Coles Child once sold almost anything: packing needles, buttons of all kinds, slate pencils, slate books, tooth-pick cases, tooth brushes, snuff boxes, Jew's harps, squirrel chains, whalebone stays, fountain pens, powder puffs, chocolate mills, powder horns, dog collars, hawk bells, fire bellows, bibles, primers, English and Dutch toys, children's trumpets, marbles and marble alleys; brass, tin, lead, pewter and wood toys: 'sold wholesale or Retail at Reasonable Rates'.

Not only was the bridge undergoing alterations at this time: in 1763 the authorities turned their attention to St Magnus Martyr. Because of the church's front the approach down Fish Street Hill to the bridge was extremely narrow; too narrow in fact for a pavement on the east side. So the westernmost bays of the aisles which projected on either side of the tower itself were docked off, leaving the tower only joined to the church on its east side. Two archways were opened in its north and south fronts, and there, running under the tower itself, was a way for pedestrians.

Soon London Bridge stood forth, cleared of its superstructure, and the medieval work completely enclosed in the new masonry added on either side to give the additional width required for the roadway. For the first time it could be seen that Peter of Colechurch's masterpiece was not absolutely level from one end to the other, but rose slightly to an apex, such as it was, at the chapel pier. Of the arches, eighteen retained their original pointed outline, while the one made by throwing two together was semicircular. In place of massive abutments the piers were decorated with panels with Gothic details, capped above the stone balustrade by wrought-iron lamps, in addition to fourteen massive stone alcoves fronting the roadway: seven on either side. Almost the only things not altered in this upheaval were the water-wheels, now occupying four of the arches at the north end.

The throwing together of two arches to give boats at least one reasonably wide opening was not without its drawbacks. Now, instead of running in almost equal volume through all the arches, the river was drawn in a cataract through the fifty-foot opening. Not only was it dangerous to craft, but there was hardly sufficient power to turn the water-wheels. Also, the current was scouring away the river bed at an alarming rate, undermining the starlings and threatening the stability of the piers.

Wisely, the authorities called in the man who perhaps knew as much as anyone about building in tidal waters: John Smeaton, designer of the newly completed Eddystone Lighthouse. Smeaton advised the dumping of a large quantity of rubble under and on either side of the central arch. This, he said, would check the current from eroding away more of the river bed, to say nothing of loosening the starlings.

For this purpose three of the recently demolished City gates were used: the seventeenth-century Cripplegate and Aldgate, and the Tudor Ludgate. It is a curious thought that today all craft coming up the Thames pass over what were the principal land gates of the City, now sunk deep into the mud. Evidently Smeaton's advice was sound, for apart from damage to the starlings caused by ice the following winter, the force of the current caused no further trouble.

By a paradox, although the bridge had been cleared of the encumbrances to the roadway, those in the river were increased when another arch at the north end was blocked by water wheels, making five in all, and in 1767 two more were added at the southern end, for the benefit of pumping water into Southwark. Now, as might be expected, since London Bridge had simply become a convenient way of getting from A to B in the shortest possible time and distance, its history dwindled to nothing.

7

On 30th October 1763 Dr Johnson added his name to the long list of those who preferred to disembark at Old Swan Stairs, walk round the end of the bridge, and then rejoin his boat: in this case taking him on a day's excursion to Greenwich. While from time to time the occasional pick-pocket and handkerchief-snatcher, common pests in the eighteenth century, plied their trade among unwary pedestrians on the bridge.

Frost Fairs during exceptionally severe winters enlived the scene above the bridge from time to time: in 1763, 1767, 1785, and 1814. But with the demolition of London Bridge in 1831–2, the flow of the river was speeded up, with the result that only on rare occasions has the Thames frozen over on its course past the City.

Slowly but surely the number of voices clamouring for the complete replacement of the bridge increased, despite the numerous prophecies of woe and disaster that would come from allowing the river to ebb and flow unhindered in its course. No longer was London Bridge the sole link between the north and south banks of the Thames. As far back as 1664 a bridge at Westminster had been mooted, but the City, fearing a loss in trade if it was built, offered Charles II £100,000—as a loan of course—to ensure the plan came to nothing. The plan came to nothing. Although the idea was revived in 1722, it was not until 1749 that the predecessor of the present bridge was built, to the fury of the watermen operating along that stretch of the river.

Now the days of the old bridge were numbered. In 1821 a Committee of the House of Commons selected a design by John Rennie Senior, and a grant of £150,000 was made towards the cost. But before the actual work could begin there were a number of legal formalities to be cleared up. Had the lease granted to Peter Maurice and his heirs by the City run its full course, that family would continue to receive payment until 2082. However, in 1701 the family had sold out to one Richard Soames, who turned it into a company; so now it is to these heirs that the Metropolitan Water Board pays £3,750 per annum in accordance with an Act passed in 1822 by which it was possible to remove the wheels under the bridge.

For the third time in its history London Bridge was rising on a new site. First came the timber bridge of Saxon and Norman times; then a few feet to the west the medieval stone bridge rose out of the tide, and now, one hundred feet still further to the west Rennie's masterpiece was to be built. With a great deal of ceremony the Duke of York laid the first stone on 15th June 1825, and six years later, on 1st August 1831, it was opened by the new king, William IV, accompanied by Queen Adelaide. Five great arches spanned the Thames, and including the wide approaches, the cost had been £1,840,438 and the lives of forty workmen. All that now remained was to demolish its six hundred and twenty-eight-year-old predecessor. For thirty-three years the medieval masons had laboured and sweated to link London with the south-east: now within twelve months their descendants had demolished the patched, rebuilt, added to and altered bridge, leaving only the starlings, like stepping stones. Soon they too had vanished.

On two occasions a night of fire saw the destruction of Whitehall Palace and Old St Paul's, but there was no drama in the last chapter of Old London Bridge. There is no grandeur in the piecemeal whittling away of the bridge: first shorn of its houses and then finally demolished. The stonework was sold for building purposes. Part of the balustrade went to enclose the approach to the pier at Herne Bay; two of the stone refuges found their way to Victoria Park in East London, while a third was moved into the courtyard of Guy's Hospital. With the exception of the medieval stone core these relics dated only from the eighteenth century. Much older is the sculptured shield bearing the three leopards of the Plantagenets with two angels as supporters, which now forms the keystone of the tower arch in Merstham parish church, after coming into the possession of the Rev. W. Jolliffe of Merstham House, one of the contractors of the new bridge.

But even in 1832 Old London Bridge had not been entirely demolished. One arch remained on the north bank, though completely hidden by buildings. Briefly it came to light in 1920 during the erection of Adelaide House on a site between St Magnus Martyr and the river. £7,000 was needed to save it *in situ*, but the money was not forthcoming, so the last of the bridge ceased to exist.

What of Peter himself? All through the centuries he had remained with his bridge, buried in the undercroft of the chapel. Then in 1832 the picks and crowbars of the demolition workers came smashing through the stone floor to where 'an enclosure had evidently been built up in a small course of firestone, to contain a person of middle stature' (*Gentleman's Magazine*). A fitting end to the whole story would be to record that Peter of Colechurch was reburied in St Magnus Martyr, as Henry Yevele had been in the pre-Great Fire church. But that was not to be. Without doubt the workmen sent him to join the river above which he had lain, through fire and flood, for six and a half centuries.

Old St Paul's

(The Church)

1

If the seventh-century inhabitants of London had not been such thoroughgoing pagans, today St Paul's and not Canterbury might be the seat of the Primate of All England. In A.D. 597 St Augustine landed in Thanet at the bidding of Gregory the Great, with the intention of converting—and in some cases re-converting—the Saxon English. In Kent King Ethelbert's wife, a Christian Frank, made his work easier, but in London the missionaries found themselves up against sturdy opposition. So Canterbury it was that became the Saint's headquarters; a temporary stay that has lasted until the present time. St Gregory himself wanted London to be the centre of England's religious life.

But at least by 604, conditions in the City had improved sufficiently for St Augustine to ordain a monk named Mellitus as its first bishop.

What buildings originally stood on the top of the hill in the centre of the old Roman city is still uncertain, but by 610 the now Christian King Ethelbert had built London's first cathedral on the site. There is no direct evidence that the site was ever occupied by a temple of Diana, but to earlier generations who believed the tradition, the dedication to St Paul was doubly appropriate. Not only was St Paul the Apostle of the Gentiles, but it was he who denounced the worship of Diana at her famous temple at Ephesus.

Mellitus was succeeded by Cedd, after the see lay vacant for over forty years—thanks to the pagans. In 654, the year of his installation as Bishop of London, he travelled by boat from Northumberland to convert the still pagan East Anglians. Where he landed at Bradwell in Essex, he founded a chapel on the foundations of the once great Roman fort of Othona. Today the first St Paul's has vanished as though it never was, but St Cedd's little chapel, simple and barnlike, still stands within a few yards of the sea at high tide.

The most notable of London's early bishops was Erkenwald, who about the year 675 became the fourth in succession to Mellitus. During his lifetime he did much for his cathedral, but as a saint after his death he helped it even more. During the Middle Ages his shrine became one of the great pilgrimage centres of England, comparable with Thomas à Becket's tomb at Canterbury, and that of St Cuthbert at Durham.

St Erkenwald and his sister St Ethelburga were the children of Offa, King of the East Angles. In addition to founding the Abbey of Chertsey in Surrey, he was co-founder with his sister of the Abbey at Barking. In the centuries to come the Abbess received the privilege of taking precedence over all the other heads of religious houses in England. About the death of the Bishop-saint there is a story, as recounted by the historian Newcourt, which would surely have appealed to Alphonse Daudet. 'There was great struggling after his death between the Canons of St Paul's and the monks of Chertsey, both challenging the body to be buried with them, but in the mean-time the people of London took away the body, and caused it to be buried in his own cathedral, where it was interred in the nave.'

By the beginning of the eleventh century there had been twenty-eight bishops at St Paul's. Of more than one it would be tactful to record he 'had transmitted nothing to posterity but his name'. Indeed, it is all that can be said. But some were of the calibre of St. Dunstan. After only a year at St Paul's the future saint became Archbishop of Canterbury. That was in 959. Two years later the cathedral (St Paul's) was burnt and rebuilt after the first of the three great fires marking the course of its history.

Among the most generous of the early benefactors was King Athelstan, crowned 924, who made over nine manors in Essex; two each in Hertfordshire and Middlesex, and one in Surrey. Many of the Saxon kings chose to be buried in the old capital at Winchester, but two who moved with the times and were interred in St Paul's were Sebba, buried 695, and Ethelred the Unready. After ruling for thirty years Sebba put down the sceptre, and 'laying aside all worldly greatness, assumed the habit of religion in this church'.

At his coronation St Dunstan told Ethelred he could foresee a reign full of misery and suffering. He did not live to see the prophecy fulfilled, but the reign was certainly miserable, both for Ethelred and his unfortunate subjects, and by the time of his death in 1017 his throne was occupied by the Danish Canute of seashore fame. The tombs of these two Saxon kings remained in the cathedral, though not in their original positions, until the overwhelming disaster of 1666.

In 1044 Edward the Confessor made a Norman, Robert of Jumièges, Bishop of London; and in 1051 he was succeeded by another, Bishop William. With the Conquest came a wave of church-building such as England had never known before. Thanks to the skilled architect-masons of Normandy, the Romanesque style crystallized with particular speed in that corner of France—in the great Abbey of Jumièges (begun 1040), and in the two abbeys at Caen. This then was the architecture, already mature at the time of the Conquest, that was to transform the cathedrals and churches of England. But even before 1066 it would have been familiar to Londoners: the Francophile Edward the Confessor's new abbey at Westminster was Norman, not Saxon.

Thanks to the influence of the Norman Bishop William, manors and privileges were restored to St Paul's that had been lost in the first upheavals following the Conquest. William of Normany signed 'a solemn charter' on Christmas Day 1066, the day of his coronation, which included his benediction on all who should augment St Paul's possessions, and a resounding curse on any who might try to diminish them. Twenty-one years later, in 1087, he died from injuries received after his horse stumbled and threw him in the streets of Mantes, a city destroyed on his orders. That same year London was also ruined by fire, and with it perished the old Saxon cathedral. Even at that date such parts of the original fabric as had survived the earlier fire of 961 could be described as venerable. They stood for four hundred and eighty-three years.

Nothing remains of that Saxon cathedral, not even a description. At Canterbury one of the precentors, Eadmer, left a record of the cathedral as it existed before the fire there in 1067, and in all probability it resembled St Paul's. A long nave of about nine bays, covered with a timber roof, aisles on either side, a semi-circular apse at each end, a choir separated from the rest of the church by a low balustrade, and a crypt beneath the east end containing relics of saints. Thanks to their being in just such a position, the tombs of Sebba, Ethelred and St Erkenwald survived the fires of 961 and 1087.

At the time of the second fire Maurice, once William's chaplain, was bishop. He was not slow to seize the opportunity of giving the capital a worthy cathedral. In that same year he began a work 'so stately and beautiful', wrote the chronicler William of Malmesbury, 'that it was worthily numbered amongst the most famous buildings; the vaults, or undercroft, being of such an extent, and the upper structure so large, that it was sufficient to contain a great number of people'.

The cathedral we know today as Old St Paul's had come into existence.

2

One of the last acts of William the Conqueror towards the City of London was a gift of stone for the new cathedral. It came from a castle, called the Palatine Tower, also ruined in the fire of 1087. But although Bishop Maurice lived another twenty years, he did not see the completion of his undertaking. In fact more than a hundred years was to elapse before it was anywhere near complete. At this time the system of administration was also being reconstructed on the lines laid down for use by some of the continental cathedrals. As well as confirming the grants of manors and privileges dating from before his time, the Conqueror transferred all ecclesiastical pleadings to the Bishop's jurisdiction, and in Henry I's time an even bigger change took place when the Bishop was given jurisdiction over church affairs in the diocese, while the business of the cathedral itself was dealt with by the Dean and Chapter.

Henry I gave the ditch surrounding Baynard's Castle, a royal residence between the cathedral and the river, to Bishop de Belmeis, so that a wall could be built along the south side of the churchyard.

The same king also decreed that ships bringing stone from Caen for the rebuilding should be exempt from toll duties, and it was at about this time Bishop de Belmeis petitioned the Pope that the Primacy should be moved from Canterbury to London, as had been St Augustine's intention five centuries earlier. But at Canterbury, Archbishop Anselm had the stronger influence with Rome, and the Primacy remained in Kent.

In 1135 yet another unfortunate reign, that of Stephen, was heralded by the burning of London. This time the damage extended from London Bridge to St Clement's Dane, and the unfinished cathedral was partly burnt. From the description in Stow's *Survey of London* it seems the apse at the east end was destroyed: 'A fire began in the house of one Aylewarde, near unto London Stone, which consumed east to Aldgate, and west to St Erkenwald's shrine, in Paul's Church; the bridge over the Thames was also burnt (p. 7) and etc: but afterwards again repaired.'

For nineteen years Stephen and Matilda skirmished for a crown neither was fitted to wear, and at this time, when 'Christ slept and his Saints also', Old St Paul's was also beset with troubles of its own. The question of who should appoint the bishops had been hammered out between Henry I and the Pope—the agreement being that the Pope should invest the new shepherds with the spiritual staff and ring, while the King held the right of choosing them and claiming their feudal homage as barons. But Stephen's reign was not more than a year old when another Anselm, nephew to the more famous Archbishop, was enthroned as Bishop of London against the wishes of the King, the Dean and many of the canons. After appeals to Rome the election was invalidated, and five years after the first protest Robert de Sigillo took his place.

But at last part of the new cathedral was ready for consecration, and on 14th November 1148, the relics of St Erkenwald were removed from the crypt and placed in the apse behind the

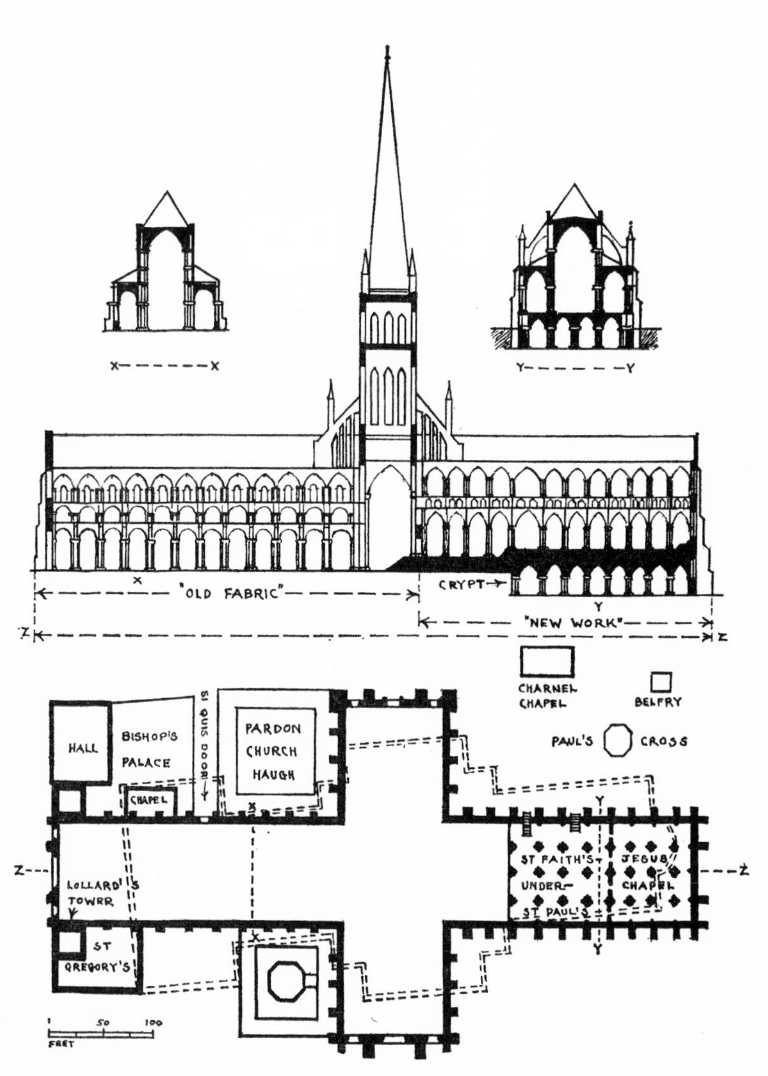

Old St Paul's before 1561. Position of present Cathedral in outline.

high altar. Although at Durham the apse was later replaced by the Chapel of the Nine Altars, the same arrangement can still be seen. St Cuthbert's shrine stands on a platform behind the altar, and marked on the floor is the outline of the original apse.

Stephen died in 1154, to be succeeded by Henry II, son of his old antagonist Matilda. Before long Old St Paul's found itself drawn into the great quarrel between the King and his one-time friend Thomas à Becket. As Archbishop of Canterbury, Becket claimed only the Pope as his liege lord, while in London Gilbert Foliot was now Bishop. Like the King he had once been friendly with Becket, but the friendship soured, and in due course he openly sided with the King. First Foliot refused to take an oath of obedience to Becket, and then further riled the Archbishop by reviving the claim that London should be the Metropolitan See. Becket was nearly as hot-tempered as the King he would not obey, and retaliated by accusing Foliot of taking bribes to allow his clergy to marry. At this Foliot declared that if the Pope would not help the Church in England against Becket, then the King and nobles would secede from the Church of Rome. This was too much for Becket, now in safety in France. At Clairvaux he pronounced sentence of excommunication against the Bishop of London.

On St Paul's Day 1166 a young Frenchman, named Berengar, entered the cathedral, went up to the altar and thrust the document at Vitalis, the priest celebrating Mass. Full of hope it was an offering, Vitalis accepted it. He soon discovered his mistake when Berengar loudly demanded he should read its contents aloud. As he opened the scroll Berengar called out: 'Know all men that Gilbert, Bishop of London, is excommunicated by Thomas, Archbishop of Canterbury, and Legate of the Apostolic See.'

In a letter describing the day's events to Becket, written by one of the assisting clergy who was sympathetic to the exile, there was an account of what happened next: 'When they heard this, many tried to hold him there and do him violence. But I made him slip away so as to avoid a riot; and as the men were leaving the church in crowds, I hid him under my cloak, and so went with him to the hostel from which he had come.'

When all this occurred Bishop Foliot was at his manor of Stepney, and strangely enough accepted the ban without protest. But before long he set out for Italy, and at Milan received letters from the Pope empowering the Archbishop of Rouen and the Bishop of Exeter to absolve him.

Shortly after, Becket returned to Canterbury, and to his murder in the cathedral by four of Henry II's literal-minded knights. Foliot was suspected of complicity in the murder, though no doubt he was as shocked (and at the same time relieved) as the King. However, he was required to swear an oath declaring he had no part in the outrage.

Meanwhile the building of Old St Paul's went slowly forward, and from time to time it was enriched in various ways. During Foliot's episcopacy, Richard de Belmeis, a nephew of the former bishop, granted the tythes of St Pancras church to the cathedral, and one Osbert de Camera 'being visited with great sickness' for the good of his uneasy soul, granted lands and houses in St Benedict's Parish, together with his ring and seal. At about the same time, when the Dean was soliciting for alms for the building work, Foliot granted a piece of land within the churchyard on which a Deanery could be built.

Richard I came to the throne in 1189. He may have been lionhearted, but also he was thoroughly irresponsible, and during his reign of ten years his English subjects only saw him on two brief occasions. They adored him. Before leaving England in 1189 he placed the governing of the country in the hands of William Longchamp, Bishop of Ely; Hugh de Puiset, Bishop of Durham; and his mother, Queen Eleanor. All might have gone smoothly had it not been for his brother Prince John, who at all times was a law unto himself.

Longchamp was undoubtedly arrogant, ostentatious and disliked by the nobles, who considered him a social inferior. On 8th October 1191, John summoned all the bishops to a council in Old St Paul's at which Longchamp—the son of a runaway French serf—was to be charged with acts of tyranny. The Archbishop of Rouen crossed the Channel to attend and take the role of arbiter. John triumphed, and the same month Longchamp left for France.

Two years later Richard was thrown into prison by the less than Holy Roman Emperor whilst crossing Austria on his way back from the Crusades. John seized the opportunity to announce that his brother was dead, and claimed the crown for himself. His mother, the old Queen Eleanor, opposed him, and together with the Archbishop of Rouen set about raising 100,000 marks; the fantastic ransom demanded by the Emperor. With brotherly devotion John pocketed a large part of it, and went off to join Philip Augustus—no friend of the English—in France. Together they offered the Emperor 150,000 marks if he would deliver Richard into their murderous hands. Fortunately for Richard the Emperor had some remnants of decency, and allowed him to return to England when the first instalment of the ransom was paid.

The ransom was a crushing burden for the whole country. The Church gave up valuable ornaments, and laymen of all classes were ordered to part with a quarter of their possessions. The raising of the ransom led to some ugly scenes in the City, and on one occasion Old St Paul's itself was nearly wrecked. The trouble was caused by William Fitzosbert, a born rabble-rouser. His family was of some importance in the City, and in his youth he took part in a crusade against the Moors: but he hated the Normans even more than the so-called infidel. On a number of occasions he harangued a large crowd at Paul's Cross, situated close to the cathedral in the angle formed by the choir and north transept.

Undoubtedly there was some truth in his charge that the burden of raising the money was unevenly imposed, but he went too far for his own good when he accused the City merchants of evading their share. For several months he remained a thorn in the side of the authorities. Then the Archbishop of Canterbury ordered his arrest. For the last time Fitzosbert rallied the mob at Paul's Cross, and after killing one of the Archbishop's men, fled with his mistress and a few followers to St Mary le Bow, where they hid in the tower.

The only way the authorities could dislodge the trouble-makers was by smoking them out. Smoking is hardly the word. The whole church was burnt in the process. Fitzosbert was

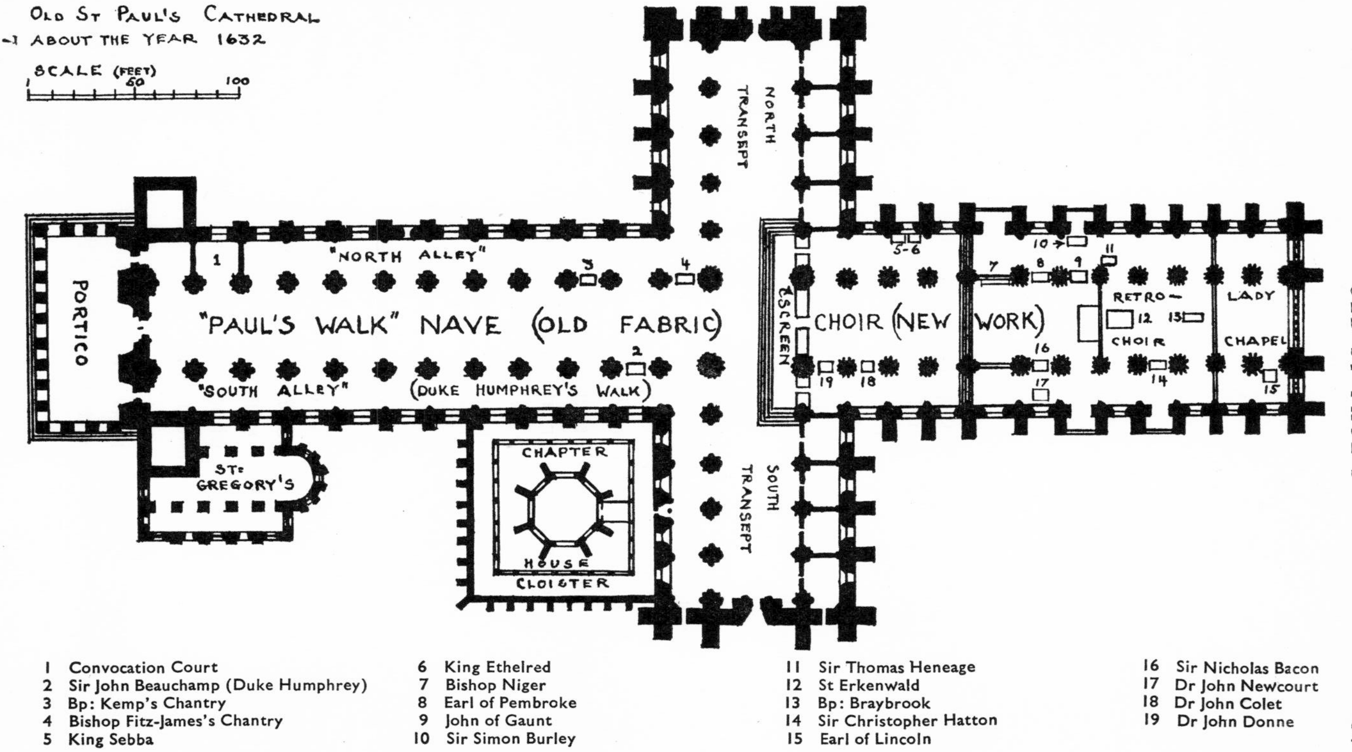
Old St Paul's Cathedral
About the Year 1632
Scale (feet)
50
100
Portico
"Paul's Walk" Nave (Old Fabric)
"North Alley"
"South Alley"
(Duke Humphrey's Walk)
St Gregory's
Chapter House
Cloister
North Transept
South Transept
Screen
Choir (New Work)
Retro-Choir
Lady Chapel
1 Convocation Court
2 Sir John Beauchamp (Duke Humphrey)
3 Bp: Kemp's Chantry
4 Bishop Fitz-James's Chantry
5 King Sebba
6 King Ethelred
7 Bishop Niger
8 Earl of Pembroke
9 John of Gaunt
10 Sir Simon Burley
11 Sir Thomas Heneage
12 St Erkenwald
13 Bp: Braybrook
14 Sir Christopher Hatton
15 Earl of Lincoln
16 Sir Nicholas Bacon
17 Dr John Newcourt
18 Dr John Colet
19 Dr John Donne

hanged in chains at Smithfield, and afterwards his followers tried to make a popular martyr of him: even claiming miraculous healing powers for the chain with which he was hanged.

With this event Paul's Cross enters recorded history for the first time as the meeting place of the Londoners: where they went to hear sermons, political and religious proclamations—or be stirred up by the Fitzosberts of this world.

3

The cathedral as it stood in the year 1200 consisted of a long nave of twelve bays (two less than Norwich), transepts and a choir. Although the eastern part was remodelled within the next eighty-five years, enough traces remained to show it was a semi-circular apse, with the aisle continued round in an ambulatory from which the chapels projected. Today the ground-plan of Norwich cathedral comes nearest to the original design, though at Old St Paul's the transepts were also provided with aisles.

The choir, completed in 1148, stood over a crypt which was only half below ground level. As a result the east end of the choir arm was raised above an impressive flight of twelve steps. On the Continent this scheme was common enough; stemming from the churches of northern Italy. North of the Alps it affected the design of the great churches of the Rhine, and even made itself felt as far away as Lund in Sweden.

The western part of Old St Paul's was unfinished when the pointed arch made its appearance. Above the triforium the walls of the clerestory, as well as the vaulting itself, were Early English. At Norwich and Tewkesbury Abbey, to give only two examples, the later vaulting was added to the already existing clerestory. The nave arcade consisted of massive piers, eleven feet in diameter, and the arches themselves sprang from small cushion capitals. Details in the form of carving were of the simplest kind, and confined to slight ornamentation round the arches. Inside, the aisle walls were decorated with round-headed arcading, while outside big round-headed windows admitted light at ground level. Above, the triforium was lit by circular windows. The buttresses were flat, and also quite plain. In the Early English clerestory above the aisles each bay was lit by one medium sized window.

The nave was between eighty-two and eighty-five feet high to the vault: about average for a great English cathedral. Outside, the roof ridge was a hundred and sixteen feet above the street level. By now Old St Paul's was substantially complete; though it still lacked a central tower, and the west front and transept fronts were unfinished.

A curious appendage was the little parish church of St Gregory. At Westminster the parish church of St Margaret was built within a stone's throw of the Abbey Church, but in the City St Gregory stood on the south side of the nave, its front adjoining the great cathedral's west end. In Saxon times a church was standing on the site, and the dedication to St Gregory, who sent St Augustine to England, suggests its early origin. During the savage and far-reaching incursions by the Danes into East Anglia in 1016, the body of Edmund, King and Martyr, was brought for safety to London from the abbey at Bury St Edmunds, and placed in St Gregory's. In A.D. 870 St Edmund had been captured by the Danes during an earlier invasion, and on refusing to forswear his religion tied to a tree and, like St Sebastian, shot to death with arrows. In 1017, when the danger had passed, his body was taken back to Suffolk, and on that journey it rested in the church at Greensted in Essex. Today St Gregory's, like the cathedral itself, has vanished, and the abbey at Bury St Edmunds is a scanty ruin, but at Greensted the little late tenth-century church made of rough-hewn oak logs still stands at the end of a narrow lane.

When St Paul's was rebuilt after the fire of 1087 St Gregory's was also built anew. Eighty feet long with a nave of five bays, aisles and an apse, it must have looked no bigger than a chapel. There was no direct access from the cathedral, nor was there a door on its west front: instead there were two entrances on the south side. One led into the nave: the other into the choir which in the Middle Ages was separated from the body of the church by a rood screen.

In 1198, the year before John came to the throne, yet another Norman became Bishop of London. William de Sancta Maria was a man with an important role to play, not only in the history of his cathedral, but also of England. By 1208 John had exasperated Pope Innocent III to the point of placing England under an interdict: outside the Roman Catholic Church. The sentence was arbitrary: falling on innocent and guilty alike. While in force, and it lay on the country for six years, no baptisms, marriages, or funerals could be held, and the churches themselves were closed. It fell to de Sancta Maria to pronounce the interdict, and feeling that discretion was the better part of valour, he and several other Church leaders left the country immediately afterwards.

When it even penetrated King John's consciousness that his aggressive attitude was getting him nowhere, he changed his tactics, and on his knees—at least metaphorically—asked the Pope for forgiveness. Back came the self-exiled bishop, accompanied by Bishop Nicholas of Tusculum. At a solemn service held in Old St Paul's in 1214, on the Saint's festival day, the Italian relaxed the ban, and once again the country's religious life began to flow. But hope of more settled times for England soon withered. Only a short while afterwards Stephen Langton, Archbishop of Canterbury, first met the barons in the abbey church at Bury St Edmunds, and again in Old St Paul's, where many of the clergy were present. Liberty, they felt, was worth any price, even that of inviting over the French Dauphin, their hereditary enemy, to rule in place of John.

The situation was certainly desperate. The Magna Carta which had been forced on the King as the key to England's freedom was declared null and void by the Pope, who, like John, was more than a little reactionary in his outlook. So it came about one day in the summer of 1216 Louis the Dauphin was welcomed into the City by an unnaturally enthusiastic populace. One of his first reactions was to attend Mass in Old St Paul's. But what course England's history might have taken if John had not ended his squalid life within the walls of Newark Castle is idle conjecture: but he did, and with his death the Dauphin returned to France. The next time French royalty—a king—attended Mass in the cathedral, it was as a prisoner of war. But that was a hundred and forty years away.

Invariably, these times of trouble had their repercussions at Old St Paul's, in that little was done either to complete or to embellish it. But in 1220 one Richard de Grenford agreed to provide timber for the choir stalls and for a belfry near the south-east corner of the cathedral. Stow wrote in his *Survey of London:* 'The Citizens claimed the East part of the Church Yard to be the place of assembly to their Folkmotes, and that the great steeple there situate was to that use their Common Bell, which being there rung, all the inhabitants of the City might hear and come together.'

About 1221 a central tower had been added to the cathedral which rose to a height of two hundred and forty-five feet: ten feet higher than the later Bell Harry at Canterbury. The design was simple. On each face three tall lancet windows admitted light into the interior, while above three shorter windows served the belfry chamber. Like the central towers at Wells, Salisbury, and Chichester, the tower of Old St Paul's gave trouble almost from the start. The massive buttresses were not part of the original scheme: when they were added it was only on the north and south faces of the tower, while the flying buttresses on all four sides would seem to date from the end of the thirteenth century. Above the tower a lead-covered spire of timber pointed up to heaven like the symbolic finger it was intended to be, giving a total height (it is believed) of four hundred and forty-nine feet.

Again it is to Norwich that one turns for a simile: Old St Paul's at this point must have been very reminiscent of the East Anglian cathedral, with an unpretentious west front flanked by two towers that were little more than large turrets, a long unadorned nave, deep transepts, a choir ending in a semi-circular apse, and above all a single spire-capped tower.

One small detail seems to have been overlooked. In a drawing of Old St Paul's during demolition following the Great Fire, a small semi-circular chapel is shown at the third bay of the eastern aisle of the South Transept (T. Wyck: *National Building Record*). It would seem to resemble those similarly placed at Canterbury (east transepts: two chapels), Gloucester and Norwich (in the latter case, north transept only). There is no sign of it whatsoever on the detailed plan prepared for Dugdale's book on the cathedral, published 1657.

To return to the description of the thirteenth-century Old St Paul's. On the north side, adjoining the nave, stood the Bishop's Palace. It consisted of a large hall, several rooms, a gallery leading to his private chapel, and a garden. Near by, on the same side adjoining the nave, stood a cloister called the Pardon Church Haugh. The name, like the date of the building, is obscure; but in Stephen's reign Gilbert Becket—father of the Archbishop—built a small chapel, in the cloister garth. But which came first?

At the south-east corner of the churchyard stood the belfry, and directly behind the east end, only separated from the cathedral by a narrow alley, stood the parish church of St Faith's. In the angle between the north transept and the choir of the cathedral was Paul's Cross.

The new king, Henry III, was only a child when he came to the throne, and there he remained for fifty-five years. Like Edward the Confessor before, and Henry VI after him, his inclinations—if not his abilities—were more suited for ruling over an abbey than a nation. The enlarging of Westminster Abbey was the Confessor's greatest achievement, while Henry III made his own fame by almost entirely rebuilding it on the model of the great cathedrals of northern France; notably the coronation church at Rheims.

If John in his time infuriated the Vatican, Henry III was sufficiently subservient for Pope Honorius to refer patronizingly to him as 'our vassal', and in 1232 Old St Paul's was the setting in which Cardinal Otho the White enlarged on the Constitutions of the English Church. Later, in 1268, these constitutions were confirmed, and right down to the Reformation they formed the basis of the Roman Catholic Church in England

During this reign Paul's Cross assumed a steadily increasing importance in the life of London. In 1236 an anonymous petition was read which accused the Governors of the City of misusing their authority. The petition, found in the King's wardrobe at Windsor, seems to have been effective, because Henry promised to investigate and put right the grievances it mentioned. On a number of occasions he himself appeared at the Cross: the first being in 1252 when he required all the citizens to swear an oath of loyalty to his son Edward (afterwards Edward I), while the last occasion was eight years later when all those over the age of twelve were required to swear an oath of loyalty to himself and his heirs.

Earlier, in 1243, the King feasted no less than fifteen thousand of London's poorer citizens in front of the cathedral. The gesture was not quite as praiseworthy as it might at first appear. The money to pay for it all came from the revenues that should by rights have gone to the Bishop of London, had there been one. In 1241 Bishop Niger died, and three years elapsed before Henry agreed to appoint a successor. By and large there was little to choose between Henry III and his Queen, Eleanor of Provence, when it came to money (p. 16).

A dramatic event which interrupted the life of the cathedral in 1250 came when a visit was paid by Boniface of Savoy, Archbishop of Canterbury. The Dean refused to submit to his authority, and when the Archbishop arrived he was not unprepared for trouble. Beneath his robes Boniface wore a cuirass. The doors of Old St Paul's were closed against him, and baffled, he had to return without entering. Almost at once excommunication followed, and for a year the Dean was outside the Church in more senses than one. When the Pope finally lifted the ban it was with the stern warning that in future Old St Paul's must obey the Archbishop as head of the Church in England.

4

Although only thirty-five years had elapsed since the scaffolding poles were finally removed from Old St Paul's, and only fifteen since the cathedral had been hallowed at a magnificent ceremony, there were plans afoot for its further improvement. They included largescale alterations, in keeping with two events then taking place. One was the development of Early English architecture, which reached its zenith with the founding of Salisbury in 1258, while the other was the devotion being paid to the Virgin Mary.

As the Middle Ages wore on, it became the custom to dedicate a large centrally placed chapel to her name, and at Old St Paul's the clergy were determined to keep abreast of the latest trends in religious architecture. In 1256 the matter was taken in hand. The scheme the authorities had in mind was nothing less than replacing the whole of the eastern limb of the cathedral. Ely seems to have been the model. There a long choir had recently been added to the Norman nave and transepts. Exactly the same procedure was followed at Old St Paul's. The design of the great Fenland cathedral influenced London on two widely separated occasions. Old St Paul's emulated its choir, and Alan of Walsingham's central octagon influenced the dome of Wren's seventeenth-century building.

Since Westminster Abbey was receiving Henry III's lavish attention it was useless for the Chapter to look to him for assistance, so most of the money came from private individuals. The easy way of encouraging the faithful in their offerings were indulgences: issued by bishops all over the British Isles, and in a few cases even further afield. In 1252 Pope Innocent III granted an indulgence of forty days to those who contributed to the building fund. In 1268 David, Bishop of Cashel (Ireland), also granted an indulgence of forty days, and in 1270 the Bishop of Brechin (Scotland) issued one for ten days. At a much earlier date, 1235, 'Henry, Archbishop of Cologne, being then in England, exciting all persons whatsoever thus to further this noble work, granted the like to them for relaxation of fifty days penance, as by his letters bearing date at the New Temple in London . . . appeareth.'

Under a new arrangement the cathedral was to be in two parts: the Norman 'Old Fabric' became the responsibility of the Bishop, while the Dean took charge of the Early English 'New Work'. The proposed extension would give the cathedral an overall length of five hundred and eighty-five feet, nearly the same as Glastonbury at the height of its glory, and twenty-nine feet longer than Winchester—today the longest medieval church in Europe.

Building operations began at the east end, which was to be square in the English fashion. Between the east end and the old

Norman apse stood St Faith's parish church and an alley connecting Watling Street with Cheapside. Both were soon to vanish as the work proceeded westwards. First a crypt resting on twenty-four piers was excavated, half below and half above ground. The western part became a successor to the parish church of St Faith's; and the eastern part, separated by a screen, formed the Jesus Chapel. The latter had its own bells in the belfry in the churchyard.

This great crypt was divided into four aisles, and the outer range of piers corresponded with those in the choir above. The new choir was in twelve bays: two more than at Lincoln or Ely (in the latter's case, before the fall of the old central tower), and each of the piers which carried the arcade was surrounded by eight freestanding shafts of Purbeck marble. Purbeck marble —in reality a stone—was probably used as at Salisbury to give contrast to the lighter-coloured freestone in the triforium and clerestory above. The fifth bay from the west was considerably wider than the others, and for no apparent reason. One theory is that there was a slight miscalculation when the site was being set out, and that particular bay had to be made wider than its fellows when the time came to link it up with the 'Old Fabric'. Here a most skilful transformation was effected by making pointed the round-headed Norman arches and clothing the piers with Purbeck shafting, so at a casual glance it all appeared to be of the same date. At the beginning of the thirteenth century the builders had crowned the nave with a simple quadripartite vault, with the ribs running diagonally, like a St Andrew's cross; and towards the end of the same century they covered the choir with the more complex tierceron vaulting, with an increased number of ribs.

An enormous rose window filled the upper part of the east end, with seven lights below. In the early morning with the sun shining through this wall of coloured glass it must have formed a glorious climax, at that time visible from the west door, along a vista of twenty-five arches. Its situation was unique in English cathedrals. Rose windows occur in the transepts at York, Lincoln, Beverley Minster, and Westminster Abbey; and in the west front of ruined Byland Abbey; but Old

St Paul's was alone among the major churches in having one at the east end. There is one at Durham, but it is an early nineteenth-century insertion by Wyatt, the arch-meddler who swept away the chantry chapels at Salisbury and wanted to do the same with the Galilee Porch at Durham, so that he could make a carriage drive right up to the west door. Wyatt's greatest achievement was, not altogether inappropriately, the enormous Folly he built for Squire Beckford at Fonthill. It collapsed within a few years of its erection.

The great east window even influenced fashion: in the next century the man-about-medieval-London was wearing 'Powles window corven on his shoes'. It is Chaucer in 'The Miller's Tale' who tells of architecture being imitated in cut leather. Later, two centuries later in fact, the little City church of St Catharine Cree, built by Inigo Jones, was given an east window which, in addition to symbolizing the saint's wheel, is supposed to have been based on the great one at Old St Paul's.

By 1283 the 'New Work' was complete, and the magnificent choir stalls and bishop's throne were in position in the first three bays east of the crossing. The High Altar was placed little more than halfway down the 'New Work', and immediately behind it stood the shrine of St Erkenwald, now more readily accessible to a large number of pilgrims than when it stood in the apse of the Norman cathedral. The very last two bays were screened off to form the Lady Chapel. In addition to the parish church of St Gregory, the last two bays of the north aisle, alongside the Lady Chapel, were adapted as a chapel dedicated to the same saint.

As in previous centuries Old St Paul's continued to receive endowments, gifts of money, land, and jewellery. Of all the gifts the strangest was a buck and a doe, offered annually by Sir William le Baud. The custom began in 1275 when the knight granted the Dean and canons a doe, on the day in winter commemorating St Paul's conversion; and a fat buck on the saint's day in summer. This offering was made in lieu of twenty-two acres of land in Essex belonging to the cathedral which Sir William wanted to enclose in his own estate. The deer was offered by the knight in person, but in later years his son Walter quarrelled with the Dean and canons, and only sent a servant to make the offering. In his history of St Paul's the seventeenth-century Dugdale relates: 'The reception of which doe and buck was, till Queen Elizabeth's days, solemnly performed at the steps of the choir, by the canons of this Cathedral attired in their sacred vestments, and wearing garlands of flowers on their heads: and the horns of the buck carried on the top of a spear, in procession round and about within the body of the church, with a great noise of hornblowers.'

By now the cathedral itself was reflected in the names of the streets hemming in the churchyard. To the west was Creed Lane and Ave Maria Lane, and to the north Pater Noster Row. But by night all was not as it should have been in so religiously named an area. In 1285 Edward I was informed that 'by the lurking of thieves and other lewd people, in the night time, within the precinct of this churchyard, divers robberies, homicides and fornications, had been oft times committed therein; for the preventing therefor the like, for the future, the said king, by his patent, bearing date at Westminster, the tenth of June, in the thirteenth year of his reign, to the honour of God and the Holy Church, and those saints whose bodies were buried therein, as also for the better security of the canons and officers belonging thereto, granted unto the said Dean and Canons licence to include the same churchyard with a wall on every side, with fitting gates and posterns therein, to be opened every morning, and closed at night.'

This wall had shops built along its outer face, and in addition to it being forbidden to burn coal in such close proximity to the cathedral, the trades which could be carried on were restricted. Butchers, goldsmiths and 'common women' were among those forbidden the precincts. Even at this early date smoke was a problem in London, and severe penalties were imposed for allowing the emission of an unnecessary amount from coal fires. In fact, in 1306 a man was executed for just that offence!

As far as Old St Paul's was concerned, the thirteenth century ended with a curse. In 1299 the Dean went to Paul's Cross to curse all those who had taken part in a most unofficial treasure hunt for a hoard of gold reputed to be hidden in St Martin le Grand in the City.

By 1300 the cathedral was substantially complete, though right up to the year of its destruction by fire it was undergoing alterations, some decorative, while others were concerned with maintaining the stability of the central tower. At this time the amount of light admitted to the interior of the 'Old Fabric' was greatly increased by inserting five light windows in the Norman aisles of the nave and on the west side of the transepts. Those on the east side (of the transepts) were rebuilt at the time the 'New Work' was in progress.

The money for all this continued to come in. Bishop de Gravesend, died 1303, bequeathed a hundred marks to the cathedral, and his successor Ralph Baldock contributed two marks annually. If Bishop de Gravesend had been content with a more modest funeral, Old St Paul's might have stood to benefit. He left instructions that £140, an enormous sum in those days, should be used for his funeral alone, without an additional £40 to endow a chantry at which a priest could recite prayers for the repose of his soul.

In addition to his grant of two marks a year, Bishop Baldock contracted with one Richard Pickerell, a citizen of London, to beautify the High Altar. The work provided consisted of a tablet 'variously adorned with many precious stones, and enamelled work; as also with divers images of metal: which tablet stood betwixt two columns, within a frame of wood to cover it, richly set out with curious pictures, the charge whereof amounted to two hundred marks.'

Although Dugdale in his mid-seventeenth-century history could write that by 1283 the main brunt of the building of the 'New Work' was over, much still remained to be done. In 1312 the pavement of the 'New Work' was 'made of good and firm marble, which cost fivepence a foot': laid down by one Adam the Marbler. Three years later much of the spire had become dangerous and was dismantled, although at the outside it could not have been a hundred years old. Almost immediately it was rebuilt, and the relics of several saints placed in the gilded cross, fifteen and a half feet high, which surmounted the two-hundred-

and-four-foot spire so that 'God Almighty, by the glorious merits of his saints, whose relics were therein contained, would vouchsafe to preserve the said steeple from all dangers of tempest.' When the spire of Salisbury Cathedral was restored in 1763, workmen found at the very top a box containing fragments of cloth: forgotten relics intended to ward off destruction by lightning. The timber and lead spire of Old St Paul's was only surpassed in height by the central spire of Lincoln, then also recently completed, which it is believed had a height of five hundred and twenty-four feet. If the latter had not been blown down in Edward VI's reign, today it would only be surpassed by the nineteenth-century spire at Ulm in Germany.

With the paying off of old scores in Edward II's reign, Old St Paul's for a short while found itself the centre of devotion being paid to an unofficial saint. Ever since the rebellious Earl of Lancaster had in 1312 ordered the execution of Piers Gaveston, the King's spendthrift favourite, Edward regarded him with bitter hatred. The tables were turned when the Earl was captured at Boroughbridge, and later beheaded outside his own castle at Pontefract. The anti-king faction regarded him as a martyr, and a much damaged fresco in South Newington parish church, Oxfordshire, shows his execution—or as some regarded it, his martyrdom. Within a short while Lancaster, who during his life had been a singularly coarse-grained individual, became an unofficial saint. Miracles were reported not only at his tomb in Pontefract Priory church, but also at a tablet put up to his memory in Old St Paul's. Both in London and in Yorkshire there were reports of the blind seeing and the lame walking unaided.

From time to time throughout the Middle Ages popular opinion made its own would-be saints. Anti-Jewish feeling made saints of the boys William of Norwich and Hugh of Lincoln; and anti-government elements did the same for Fitzosbert and the Earl of Lancaster. When Edward II heard of the veneration being paid at the tablet in Old St Paul's he ordered it to be removed, together with the candle kept burning before it.

The year of Edward II's death, 1327, also saw the completion of the 'New Work' at Old St Paul's. For the first time Mass was celebrated at the High Altar, and as in many great abbey churches, the Dean and canons had the exclusive use of the choir, while the laity attended services in the nave. A year before the remains of St Erkenwald had been moved at the dead of night, to avoid the attentions of the merely curious, to a magnificent new shrine immediately behind the stone screen separating the choir from the saint's chapel. This shrine was paid for out of the rings and jewellery bequeathed by one of the canons, and 'the Dean and Chapter bestowed no small cost in the adorning thereof with gold, silver and precious stones'. This was the great age for the veneration of relics; from the head of St John at Constantinople to the Magi in a casket—first at Milan and then as the spoils of war in Cologne. It was also the age of the exploitation of the faithful by the sellers of Chaucer's 'piggies bones': relics that had in all probability come from the next village rather than the Holy Land. A few that were collected together in nearly every great church in Christendom might be genuine, but many were blatantly false. Old St Paul's was no exception. There the list included the arms of St Mellitus, a knife of Our Lord, hair of Mary Magdalen, milk of the Virgin, blood of St Paul, the hand of St John, a piece of the True Cross and the bones of a few of the eleven thousand virgins who accompanied St Ursula on her ill-fated Rhine journey.

Although the cathedral was complete in itself, it still lacked a chapter house and a cloister. Then in 1332 the master mason William Ramsey was called in to design both these buildings. Ramsey, active from about 1326 to 1349, was the leading architect in England. At that time though the term architect as it is understood today had not yet evolved. Ramsey combined the roles of draughtsman, designer, and master mason. Before working at Old St Paul's he had been employed on St Stephen's Westminster—the crypt still survives—and more than anyone he was responsible for developing the clean upward soaring lines of the Perpendicular style out of the aptly named Decorated.

At this time, the early years of the fourteenth century, the south transept of Gloucester Abbey (as it then was) was going up in the new style; but the Chapter House at Old St Paul's was the first building to be erected which was a complete and individual structure. Owing to the restrictions of the site between the nave and the south transept, the cloisters were only ninety-five feet square, with the chapter house placed in the centre. This was unique among English cathedrals. Another feature without parallel was the cloister itself: in two storeys, with both levels open to the weather.

The arches in the lower range had heavy cusping, but no tracery, while those above were divided into two lights, with embryonic Perpendicular tracery in the heads. Like the chapter house at Wells, Ramsey's creation was in two storeys, but at Old St Paul's the undercroft was open on all eight sides. Above, the great room where the Dean and canons met once a week to discuss the business of the cathedral measured thirty-two and a half feet across. Seven sides were filled with large windows, and the eighth by the entrance along a gallery from the upper walk of the cloister. Outside, the chapter house was supported by eight massive buttresses, and the tracery of the windows carried down into the stonework below, to divide up the wall surface into a series of panels. The pinnacles on the tops of the buttresses were carried up only a few feet above the parapets, and then stopped abruptly, giving the impression they were never finished. Two surviving works by William Ramsey are the presbytery of Lichfield Cathedral and the medieval core of Penshurst Place in Kent: though the latter is only attributed to him.

However well English fortunes might be doing in France during the Hundred Years War, there was one invader from that country who could not be resisted. Throughout the summer of 1348 the Black Death spread westwards into Europe from the Crimea. From France it came to the Channel Islands, and from there into Dorset. In November it reached London, and before its course was run a year later over fifty thousand had died in the City alone. Among those carried off was William Ramsey himself.

London, Paris, Florence: all were hit with equal severity. Boccaccio's description of the plague-emptied streets of

Florence in the 'Prologue' to the *Decameron* applied equally well to London. 'The condition of the common people (and belike, in great part, of the middle class also) was yet more pitiable to behold, for that these, for the most part retained by hope or poverty in their houses and abiding in their own quarters, sickened and died by the thousand daily and being altogether unattended and unsuccoured, died wellnigh all without recourse. . . . And an infinite number of times it befell that, two priests going with one cross for someone, three or four biers, born by bearers, ranged themselves behind the latter, and whereas the priests thought to have but one man to bury, they had six or eight, and whiles more.' But at last the Plague did die away, leaving few families that had not lost at least half their members, and in the country as a whole the population had shrunk from four million to just over two and a half million.

Many years passed before the memory of the Plague was erased, and it lingered longest in church art. Before 1348 there had been a cheerful confidence in the tomb sculpture that portrayed the tranquil figures, their hands together in prayer, looking peaceful and without blemish. But slowly a new and darker trend was appearing. During the eighteen months the Plague lasted, men saw too much of death in a most shocking form not to be influenced by it. This obsession with physical death, for that was what it amounted to, made itself felt on both sides of the Channel. In the succeeding centuries it was to leave its mark on several of the tombs in Old St Paul's, as well as in the Cloisters of the Pardon Church Haugh.

Another curious and unpleasant feature that came into prominence at this time were the Flagellants, those men who for the sins of the world—and it must have sinned mightily to be punished with so terrible a plague—travelled from place to place doing penance by scourging themselves and each other with whips.

'About the feast of St Michael in the year 1349', wrote Stow, 'more than a hundred and twenty persons of Zealand in Holland, coming through Flanders unto London, sometime in the church of St Paul, sometime in other places in the City twice a day, in

The massive Norman nave of Old St Paul's. (Finden, after Hollar)

The 'New Work', the Early English choir-arm of Old St Paul's, added in the 13th century. (Finden, after Hollar)

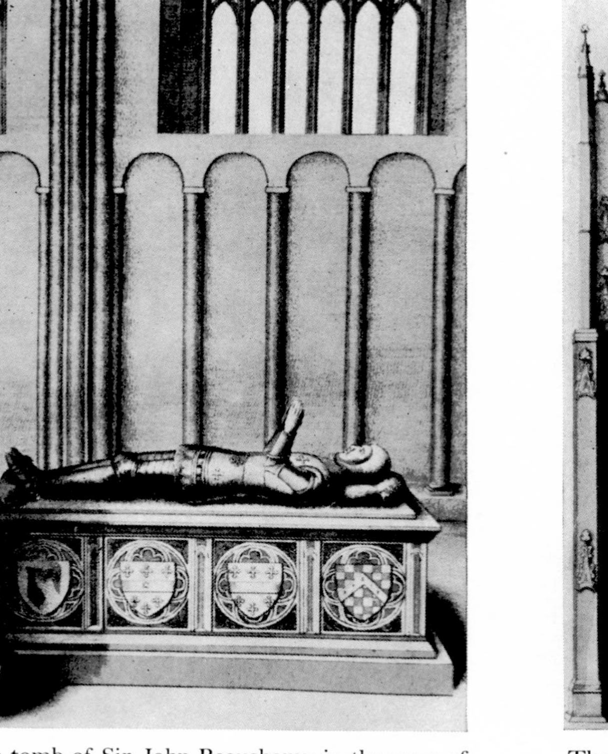

The tomb of Sir John Beauchamp in the nave of Old St Paul's. (Finden, after Hollar)

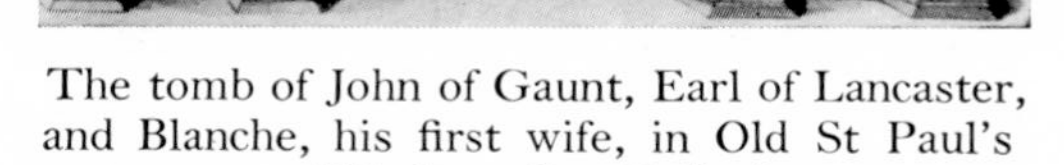

The tomb of John of Gaunt, Earl of Lancaster, and Blanche, his first wife, in Old St Paul's (Finden, after Hollar)

the sight of all people, from the loins unto the heels covered in a linen cloth, all the rest of their bodies bare, having on their heads hats, with red crosses before and behind, every one in their right hand a whip with three cords, each cord having a knot in the midst, beat themselves on their bare bloody bodies going in procession, four of them singing in their own language, all the others answering them.'

If the Middle Ages was like some great tapestry, rich with the colours of heraldry, gules was also the colour of blood.

5

As the fame of St Erkenwald spread, the shrine itself grew in magnificence, and goldsmiths and jewellers lavished their arts upon it. In 1339 'there were certain covenants made betwixt the then dean and chapter, and three goldsmiths of London, whereby they were retained to work upon it for no less than a whole year (beginning at Candlemas), one of them at the wages of 8s. by the week, and the other two at 5s. a piece'. The silver-plated wooden chest that enclosed the bones of the saint was surmounted by a painted wooden canopy, adorned with carvings of saints and angels, while the whole shrine was surrounded by a stout iron railing five feet ten inches high, which weighed three thousand four hundred and thirty-eight pounds, and at the rate of 4d. a pound, cost £64 2s.

Among the many visitors to the shrine was King John II of France, a semi-prisoner in the Tower after his capture by the Black Prince at Poitiers. On several occasions he left the fortress to visit the City, and in 1360 he rode to Old St Paul's, where he heard Mass and made several very handsome offerings. He 'laid down at the Annunciation Twelve Nobles; at the crucifix, near the north door, twenty-six florin nobles; at his first approach to the High Altar, four basins of gold, and at the hearing of Mass, after the offertory, gave the dean, then officiating, five florin nobles, which the said dean and one John Lyllyngton (the weekly petty canon), his assistant, had. All which being performed, he gave, moreover, in the chapter house, fifty florin nobles, to be distributed amongst the officers

8

of the church.' In addition he offered the additional sum of twelve nobles at the shrine of St Erkenwald.

King John, called the Good, was a man of extraordinary honour. In 1363 he was allowed to return home to raise the money for his ransom, leaving his son Louis as a hostage with the English at Calais. Louis escaped, whereupon King John surrendered himself saying: 'If good faith were to disappear from the rest of the earth, it should still be found in the hearts and mouths of kings.'

By the middle of the fourteenth century Old St Paul's was well filled with tombs and chantry chapels. The chests that held Sebba and Ethelred—saved from the old cathedral, were placed in recesses in the thickness of the aisle wall on the north side of the choir. Most of the earlier tombs in the Norman cathedral commemorated bishops, as did some of the first to be erected in the New Work: including the simple tombs of Bishops Chishull, Wengham, and de Fauconberg. More impressive were those of Bishop Niger, died 1241 and canonized soon after, and Hugh de Lacy, Earl of Lincoln, died 1310. Bishop Niger's tomb stood between two piers on the north side of the choir, and consisted of a tomb chest set behind three small arches, and above a stone screen of delicate tracery. The Earl of Lincoln lay in effigy wearing a loose surcoat over chain-mail; his feet on a lion and at his head two angels. In the niches surrounding the tomb were twenty-four weepers; little standing figures in various attitudes of grief.

A monument for long attributed to a man who died nearly a century after its erection was that to Sir John Beauchamp, one of the founder knights of the Order of the Garter, died 1360. His tomb stood on the south side of the nave, and right up to the destruction of 1666 was referred to as 'Duke Humphrey's tomb'. The real Humphrey, Duke of Gloucester, died in 1447 and lies beneath a magnificent tomb in St Alban's cathedral.

In addition to the tombs of the early Middle Ages, and numerous brasses, mostly of church dignitaries, Old St Paul's was rich in chantry chapels. At one time there were no less than seventy-six chantries at which priests would recite prayers for the benefit of the souls of the founders and other named friends and relatives. In addition to chapels that formed part of the structure of the cathedral itself, there were those singularly beautiful little structures, only a few feet square, that for the most part were placed between the piers of the arcades. In addition to the founder's tomb they contained an altar; all in a tiny space. According to Dugdale, the oldest chantry in Old St Paul's was probably that founded in Henry III's reign, which consisted of one priest who celebrated divine service for the soul of Master John de London, and the souls of all faithful deceased. Usually the endowment of the chantries came from rent for properties bequeathed to the cathedral for that purpose; as did Ralph Donion in 1317, who left a hundred marks to purchase property that would yield an income 'to sustain a priest daily celebrating in this church for his soul, and the souls of all his parents.'

This system of providing a living for a priest who had no other duties was open to abuse, and in his description of the Poor Parson in the *Canterbury Tales*, Chaucer wrote:

> 'He sette not his benefice to hire,
> and lette his shepe acombred in the mire,
> and ran unto London, unto Seint Poules,
> to seken him a chantry for soules.'

Some of these chantries were served by two priests; Bishop Stephen de Gravesend founded such a one in 1360 for himself and his uncle, an earlier Bishop of London. He also left instructions that the marble slab covering his grave should be no higher than the surrounding pavement. His personal estate, consisting of books, household goods, corn, and cattle, was worth two thousand marks, and from this £140 was to go on funeral expenses and for distributing to the poor. He also left £10 for the founding of a chantry and for keeping the anniversary of his death.

The next bishop in succession is Michael de Northburgh. He was equally particular in the ordering of his funeral. 'He directed that twenty poor men should be clothed in gowns of black, white or grey cloth; every of them holding in his hand, about the hearse, a torch of at least six pounds weight in wax.'

A curious legacy left by this Bishop to the cathedral was a thousand marks to be put in a chest kept in the treasury, from which a poor layman might borrow £10 against a suitable pledge. The Dean and principal canons could borrow £20, the Bishop between £40 and £50, and noblemen and citizens £20. The loan was valid for a year, and if the pledge was not redeemed after that, the preacher at Paul's Cross would declare that it would be sold in fourteen days' time. The chest had three keys: one kept by the Dean, the second by the eldest canon resident and the third by the Warden of the Old Fabric.

The view down the whole length of the cathedral remained uninterrupted until the middle of the fourteenth century when a great stone screen was erected across the entrance to the choir. A large doorway in the centre gave admittance to the choir, and smaller ones on either side led into the aisles, while the top of the screen was wide enough to hold two small altars. Somewhat similar screens remain at York and Canterbury, and also in several collegiate churches—Tattershall in Lincolnshire and Edington in Wiltshire, to name two. The Old St Paul's screen was completed with figures of Christ on the Cross and Mary and John: the group that made up the rood.

The finest of the medieval tombs was that designed by Henry Yevele for John of Gaunt and Blanche, his first wife. Henry Yevele, now the leading architect in succession to William Ramsey, lived from about 1320 to 1400. A man of culture, he could claim Chaucer as a friend, and for those days he was widely travelled, having been as far afield as Florence. At his death he was a man of property, owning several manors and having his private chapel. On his epitaph in St Magnus Martyr he was proud to claim he had been freemason to three kings: Edward III, Richard II, and Henry IV. Amongst those works attributed to him are the west gate and the cathedral nave at Canterbury, the Bloody Tower, and in Westminster Abbey the tombs of Edward III and Richard II. Blanche, Duchess of Lancaster, died in 1374 from plague, and her husband commissioned a tomb for both of them in Old St Paul's. Beneath a soaring canopy of alabaster the Duke lay in effigy beside his wife, and attached to one of the little piers was his helm, surmounted by his crest, his lance and a leather-covered target. Henry Yevele was a highly paid craftsman: one instalment alone to him and Thomas Wreck, a fellow master mason, amounted to £108, while the total cost was £486, well over £10,000 at modern rates!

Already there were murmurings against what might be described as the rigid thought-control of the laity by the Church, and the latter was not slow to react. Early on the morning of 23rd February 1377 John of Gaunt himself was present at an ecclesiastical court held in the cathedral when John Wycliffe was summoned to appear on a charge of heresy. His heresies consisted of attacking the sale of indulgences, the worship of relics, and wishing for the service in the native tongue. Wycliffe's great achievement was the first full translation of the Bible, for at this date only a few people of sufficient importance, either religious, political, or social, were allowed translations under a specially granted licence from the Church. Within a few years the possession of Wycliffe's Bible by an unauthorized person was a capital offence.

This then was the man facing the Archbishop of Canterbury, the Bishop and the clergy in the Lady Chapel of Old St Paul's that early winter's morning. The hearing soon degenerated into a quarrel between Gaunt, who supported Wycliffe, and Bishop Courtney. The crowd in the nave became out of hand when the rumour was spread that Gaunt threatened to drag the Bishop out of the cathedral by his hair. While all this was going on, Wycliffe slipped away, and the meeting broke up in disorder. In later years he retired to the rectory at Lutterworth in Leicestershire, where he continued his writings and laying the foundations for the English Reformation, a century and a quarter before Martin Luther erupted into life in Germany.

This same year, 1377, saw the great procession of Richard II passing Old St Paul's as he went from the Tower to Westminster. The procession, which from his reign until the time of Charles II became a feature of the pre-coronation festivities, took three hours to cover the few miles separating the two points. At the end of the lengthy service in the Abbey what the spectators outside saw was a very tired small boy of ten being carried to Westminster Palace on the shoulder of his tutor, Sir Simon Burley. On the way Richard lost one of his red velvet shoes. Some regarded this as an ill omen, as well it might have been, but on that day neither the tutor nor his charge would have believed possible the tragedy and disaster that lay ahead for both of them; and that for Richard the most hypocritical scene of all would be played out in Old St Paul's.

The first major trouble came with the Peasants' Revolt. But the events of June 1381 only concerned Old St Paul's when when Simon of Sudbury, once Bishop of London, was beheaded by the mob on Tower Hill (p. 25). Six years later Richard attended High Mass in great state, but by now his fortunes were on the downward trend. In 1387 Sir Simon Burley, now Vice-Chamberlain, was tried by a thoroughly rebellious Parliament on a trumped-up charge of corruption, and in due course beheaded.

As was frequently the case in the Middle Ages, and later for that matter, after Burley's execution his family were allowed to put up a fine tomb to his memory in Old St Paul's. Those in power, having achieved their object, could now afford to be magnanimous. The tomb stood against the wall of the north choir aisle: a beautiful piece of fully developed Perpendicular work which may also have been the work of Henry Yevele.

Richard de Preston, a citizen of London, made a curious present to St Erkenwald's shrine at about the time these happenings formed the prelude to worse and more unscrupulous events. In 1392 he 'gave to this Shrine his best sapphire stone, there to remain for curing of infirmities in the eyes; appointing that proclamation should be made of its virtues.' Two other additions to the cathedral in the fourteenth century were a clock, set up in 1345, and a statue of the Virgin Mary placed in the nave a year later. The clock, which cost £6, had the figure of an angel which pointed to the hour. At some time in the cathedral's history there were figures of mechanical men, probably similar to Jack Blandifer at Wells, who struck the hours and were in fact called Paul's Jacks.

By now both the century and Richard II's reign were coming to an end, and in 1399 John of Gaunt, a younger son of

Edward III, died and was buried beside his wife in the tomb commissioned a quarter of a century before, which stood close to the High Altar on the north side of the sanctuary. He left behind a son, Henry Bolingbroke, cousin to the King he now intended to supplant. That same year saw Bolingbroke praying most devoutly in Old St Paul's for the deposition of Richard, and before long his cousin had been betrayed into his hands at Flint Castle. In his misery Shakespeare makes the wretched King exclaim: 'For God's sake, let us sit upon the ground, and tell sad stories of the death of kings:—How some have been depos'd, some slain in war; Some haunted by ghosts they have depos'd; Some poisoned by their wives; some sleeping killed; all murdered.' Richard, in all probability, was murdered, and soon after, his cousin together with his followers were spreading sheets of cloth of gold over his coffin as it stood in front of the High Altar in Old St Paul's. Henry Bolingbroke, now Henry IV, was even weeping.

With his enemy safely buried in the long since destroyed Dominican church at Abbots Langley in Hertfordshire (Richard II was later removed to Westminster Abbey), Henry IV of the small eyes set in a heavy face, could think of his own coronation. In at least one respect he emulated his predecessor—by going in procession from the Tower, past Old St Paul's to Westminster. Wrote the French chronicler Froissart of the day's events in October 1399: 'He passed through the streets of London, which were all handsomely decorated with tapestries and other rich hangings: there were nine fountains in Cheapside and other streets he passed through, that ran perpetually with white and red wines. The whole cavalcade amounted to six thousand horse, that escorted the duke from the Tower to Westminster.'

6

While the new king was consolidating his position on the throne, and warring with great families like the Percies who threatened to look too lofty in his commonwealth (London Bridge, p. 30), in the Church itself events were casting the flickering shadows of Smithfield before them. The threat of burning was brought nearer those holding views considered heretical in 1401 when the writ 'De Heretico Comburendo' came into force. It was aimed at stamping out the Wycliffists and the Lollards. The latter found most of their supporters among the poorer classes who gathered together for secret Bible readings, and that same year a priest named William Sautree was sentenced to death at a convocation held in Old St Paul's. The Convocation Court, which dealt with such matters, was situated inside the cathedral itself: the second bay from the west end of the north aisle of the nave being screened off for the purpose. In later years the small tower on the south side of the west front acquired the name the Lollards Tower, because prisoners charged with Lollardry were from time to time confined there.

Although Henry IV had another two years to rule, in 1411 a chantry was founded for him in accordance with John of Gaunt's will. Two priests served it 'for the good estate of the said king Henry IV, during his life in this world, and for his soul, after his departure hence'.

Throughout most of the cathedral's existence the authorities were harassed by those who used the building for any purpose except the right one. At all times the citizens of London were an independent crowd with a contempt for restriction, but they went too far in their conduct in Old St Paul's. As early as 1411 the Bishop found it necessary to issue a proclamation forbidding wrestling in the sanctuary, on pain of a fine and forty days imprisonment. But obviously it was not seriously enforced, and with the passing of time the abuses grew worse, not better.

Henry V came, conquered half France, and in August 1422 died at Vincennes. Slowly, and in a great procession, his body was brought back to England (p. 32), and three months after his death the coffin was carried into Old St Paul's and placed before the High Altar. All the great ones of Church and State were present, including the whole of Parliament. Then the next day, 11th November, the procession formed up for the last time when it set out for Westminster Abbey.

His son Henry VI was only two years old at the time of his accession, and as far as his mind was concerned, he never really grew up. Like Edward the Confessor before him, he would probably have been much happier could he have concerned himself only with God and left man, in the shape of his subjects, to their own devices. But like Richard II he was destined to become the tool of those around him, and as with the earlier king, the last act was played out in front of the High Altar in Old St Paul's.

During his reign the cloisters of the Pardon Church Haugh, on the north side of the cathedral, were decorated with a series of panels representing the Dance of Death. Since the Black Death, itself a dance of death like some nightmarish Pied Piper with all Europe in its train, men's minds had been dwelling more and more on the subject.

The Dance of Death was totally different in conception from that of the nineteenth-century romantics: death dancing in a churchyard with a number of fellow skeletons—quite an innocuous character in fact. In the iconography of the Middle Ages, Death, like the Devil, was a gentleman, even if he did not always behave like one. There was no escape: at Perigueux in France 'Memento Mori' was carved on the back of a fireplace in a private house, while at Rouen a pitcher has survived with the inscription 'Remember Death, poor foolish one'. A book was published entitled *Ars Moriendi: The Art of Dying*. Death had become an obsession, and this attitude was strongly reflected in the art of the Church. At Kermaria in Brittany a complete Dance of Death survives in the nave of the parish church; and at the Chaise Dieu (a corruption of Casa Dei—the House of God) in the Auvergne, another is painted around the apse.

London was no exception. At Old St Paul's a Dance of Death was commissioned and paid for by John (or Jankyn) Carpenter, the clerk to the City of London and one of the executors of Dick Whittington's will. There were thirty-six painted panels, copied from a series in the cloisters of St Innocent in Paris. These panels depicted Death, in the form of skeletons, pairing off with men from all walks of life. The Pope, the Emperor, the Cardinal, the King—down the scale to the Burgess and the Monk; even the usurer was not forgotten. The Minstrel, the Labourer, the Young Child, the Clerk and last of all the

Hermit. Underneath each panel were two verses, each of eight lines. In the first Death addresses his victim, and in the second the victim replies. One, the Cardinal, grieves that never again will he 'clothed be in grise nor ermine unto my degree', while the labourer tells 'I have wished after death full oft, Albe that I would have fled him now'.

The verses ended with a little envoi by the translator:

> 'Have me excused, my name is John Lydgate,
> Rude of Language, I was not born in France,
> Her curious metres to translate,
> Of other tongue have I no suffience.'

John Lydgate was a monk of Bury St Edmunds, and some of his verses survive painted on the roof of the Clopton Chantry in Long Melford church. Two panels from a Dance of Death remain in another great parish church, that at Newark in Nottinghamshire. Lydgate was the poet laureate of his day: providing verses made to measure—like Browning's composer Galuppi he was 'good alike at grave and gay'—and an important occasion he commemorated was the arrival of Henry VI's French bride at Old London Bridge (p. 36).

When only five years old the as yet uncrowned Henry VI came to Old St Paul's. 'The King, with the Queen his mother, came through the City from Windsor: and when he came to the west door of Pauls, the Lord Protector took him out of the chair, and so led him upon his feet, between the said Lord Protector and the Duke of Exeter, unto the steps going into the choir, from whence he was born unto the High Altar, and there kneeled in a travers (curtains hung up to make a small room-like apartment) prepared for him. And when he had done there he went to the Rood of the north door, and there made his offerings: he was then born into the churchyard, and there sat upon a fair courser, and so conveyed through Cheapside, and the other streets of the City, unto St George's Bar.'

The figures of the Crucifixion that made up the rood near the door into the north transept were particularly celebrated, and by a decree of 1410 the Dean and canons had the benefit of offerings made there.

In the summer of 1441 the inhabitants of the City flocked to Paul's Churchyard to see a necromancer doing penance. Roger Bolingbroke himself was of no great consequence, but caught in the same web was Eleanor Cobham, the King's aunt by marriage; Thomas Southwell, a Canon of St Stephen's Westminster, and Margaret Jourdain. The latter was a witch from Eye near Westminster. Eleanor Cobham, wife of that Duke Humphrey who in later years was thought to be buried in Old St Paul's (p. 141), had procured Roger Bolingbroke's services to try and kill the King with witchcraft; but all came to nothing 'And the five and twentyth day of July, being Sunday, Roger Bolingbroke, with all his instruments of Necromancy, that is to say, a chair painted wherein he was wont to sit, upon the four corners of which chair stood four swords, and upon every sword an image of copper hanging, with many other instruments, he stood on a high scaffold in Paul's Churchyard, before the cross holding a sword in his right hand and a sceptre in his left, arrayed in a marvellous attire, and after the sermon was ended by Master Low, Bishop of Rochester, he abjured all articles belonging to the craft of necromancy or missowning to the faith, in presence of the Archbishop of Canterbury, the Cardinal of Winchester, the Bishop of London, Salisbury and many other.'

Bolingbroke was examined by the Council, confessed to witchcraft, and blamed Eleanor Cobham for all his misfortunes. At this unexpected turn of events the Duchess fled to Westminster Abbey for sanctuary, but eventually she too was tried, on a charge of treason, along with the witch. Eleanor Cobham threw her female accomplice to the dogs in an effort to save her own life; declaring Margaret Jourdain was a witch who in the past procured her the love of her present husband, the Duke of Gloucester. But this confession of other people's sins could not altogether save her and 'On Monday 13th November she (Eleanor Cobham) came from Westminster by water, and landed at the Temple Bridge, from whence with a taper of wax of two pounds in her hand, she went through Fleet Street, hoodless (save for a kerchief) to Pauls, where she offered her taper at the High Altar.'

On Wednesday she walked through the City to Christ Church, Aldgate; and on the Friday she was made to go to St Michael's Cornhill, accompanied by the Lord Mayor, sheriffs and guilds. Later she was sent into exile, first in Chester and then in Kenilworth Castle. Meanwhile both Roger Bolingbroke and Margaret Jourdain had been put to death.

If the Bishop and clergy were the keepers of London's conscience, Paul's Cross was the pulpit where all manner of items were dealt with; from the reading of Papal pronouncements to the castigating of outlandish fashions, and where sinners of one kind or another did penance. In 1417 Lord Strange and Sir John Trussel were excommunicated for instigating a fight in St Dunstan's in the East which led to bloodshed; while in 1457 the Bishop of Chichester went there to recant the heresies with which he had been charged. 'I, Reginald Pecocke, Bishop of Chichester, unworthy of my own power and will, without any manner of coersion or dread, confess and acknowledge that I here . . . have held, written and taught otherwise than the Holy Roman and Universal Church teacheth, preacheth or observeth.' Stow concludes his account of the Bishop's statement: 'I have openly assented, that my said books, works and writings be deputed unto the fire, and openly burnt in example and terror of all others.'

To run on a few years into the reign of Edward IV: in 1464 the clergy at Paul's Cross were then denouncing trends in fashion. In addition to the side-saddle, Anne of Bohemia (Richard II's queen) introduced a most extravagant fashion. 'By her example, the English people had used peaked shoes, tied to their knees with silken laces, or chains of silver or gilt, wherefore in the 4th of Edward IV, it was ordained and proclaimed that beaks of shoon and boots should not pass the length of two inches, upon pain of cursing by the clergy, and by parliament to pay twenty shillings for every pair. And every cordwainer (shoemaker) that shod any man or woman on the Sunday to pay thirty shillings.' That was in 1464: in 1469 an edict from the Pope was read at Paul's Cross denouncing these shoes—evidently the fashion had not died a natural death in spite of the threat of cursing, to say nothing of a fee of twenty shillings. It was not so much the worldly vanity of these shoes that exasperated the Church, but the fact the wearers would not go down on their knees properly to pray. Had they done so it would have meant spoiling the elongated toes, and human nature being what it is, it was the prayers that went by the board. But then, all through the ages, people have been prepared to make sacrifices in the cause of fashion.

Not for long was the spire of Old St Paul's destined to remain free from trouble. At two o'clock in the afternoon of 1st February 1444 it was struck by lightning, and set alight halfway from the top. Soon the fire was under control, and thought to be out. But at about nine in the evening it blazed up again 'and did much hurt to the lead and timber, till, by the great labour of the Mayor and people that came thither, it was thoroughly quenched'. The damage must have been considerable, for the repairs were not completed until 1462. On that occasion when a gilded weather-cock was being set in place, the rope broke, killing one of the workmen, and damaging the cock itself. Finally it was fixed in place by one 'Burchwood, the king's plumber'.

Some sixty years earlier, in 1382, it was Paul's Cross that was damaged by lightning, and in 1448 the whole structure was rebuilt by Thomas Kemp, who in two years' time became Bishop of London. In wet weather the sermons usually given at Paul's Cross were delivered in the 'Shrouds'. That was the popular name given to the crypt beneath Old St Paul's. The eastern part contained the Jesus Chapel (its bells hung in the Tower in the churchyard, and were called the Jesus Bells), while the western half was dedicated to St Fidei in Cryptis, to give its Latin designation. Cryptis become corrupted to Crowds, and from Crowds to Shrouds. Indeed, there was a great deal of truth in the seventeenth-century Fuller's simile that Old St Paul's was a mother church with one (St Gregory) in her arms, and another (St Faith's) in her womb.

The probable appearance of the cathedral at this date has come down to us in a graffitus scratched on the stonework in the tower of Ashwell parish church in Hertfordshire sometime after the third quarter of the fourteenth century. Without doubt that humble scratching is the oldest, and apart from a medieval seal, the only real record of the cathedral at the height of its glory. Above all rises the tower and great spire: four tall pinnacles at the corners of the tower, which even at this early date is supported by massive flying buttresses that were so distinctive a feature right down to the time of the Great Fire. Even the rose window at the east end is there, as well as the bell tower in the corner of the churchyard: the latter was squat, and like the central tower capped with a spire and pinnacles.

Not only were those who preached at Paul's Cross men connected with the cathedral: 'considerable contributions were raised, among the nobility and citizens, to support such preachers as were called to town from either of the universities. In particular, the Lord Mayor and aldermen ordered that every preacher who came from a distance, should be freely accommodated, during five days, with sweet and convenient lodgings, fire, candle, and all necessaries: and notice was given by the Bishop of London, to the preacher appointed by him, of the place he was to repair to.'

By 1452 the differences between York and Lancaster had become a rift which despite appearances went on widening until it was war: the Wars of the Roses. Henry VI and the Duke of York were reconciled at a meeting in Old St Paul's—for what it was worth. Within three years the two factions were fighting at St Alban's. Empty though the reconciliation was, the procession into the cathedral was impressive. The rival nobles walked in pairs: the Duke of Somerset hand-in-hand with the Earl of Salisbury, followed by the Duke of Exeter extending an equally insincere hand to the Earl of Warwick, and so on. After the peers came the King, the Queen and the Duke of York, all apparently on the friendliest terms. Another attempt was made in 1460 in front of the High Altar to patch up the peace between the two parties. On this occasion it was an even greater farce than before. By now the King was Warwick's prisoner, and after listening to his oath of loyalty Henry VI had to agree to a decree disinheriting his own son (Prince Edward) in favour of the Duke of York (later Edward IV).

Little time was wasted, and on 28th June of the next year the Duke was crowned as Edward IV, and Henry VI was deposed and made a prisoner in the Tower. The day after the coronation in Westminster Abbey, Edward 'went crowned in St Paul's church in London, in the honour of God and St Paul, and there an angel came down and censed him, at which time was so great a multitude of people in Paul's as ever was seen in any days.' On great occasions it was the custom to let down a censer through a hole in the middle of the vaulting of the nave which could be swung backwards and forwards.

Ten years pass, and a change of fortune brings Henry VI out of his prison. This came about when the Earl of Warwick, feeling he had been insufficiently rewarded by Edward IV, turned traitor to the man he had helped on to the throne. But the change of alliance did him little good. After the Battle of Barnet 'on the morrow after Easter Day, were the bodies of the Earl of Warwick and the Marquis Montagu (his brother) laid naked in Pauls Church, that all men might see them, for the space of three days, and then buried at Bissam Priory in Berkshire'.

Soon it was Henry VI's turn to come for the last time to the cathedral. On 21st May 'King Edward came to London, with thirty thousand men: and the same night King Henry was murdered in the Tower of London. On the morrow he was brought, through Cornhill, from the Tower with a great company of men, bearing weapons as they should have led him to some place of execution, to St Paul's church in London, in an open coffin, where he bled: thence he was carried to Black Friars, and there bled: and thence to Chertsey Abbey in a boat, where he was buried.' Later his body was removed to St George's Chapel, Windsor.

During the Wars of the Roses practically no building work was carried out at Old St Paul's, apart from restoring the spire. Inside, the cathedral was now complete, glowing with subdued light filtered by the stained glass into patterns of colour slowly moving across floors and walls. In addition to the glittering Shrine of St Erkenwald, there were pin-points of light from the hundreds of candles burning before more than thirty altars.

The Bishop, the Dean, the greater canons, the minor canons and the priests who served the numerous chantry chapels all had their part to play in the life of the cathedral. A feature in the interior were the guilds, founded for the purpose of providing a priest to say masses for the good of their members' souls. In 1469 the Guild of the King's Minstrels was granted a charter, and in return they were bound to pray for the King and Queen; at that date Edward IV and Elizabeth Woodville.

'Farewell sour annoy, for here begins, I hope, our lasting joy'; exclaimed England's second or third merriest monarch at the end of *Henry VI, Part Three.* In reality Edward's joy lasted until 1483 when the flames of his candle met in the middle. After his death his last mistress, Jane Shore, attached herself to Lord Hastings. But this little idyll was not destined to last for long. When Richard, Duke of Gloucester, suspected Hastings' allegiance he sent the unfortunate peer to instant execution, and charged Jane Shore with being his accomplice.

A different fate was decreed for her; that of doing penance at Paul's Cross. One Sunday she was taken there in procession, walking in front of a cross, with a taper in her hand, and wearing only a kirtle. The stares of the crowd made her blush: 'which cast a comely red in her cheeks . . . and many good folk that hated her living, and were glad to see sin corrected, yet pitied they more her penance than rejoiced at it'.

Soon after this event Paul's Cross was the setting for one of the most dramatic scenes in the history that was then in the making. Richard, Duke of York, had just put forward his claim to the throne. Whether or not he was the 'bottled spider' of the Dowager Queen Elizabeth's well-turned tongue—or simply the victim of later Tudor propaganda—the fact remains he did not hesitate to use the foulest of arguments to gain his ends. On his orders Dr Shaw, the Lord Mayor's brother, delivered a sermon at Paul's Cross declaring that neither the late King Edward IV nor his brother Clarence had been legitimate, though of course Richard was. In other words, Gloucester ordered the public defamation of his own mother. As if that was not enough, Dr Shaw went on to add that because Edward IV's marriage was bigamous his children were illegitimate, and

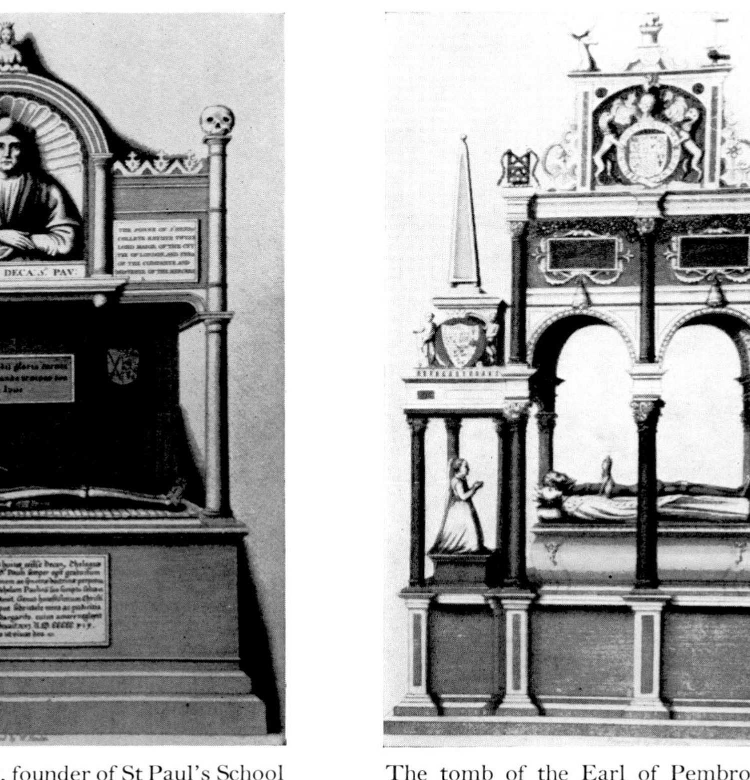

The tomb of John Colet, founder of St Paul's School in 1509, in Old St Paul's. (Finden, after Hollar)

The tomb of the Earl of Pembroke and his wife in Old St Paul's. (Finden, after Hollar)

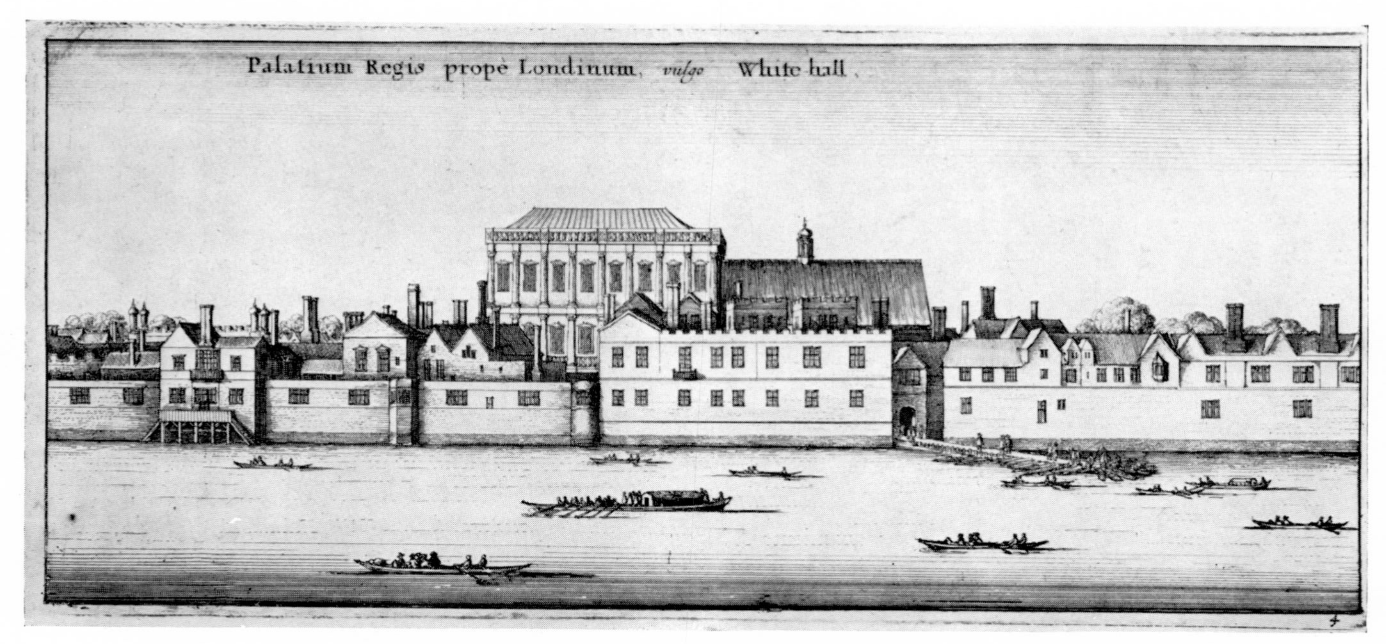

Old Whitehall Palace from the Thames, about 1645, by Hollar.

therefore barred from the throne. 'Bastard slips should never take deep roots', was Shaw's elegant phrasing.

At this point in the sermon Richard himself should have come riding by Paul's Cross, to receive the acclamations of his new subjects. But because of the crowded streets on his way to the cathedral he was late, and Dr Shaw was forced to go on to talk of other matters. When Richard did appear, and he returned to his statements about the old Queen's virtue, the future king was received in deadly silence.

Before many weeks passed the little princes had been murdered in the Tower, and now Richard himself was riding by Old St Paul's in the coronation procession originally intended for the elder of the two boys. But two years later England rid herself of the last Plantagenet king at the Battle of Bosworth Field, and now Henry VII wore the crown found hanging on a thorn bush. As soon as the first Tudor reached London he 'came with great pomp to St Paul's where he offered his three standards, one of St George, the second a Red Dragon, the third a Dun Cow. After prayers said, and Te Deum sung, he departed to the bishop's palace, where he sojourned a season.'

Within two years of that first visit to Old St Paul's, Henry VII was again at the cathedral. This time the service was to mark the successful crushing of the pretender Lambert Simnel. Instead of having him executed, Henry showed just how lightly he took his would-be rival's claim to the throne by employing him in his kitchen. Another who fared badly by comparison was the young Earl of Warwick, son of the Duke of Clarence. Rumours spread that he was not a prisoner in the Tower, but free, and preparing to depose Henry VII. To scotch this story the King ordered the youth to go from the Tower to hear Mass in Old St Paul's, where he was to be allowed to talk with other nobles in the congregation. In this way peer and commoner alike could see for themselves that he was indeed a prisoner. The visit to the cathedral was the earl's last day of semi-freedom: until his execution—to clear the way for the marriage of the King's elder son Arthur to Katharine of Aragon (p. 40) —he remained behind the walls of the Tower, because his

Plantagenet blood automatically made an enemy of him to the Tudor dynasty.

Few additions were made in Old St Paul's during these last years of the fifteenth century, but what was perhaps the finest brass in the cathedral was placed in the south aisle of the 'New Work' in 1485, to commemorate Dr John Newcourt, a canon of St Paul's. The Annunciation was engraved on a panel above the canon in his robes; while on either side were twelve small figures.

An event hailed throughout Europe was the expulsion from Spain of the last of the eminently civilized Moors. The unification of Spain was to have most dangerous results for England in the next century, but now, on 6th April 1492 'Hugh Clopton, Mayor of London, his brethren and aldermen, sheriffs and companies of the City in their liveries assembled in the Cathedral Church of St Paul, where Dr Morton, Archbishop of Canterbury and Chancellor of England (of "Morton's Fork" fame), made them an oration, declaring how the king of Spain had won the great and rich city and country of Granada from the Moors, for the joy whereof Te Deum was sung with great solemnity.'

7

The great event that began the sixteenth century at Old St Paul's was the marriage of Prince Arthur and Katharine of Aragon on 21st November 1501. If the young princess's entry into the City was magnificent (p. 41) the wedding ceremony itself was spectacular. Stands were erected in the nave for the more important of the guests, and in the tapestry-hung choir the marriage itself took place on a raised platform, similar to the one set up in the 'theatre' in Westminster Abbey in medieval times for the actual ceremony of crowning. The Archbishop of Canterbury united the young couple, assisted by the Spanish Legate and nineteen bishops and abbots. After the wedding it fell to the Duke of York to conduct Katharine to the banquet at the Bishop's Palace. Within weeks, however, all was brought to nothing when the sixteen-year-old prince died at Ludlow. Later Katharine married that young Duke of York. By then he had become Henry VIII.

Two men of vastly different temperament now directed the life of the cathedral. One was Richard Fitz-James, who as Bishop demanded unquestioning acceptance of everything concerning the Church. The other was Dr John Colet, Dean from 1505 to 1519. He represented the New Learning, as expounded by Erasmus, and in due course Fitz-James charged him with heresy, but neither the King nor Archbishop shared his intolerant ideas, and the accusations came to nothing. Indeed, Henry said of the Dean: 'Let every man have his doctor, this is mine.'

Dr Colet's great memorial was St Paul's School, which he founded in 1509 in the shadow of the cathedral. It was for one hundred and fifty-seven; the same number as there were fishes in the miraculous draught. His other memorial, in the south aisle of the choir, consisted of a half-figure of himself in a niche above a skeleton laid out on a mat in the lower compartment. The carving suggests the whole monument may have been of wood. At Steeple Langford in Wiltshire there is a somewhat similar half-figure of a seventeenth-century rector, and at Worsborough in Yorkshire a remarkable memento-mori tomb entirely in wood, dating from 1522. As on a number of other tombs in Old St Paul's (and throughout the country) small skulls formed a decorative motif, to say nothing of bones, mattocks and spades. Like Thomas Love Peacock's character Mr Flosky in *Nightmare Abbey* the sixteenth- and seventeenth-century sculptors had a very fine sense of the grim and the tearful.

The erection of a new chapel of almost unparalleled splendour at the east end of Westminster Abbey was Henry VII's great extravagance, but at the time of his death in 1509 it was unfinished, so for a short while his body lay in Old St Paul's, before going to Windsor for temporary burial.

Not long after yet another coronation procession was passing Old St Paul's as the eighteen-year-old Henry VIII rode from the Tower to Westminster. The City excelled itself: many of the streets were hung with tapestries, and on the south side of Cheapside—a particularly prosperous area—it was cloth of gold that the merchants hung out. 'The priests and the clerks in rich copes, with crosses of silver, censing his grace and the queen also as they passed. The Queen Katharine was sitting in her litter, borne by two white palfreys trapped in white cloth of gold; her person apparelled in white satin embroidered, her hair hanging down to her back, and on her head a coronal set with many rich orient stones.'

Some twenty years later preachers would be arguing for and against her divorce at Paul's Cross, while Anne Boleyn, safe in the King's favour, would be making the ageing Queen's life miserable with slights and pin-pricks.

Nearly all Henry VIII's visits to Old St Paul's were accompanied by the pageantry he loved so well. On 21st May 1514 he went there to receive a sword and cap of maintenance bestowed by Pope Leo X. After a brief oration by the Papal envoy the 'King next knelt at the High Altar, and two noblemen girded him with the Sword; and on his head they placed the cap, which by reason of the length covered his whole face. The procession then commenced making the entire circuit of the church. It was a fine sight to see the King and the handsome nobility of England in most pompous array. All bore such massive gold chains that some might have served for fetters for falcons' ankles, and sufficed for their safe custody, so heavy were they and of such immense value. The King wore a gown of purple satin and gold in chequers, and a jewelled collar worth a well of gold, his cap being of purple velvet with two jewelled rosettes, and his doublet of gold brocade.' So wrote the Venetian Ambassador.

Yet another of these great occasions at the cathedral was the Mass to celebrate the proclamation of Charles V—nephew to Katharine of Aragon—as Holy Roman Emperor; and in 1525 came proof of just how empty were oaths of friendship sworn between Henry and Francis I of France. To mark the capture of the French king by Charles V at the Battle of Pavia, Henry ordered a celebratory bonfire to be lit outside the cathedral, while inside a Te Deum was sung in the presence of the Court and both Houses of Parliament.

Beneath all the outward pageantry everything was not well for Rome. More and more people were being caught up in the spirit of the Reformation, which had recently received fresh impetus from Germany. As far back as 23rd July 1499 twelve Lollards who had recanted were made to do penance at Paul's Cross, surrounded by faggots, as a sinister warning that others would be less fortunate in the future. Much the same methods were employed at a ceremony in the cathedral itself in 1527 when Wolsey and thirty-six bishops and abbots were present when six recanted Lutherans were brought from the Fleet Prison to Old St Paul's; one carrying a taper and the others bundles of faggots. After kneeling and confessing their sins in front of the clergy, who were seated on a platform with the resplendent Wolsey in their midst, the six Lutherans were made to throw their faggots on a fire burning inside the north transept. The oppressive ceremony ended with the burning of heretical books and the absolution of the six, who were then received back into communion.

Soon Henry himself was attacking the Church in England. He, who had been given the title of 'Fidei Defensor' by the Pope. The King wanted two things: a male heir and to turn Anne Boleyn from a mistress into a wife. Only a few years before the Pope had freed Henry's own sister Margaret from her marriage vows, and now he hoped Rome would perform the same kindness for another member of the family. But Henry was reckoning without Katharine of Aragon's nephew Charles, who now held the Pope a prisoner in the Castel San Angelo in Rome. He had no intention that his aunt should be discarded like an old glove, so no divorce was forthcoming.

Eventually the Tudor took matters into his own hands, and in 1533 one of the items agreed at the King's Council was: 'Therefore, that order be taken that such as shall preach at Paul's Cross from henceforth, shall continually from Sunday to Sunday preach there, and also teach and declare to the people, that he that now calleth himself Pope, nor any of his predecessors, is and were but only Bishops of Rome, and hath no more authority and jurisdiction by God's laws within this realm than any other foreign bishop, which is nothing at all. . . . And that the Bishop of London may be bound to suffer none others to preach at St Paul's Cross, as he will answer, but such as will preach and set forth the same.'

Among those made to do penance at Paul's Cross at this time, 1534, for speaking against Henry's divorce was Elizabeth Barton (p. 44), the self-styled Maid of Kent. Also about this year—Stow does not give the exact date in his *Survey of London*—both St Michael's Cornhill and Paul's Cross were struck by lightning. 'At the same time certain main timber posts at Queen Hythe were scratched and cleft from top to bottom; and the pulpit in Paul's Churchyard was likewise scratched, cleft, and overturned.'

Almost at once following the Act of Supremacy which declared Henry, and not the Pope, as head of the Church in England, he began his headlong career—aided and abetted by many of his courtiers—of spoliation and legalized thieving from the treasuries of cathedrals and churches up and down the country. To him the looting of shrines such as St Erkenwald's at Old St Paul's and Thomas à Becket's shrine at Canterbury were simple ways of filling the royal coffers and rewarding lucky favourites.

Among the greater churches Old St Paul's was comparatively fortunate: none of the estates with which it was endowed were confiscated, and apart from the stripping of the shrine and the taking down and burning of the rood in the north transept, the fabric of the cathedral remained unharmed. One little incident connected with Old St Paul's is typical of Henry in his later years. One day when gaming with Sir Miles Partridge he wagered the four 'Jesus Bells' hanging in the tower in the churchyard on a single throw of the dice. He lost, and Sir Miles could hardly wait to convert them into cash: they were broken up as they hung, and the metal sold for what it would fetch. In the next reign, when he happened to be playing a political game of chance, he lost everything, including his head.

That next reign was Edward VI's, and his coronation on 20th February 1547 marked the beginnings of the ten stormiest years in the history of Old St Paul's. During his lifetime the cathedral was stripped of nearly all that had been added for its adornment in the past four hundred years, and in the reign of his half-sister—Mary Tudor—the Protestant bishop and one of the canons were burnt at the stake, and others of the clergy deprived of their offices by the Catholic faction; by then once again all-powerful.

The chronicler Holinshed recorded the scene as the nine-year-old king passed Old St Paul's, on the eve of his coronation, on his way to Westminster. 'As he passed on the south part of Paul's churchyard, an Argosine (inhabitant of Aragon) came from the battlements of Paul's Church upon a cable, being made fast to an anchor by the dean's gate, lying on his breast, aiding himself neither with hand nor foot, and after ascended to the midst of the cable, where he tumbled and played many pretty toys, whereat the king and the nobles had good pastime.'

That same year the heavy hand of the reformers was laid on the cathedral. 'The 17th November was begun to be pulled down the Rood in Paul's Church, and then the like was done in all the churches in London, and so throughout England.' The fact that two men were killed while trying to remove the great cross over the screen must have given rise to a certain amount of satisfaction in some quarters. Nearly ten years earlier another rood figure had been the cause of much scandalized conversation in Ave Maria Lane, Paternoster Row, and elsewhere in the City. Then John Hisley, Bishop of Rochester, had exhibited the fraudulent rood of Bexley at Paul's Cross. 'Wherein a man should stand enclosed, with an hundred wires within the Rood, to make the image goggle with the eyes, to nod with his head, to hang the lip, to move and shake the jaws, according as the value was of the gift which was offered. If it were a small piece of silver, he would hang a frowning lip; if it were a piece of gold, then should his jaws go merrily.' After exposing the rood for what it was, it was broken up in front of the crowd gathered about the cross.

Whether it was the great cathedral on Ludgate Hill, or the little chapel on Old London Bridge, all were visited by the Commissioners. Following an Order in Council of 1548 they visited Old St Paul's to see that all figures were removed 'as being things corrupt, vain and superstitious.' The Duke of Somerset, like the Duke of Northumberland, abused his office for his own ends, and among much to his discredit was the shameless way he plundered old buildings and used the materials for Somerset House, his palace in the Strand. Several of the additions on the north side of Old St Paul's became quarries for his own aggrandizement; including the cloister which contained the Dance of Death, and above its east walk, a fine library: two detached chapels and the Charnel Chapel. The latter was built about 1282. This last chapel included the tombs of three lord mayors, and from time to time when bones were removed from the churchyard as it became overfull, they were placed in the vault. Now at its demolition no less than five hundred tons of long-departed Londoners were removed in one thousand cart loads and 'laid on a moorish place, with as much soil to cover them as did raise the ground for three windmills to stand on, which have since been built there'. The moorish place was later called Bone Hill, which in due course became Bunhill, and today Finsbury Square stands somewhere near the site.

Eventually the Catholic and Protestant members of the Council sank their differences and united to oust Somerset from office, and in due course he made the short journey to Tower Hill.

As might be expected, the cathedral treasury did not escape the attentions of the Commissioners—since it consisted of a wealth of exquisitely wrought objects of great value and beauty. In addition to crosses, crosiers, monstrances, ampullae, plates and bowls of silver and silver-gilt; many set with precious stones and inlaid with enamel, there were the reliquaries housing the tangible relics of religious history (some it must be admitted of more than doubtful authenticity) gathered from the four corners of Europe throughout the whole of the Middle Ages. These reliquaries must have formed the most striking part of the whole priceless collection. Perhaps most notable would have been a silver-gilt reliquary of St Lawrence, decorated with stones and pearls, which stood on the backs of four lions; and a crystal reliquary set in silver-gilt and decorated with two angels containing relics of St Swithin, and Sts Cosman and Damian, St Mary and stones from the Holy Sepulchre and Calvary. Two others were reliquaries of crystal set in silver-gilt enamelled, with tiny figures of the Crucifixion on the top; while yet another—standing on three lions—contained milk of the Virgin, and was ornamented with figures of Sts Peter and Paul. The skull of St Athelbert, king and martyr, was enclosed in a head of silver-gilt, on which was a crown set with sixteen large stones. These were only a few of the treasures at Old St Paul's. More curious, but less valuable, were several poma, apple-shaped balls of silver that could be filled with charcoal or hot water to warm the hands of the celebrant during exceptionally severe weather. But within weeks, maybe days, all had been broken up, the stones removed and the metal melted down, leaving only their descriptions to fill a later generation with a sense of the futility of it all.

At Old St Paul's the vestments were as magnificent as they were numerous, and in their way they rivalled the Treasury. As far back as the beginning of the fifteenth century the collection included a hundred and seventy-five copes, fifty-one chasubles and ninety-two tunicles in red, blue, green, yellow black, white, and purple.

At this time the Bishopric of Westminster was abolished: the Abbey's career as a cathedral only began after the Dissolution of the Monasteries; and at the same time Edward VI transferred the Manor of Paddington from the Abbey of St Peter, Westminster, to Old St Paul's. From that action the expression 'to rob Peter to pay Paul' came into currency.

Even now Mass was still being celebrated in a number of the chapels. However, in 1550 steps were taken to put a stop to the practice. 'Order had been given in June the last year, from the Council to Bishop Bonner against the use of Mass said privately in some of the chapels in St Paul's, under the name of Our Lady's Communion: and that for the future, the Communion should be celebrated nowhere else but at the High Altar, and at no time else but at the times when High Masses used to be said. Yet still, to this time even under Ridley who is now Bishop, the Communion was celebrated with such superstitious as thought it were a Mass.' In 1548 Cranmer, assisted by eight bishops, had celebrated a Requiem Mass in Old St Paul's for Francis I of France, recently dead. But slowly, for all its anomalies, and out of the doctrinal upheavals and uncertainties, the Church of England was taking shape.

'The 1st of November 1552', wrote Stow, 'being the feast of All Saints, the new Service Book called of Common Prayer, began (to be used) in Paul's Church, and the like throughout the whole City . . . . and at afternoon he (Bishop Ridley) preached at Paul's Cross, the Lord Mayor, Aldermen and Crafts in their best liveries being present: which sermon, tending to the setting forth of the new late made Book of Common Prayer, continued till almost five of the clock at night.'

Soon the Protestant Edward VI was to die and be succeeded by his half-sister Mary Tudor. According to custom she rode in procession from the Tower, past Old St Paul's, to Westminster, on the day before her coronation. She travelled in an open chariot, drawn by six horses, and followed by a second carrying Princess Elizabeth and Anne of Cleves; the latter now the sole survivor of Henry VIII's matrimonial ventures. In Cheapside the Queen was presented with a purse containing a thousand marks in gold, and at Old St Paul's the royal party stopped to watch 'one Peter, a Dutchman, that stood on the weather-cock of Paul's steeple, holding a streamer in his hand of five yards long, and waved thereof, stood sometimes on the one foot and shook the other, and then kneeled on his knees, to the great marvel of all people. He had made two scaffolds under him, one about the cross, having torches and streamers set on it, and another over the ball of the cross, likewise set with streamers and torches, which could not burn, the wind was so great. The said Peter had sixteen pounds, thirteen shillings, four pence for his cost, and pains, and all his stuff.'

Within the cathedral itself not long elapsed before 'the service began again in Latin in Paul's Church, after the service of Sarum', while two customs reinstituted at this time—and finally abolished under Elizabeth I—were the choir singing on the top of the tower, and the Boy Bishops. 'On St Katharine's Day, after evensong, began the choir of Paul's to go about the steeple singing, with lights, after the old custom.' Today the tradition is still kept alive at Oxford where early on May Morning choristers sing from the top of Magdalen College Tower; and also from the top of the central tower of Durham

Cathedral on the anniversary of the defeat of the Scots at Neville's Cross outside the city in 1346.

Far more extraordinary were the Boy Bishops. They may have originated in the Middle Ages as far as the Christian Church is concerned, but their roots would seem to go back to the Saturnalia of Ancient Rome, where for a brief spell the roles of master and servant were reversed in a bibulous debauch. Every St Nicholas Day, 6th December, one of the choir boys was elected by his fellows to be Boy Bishop, and on 28th December, the Feast of the Holy Innocents, he was dressed in miniature robes and a mitre and allowed to preach a sermon, and even to give the benediction. At Old St Paul's two small mitres were included among the vestments. The custom was widespread, and the order of service for Boy Bishops is preserved in the library of Salisbury Cathedral.

At a steadily increasing rate the Queen was dissipating the goodwill of the ordinary people. In the early part of her reign it was not so much the question of religion, as her marriage to Philip of Spain. Some at least of those around Mary Tudor realized the idea of a Spanish king as her husband was equally repugnant in manor house and ale house alike.

Shortly before Philip's arrival Bishop Gardiner did his best at Paul's Cross to convince the Londoners only good could come from the match. Soon Philip was at Old St Paul's in person. On 18th October 1554 he visited it to hear Mass celebrated by a Spanish bishop and sung by Spaniards. The next year he again visited the City, this time with Mary Tudor at his side, to attend a pageant. Outside the cathedral one of the boys from St Paul's School, dressed in cloth of gold, presented him with a Bible, which 'he received very gently'. There were also acrobatics for the entertainment of the royal couple. 'A fellow slipping upon a cord as an arrow out of a bow, from Paul's steeple to the ground, and lighted with his head forward on a great sort of feather beds: and after he climb up the cord again and done certain feats.'

Now, day by day, the tension between the two religious factions grew: at Paul's Cross a knife was thrown at the Queen's chaplain which only just missed him, and stuck quivering in the side of the pulpit. On another occasion a dead cat with its head shaved like a priest's, and with a wafer fixed between its paws, was found hanging in Cheapside.

Once again Bonner was Bishop of London, while his predecessor Ridley was now in prison. Reunion with Rome came about in 1555, and from then on the number of those burnt as heretics increased sharply. Among them was Ridley himself, burnt in the town ditch at Oxford together with Latimer, while John Rogers, a Canon of Old St Paul's, was burnt at Smithfield.

It was all part of Mary Tudor's personal tragedy, to say nothing of the tragedy for her subjects, that she could bear no children: to her it seemed like a divine punishment for England's heresy. By a twist of fate word spread round the City in April 1555 that she had actually given birth to a son, and the bells of Old St Paul's pealed out in celebration. But it was only a rumour, and at Hampton Court the cradle remained empty.

During these years an abuse that became progressively worse at Old St Paul's was the habit of taking short cuts from one side of the churchyard to the other by going through the cathedral: to say nothing of loitering and transacting business in the nave. As far back as 1386 Bishop Braybrook, whose grave was marked by a fine brass, made it an offence punishable by excommunication to buy and sell, to throw stones, relieve nature, shoot arrows, or play ball in or around the cathedral. But by the middle of the sixteenth century the enforcing of these regulations had become very lax: in 1555 the Lord Mayor issued a proclamation forbidding the cathedral to be used as a thoroughfare or a market. 'Vessels full of Ale and Beer, great Baskets full of Bread, Fish, Flesh and Fruit and such other things' were among the items listed. Even worse were 'Mules, Horses and other beasts' led through from time to time. In addition to confiscation of the goods carried the penalties were three shillings and fourpence for the first offence, six shillings and eight pence for the second, ten shillings for the third, and two days' imprisonment—as well as the ten-shilling fine—for subsequent offences. But obviously these penalties were no more strictly enforced than the earlier rulings, and by the end of the century the nave had become a recognized meeting place both for the gallants and the riff-raff of the town.

Yet the religious life went on, literally in front of this annex of Cheapside. A new rood was set up over the entrance to the choir; in place of the one removed in Edward VI's reign. But after Mary Tudor's death it, and all such figures, were ordered away, and the enforcement was all but nationwide. Two extraordinarily interesting roods from this time do survive—the figures of Christ on the Cross with St Mary and St John—in the parish churches at Ludham in Norfolk and Winsham in Somerset. They are both makeshift paintings executed on the boards that had formed the backing to the original carved figures. At Old St Paul's the replacing of the rood was only a very small reparation compared with Protector Somerset's demolition of the cloister and chapels on the north side of the cathedral. By now the Palace must have become sadly dilapidated, and in 1556 Bishop Bonner leased it out to a private citizen; preferring to live at either Fulham or Stepney, his other London residences.

8

The advent of Elizabeth I as queen meant more settled times for England; but Old St Paul's was not to know peace for long. In 1561 fire seriously damaged the whole building. Today we can read all about it, not in a news-sheet, but in a pamphlet published only six days after the outbreak, giving all the details: 'Imprinted at London at the West End of Church at the Sign of the Hedgehog, by William Seres.'

'Between one and two of the clock at afternoon, was seen a marvellous great fire of lightning, and immediately ensued a terrible hideous crack of thunder, such as seldom hath been heard, and that by estimation of sense, directly over the city of London. . . . For divers persons in time of the said tempest being on the river of Thames, and others being in the fields near adjoining to ye City, affirmed, that they saw a long and a spear pointed flame of fire run through the top of the broach or spire of Paul's steeple from the east westward. . . . Between four and five of the clock a smoke was espied, by divers (persons), to break out under the bowl of the said shaft of Paul's.'

The Bishop was at once informed, and the Lord Treasurer was hastily sent for. Within a quarter of an hour the cross fell, together with the eagle, setting fire to the roof of the south transept. Everyone seemed to be offering advice at once, and very bad some of it was too. 'Some there were pretending experience in wars, that Councilled the remnant of the steeple to be shot down with canons, which council was not liked.' But before any effective method of fighting the fire could be put into practice: 'Ye labourers also being troubled with ye multitude of idle gazers, the most part of the highest roof of the church was on fire.' Within an hour the spire had burnt down to the battlements, and the roofs of the choir, the north transept and the nave were in flames. Such was the situation that those fighting the blaze were advised to leave the cathedral to its fate, and concentrate on saving the Bishop's Palace and preventing the flames spreading to the jumble of narrow streets which came particularly close to the churchyard on the north-west side. This was done, and the fire was prevented from spreading, but by evening when the wind dropped only the roofs of the aisles of the New Work and small areas of the transepts remained. The rest had been totally destroyed and the lead melted. But what was most remarkable was that no other buildings caught fire: 'By the violence of the fire burning coals of great bigness fell down almost as thick as hailstones, and flawes (flakes) of lead were blown abroad into the gardens without ye city, like flawes of snow in bredth, w'out hurt, God be thanked, to any house or person.'

The Queen saw the blaze across the fields that separated her palace at Greenwich from the City, and 'As soon as the rage of the fire was espied by her majesty and others in the court, of the pityful inclination and love that her gracious highness did bear to ye said church, and the city, sent to assist my Lord Mayor for the suppressing of the fire'. About five hundred helped in the operation that 'laboured in carrying and filling water, and divers substantial citizens took pains as if they had been labourers, as did also divers and sundry gentlemen, whose names were not known to the writer hereof'.

Inside the cathedral the vaulting was pierced in one or two places, but compared with what might have been, the damage was slight. The chief object to suffer damage was Bishop Fitz-James's chantry, which stood in the nave and was wrecked by falling timbers.

A curious incident connected with the burning was a statement made many years later by an old plumber when on his deathbed. In it he took the blame for the disaster on himself. According to his statement he was working on the spire on the day in question, and went off to get his midday meal, leaving a pan of coals and other fuel still burning. When he returned he found the dry timbers were well alight, and as he could not quench the fire he slipped away, saying nothing. But according to William Seres, the author of the pamphlet on the burning of the steeple: 'It is proved that no plumbers or other workmen laboured in the church for six months before.' So what was the truth of it all?

The work of making good the damage was put in hand immediately, and within two months a temporary roof was on the cathedral, and by the middle of the next year this in its turn had been replaced by a permanent oaken structure brought by sea from Yorkshire. The Queen contributed handsomely to the £6,000 repair bill by giving 1,000 marks, and timber to the same value, but fortunately for London Sir William Cecil would not agree to Bishop Grindal's suggestion that the lead for the new roof should come from St Bartholomew's, the finest Norman church in the City, and that matter for miles around. The Bishop's argument in favour of this vandalism was 'What is more reasonable than that the children should clothe their naked parents?' Like many a politician's emotional statements, it sounds reasonable enough until the cold light of common sense is brought to bear upon it.

The spire was never rebuilt, although several plans were drawn up and models made, but as late as June 1576 the Queen was taking an active interest. In that month she demanded to know what the Lord Mayor was doing in the matter. Her statement was typical: if his reply was not satisfactory she 'would have the Mayor and six of the best of his brethren before her upon the very next Sunday following, though she were then in a progress, and some distance from London. But however, after all, greater state matters obstructed and deterred from this undertaking. And so it lay neglected ever after.'

Another of her subjects to feel her tongue was Dean Nowell. On the occasion when Queen Elizabeth visited Old St Paul's for a service on New Year's Day, 1562, he put a prayer book, enriched with coloured engravings, in her pew. After the service the Queen swept into the vestry and demanded an explanation of this idolatrous and Roman thing. The Dean, in a dither at this display of Tudor wrath, explained he meant no harm by it. The Queen was mollified, but before dropping the subject she loudly prayed God to grant him more wisdom for the future; and with that swept out of the cathedral.

Although the authorities might fulminate against the financial transactions carried on inside Old St Paul's, it is not without its humour that in 1569 England's first public lottery was held outside the west door. In all there were forty thousand lots at ten shillings each, for prizes of plate, and the money raised went towards the restoration of harbours and havens around the coasts. It was successful, and in 1586 another was held. This time, with the threat of a Spanish invasion hanging over the country, the prizes were distinctly useful. 'Rich and beautiful armour: a house of timber and board was erected at the great West Gate of St Paul's for the purpose.'

By 1570 Elizabeth and England might have parted from Rome, but the Pope had no intention of returning the gesture. He issued a Bull releasing her subjects from their allegiance—which also declared her bastard and heretic. One John Felton actually nailed the objectionable document to the door of the Bishop's Palace at Old St Paul's; and later he was hanged for his pains, in the churchyard itself near the scene of his exploit.

Many Roman Catholics found themselves with their loyalties divided between their allegiance to their spiritual and temporal leaders, and as a result men of the quality of Father Campion and Father Garnet were executed for mixing politics with religion.

As the Counter-Reformation moved into action in Europe, so England's relations with Spain deteriorated, and in 1587 came the climax. After staving off the demands of Parliament for nearly ten years Elizabeth finally agreed to the execution of Mary Stuart, the centre of so many Catholic plots. A man much concerned with the Scottish queen's last months was Sir Christopher Hatton, later to have the most grandiose of monuments in Old St Paul's. In October 1573 Peter Burchett, a Gentleman of the Middle Temple, stabbed a man in the Strand, thinking it was his arch-enemy Hatton. In point of fact it was none other than Admiral Hawkins, who was Hatton's double. Elizabeth was enraged at an attempt on her favourite's life, and demanded Burchett should be hanged forthwith under martial law.

Eventually she was persuaded this would be illegal, and since the man was also charged with heresy, he was lodged in the Lollard's Tower at the west end of Old St Paul's. Later he was removed to the Tower—where he killed one of his warders with a piece of firewood—and eventually hanged in the Strand, near where he attacked Admiral Hawkins.

Much earlier, during Henry VII's reign a man named Hunn committed suicide in the Lollard's Tower by hanging himself with his girdle, after being imprisoned there for refusing to pay a mortuary fee to the priest who buried his child.

Among those concerned with Mary Stuart's execution who are entwined—if only slightly—in the history of the cathedral is Richard Fletcher. In his official capacity as Dean of Peterborough he was among those in the great hall of Fotheringhay Castle that February morning. Politely but very firmly Mary Stuart put him in his place when at the last minute he tactlessly tried to convert her to Protestantism. Seven years later, in 1594, he became Bishop of London; but died within two years—from taking too much tobacco, so the historian Campden declares.

After Mary's death Philip of Spain waited no longer, and the Armada set sail to deal with England as the Duke of Alba had dealt with the hapless Netherlands. A ratio of a hundred and eighty priests and only eighty-five surgeons among sixty galleons was only one miscalculation, and before long Elizabeth was riding in a chariot drawn by four horses to the service of thanksgiving in Old St Paul's. 'The preacher at Paul's Cross moved the people to give God thanks for the overthrow of our enemies the Spaniards, and there were showed eleven Ensign, or Banners, taken in the Spanish ships by our men. These Ensigns were set upon the lower battlements of Paul's Church before the preacher and the audience, which was great, all saving one streamer, wherein was an image of Our Lady with her son in her arms etc: and this was held in a man's hand over the pulpit.' Later the flags were set up on Old London Bridge, on the Great Stone Gate overlooking Southwark.

In 1592 Sir Christopher Hatton came to the cathedral for the last time. He had played the courtier to perfection, and at his death was Keeper of the Great Seal, Lord Chancellor and a Knight of the Garter. The funeral, like his living, was on a grand scale. One hundred poor people, suitably clad, were in attendance during the service, together with four hundred gentlemen and yeomen, the lords of the council and eighty gentlemen pensioners. Hatton's tomb stood on the south side of the retrochoir, was at least twenty-five feet high, with two enormous obelisks on either side, and must have been just a little vulgar. In fact it gave rise to at least two couplets.

'Philip (Sidney) and Francis (Walsingham) have no tomb
For great Christopher takes all the room'

and

'Three years together in this town hath been,
Yet my Lord Chancellor's tomb he hath not seen.'

Certainly Sir Philip Sidney, who died a few days after being wounded at Zutphen in 1586, had only a simple wooden tablet as his memorial. It bore the famous inscription:

'England, Netherlands, the Heavens and the Arts
The Soldiers of the World, have made six parts
Of noble Sidney; for none will suppose
That a small heap of stones can Sidney enclose.

His body hath England, for she it bred,
Netherlands his Blod in her defence shed,
The Heavens have his soul, the Arts his Fame,
All soldiers the grief, the World his good name.'

The other great man mentioned in the couplet was the Queen's wise old counsellor-fox Sir Francis Walsingham. At this time the cathedral almost surpassed the Abbey as the burial place for the great in statesmanship, soldiering, art, and science. Here Sir Nicholas Bacon was buried in 1579 in a curious tomb which showed his two wives side by side in effigy, while he himself lay above and between them. But of all the tombs erected since Henry Yevele's great work for John of Gaunt, the finest was the Earl of Pembroke's, on the north side of the sanctuary. The earl's sympathies lay with Mary Stuart, so perhaps it was as well he died honourably in 1561, before the intrigue and plotting dragged him down, as it did the Duke of Norfolk and so many others. The large but graceful monument was supported on twenty Corinthian columns. In the centre, beneath a tall canopy, lay the earl and his wife, and at their head and feet kneeled their sons and daughter. It was thanks to the elder son that the monument was erected some eleven years after his father's death. On the same side of the New Work was the tomb of Sir Thomas Heneage and his wife: a smaller but none the less fine monument of 1594.

For Old St Paul's the most turbulent century it had seen was to end on a note of triumph: 'On the 17th of November, 1598, a day of triumph for the long and prosperous reign of her Majesty at London. The Pulpit Cross in Paul's Churchyard was new repaired, painted and partly enclosed with a wall of brick: Dr Fletcher, Bishop of London, preached there in praise of the queen, and prayed for her majesty before the Lord Mayor, Aldermen, and citizens, in their best liveries. Which sermon being ended, upon the church leads the trumpets sounded, the cornets winded, and the choristers sung an anthem. On the steeple many lights were burned: the Tower shot off her ordinance, the bells were rung, bonfires made.' In the sixteenth and seventeenth centuries the term steeple was used to describe a tower, whether or not it had a spire. In the case of Old St Paul's, from 1561 until its final destruction only a low pyramidal roof capped the great central tower.

That was in 1598 that it rang with the music of a great occasion. In that same year Paul Hentzner visited the City and its cathedral during his stay in London, and his impressions are among the very few surviving accounts of what the intelligent traveller thought of Tudor England. However, one cannot help regretting that in the case of Old St Paul's he chose to copy down so many of the epitaphs in their entirety, instead of giving more of his own impressions of the cathedral itself.

'The cathedral of St Paul was founded by Ethelbert, King of the Saxons, and being from time to time re-edified, increased to vastness and magnificence, and in revenue so much, that it affords a plentiful support to a bishop, dean and precentor, treasurer, four archdeacons, twenty-nine prebendaries, and many others. The roof of this church, as of most others in England, with the adjoining steeple, is covered with lead. [The information about the detached belfry in the churchyard possibly having a spire at this date is interesting: there seems no other record of it.]

'On the right side of the choir is the marble tomb of Nicholas Bacon, and with his wife. Not far from this is a magnificent monument, ornamented with pyramids of marble and alabaster, with this inscription:

> Sacred to the memory of Sir Christopher Hatton. William Hatton, Knight, his nephew by his sisters side, and by adoption his son and heir, most sorrowfully raised this tomb, as a mark of his duty, etc:

'On the left hand is the marble monument of William Herbert, Earl of Pembroke, and his Lady: and near, is that of John, Duke of Lancaster. A little further, almost at the entrance to the choir, in a certain recess, are two small stone chests, one of which is enscribed "Here lies Sebba, King of the East Saxons, who was converted to the faith by St Erkenwald, Bishop of London, A.D. 677." On the other: "Here lies Etheldred, King of the Angles, son of Edgar." On whom St Dunstan is said to have denounced vengeance, on his coronation day. All of which came to pass, as predicted by the saint; for after being worsted and put to flight by Sueno, king of the Danes, and his son Canute, and at last closely besieged in London, he died miserably in A.D. 1017, after he had reigned thirty-six years in great difficulties.

'There is besides in the middle of the church a tomb made of brass, of some bishop of London, named William, who was in favour with Edward, King of England, and afterwards made chancellor to King William. He was Bishop sixteen years, and died in 1077. Near this is the following description:

Virtue survives the funeral:
To the memory of Thomas Linacre, an Eminent Physician.
John Caius placed this monument, etc:

'Thomas Linacre, physician to Henry VIII, a man learned in the Greek and Latin languages, and particularly skilful in physic, by which he restored many from a state of languishment and dispair to life . . . he went into orders a few years before his death, and quitted this life full of years, and much lamented, A.D. 1524, on the 20th of October.

'There are many tombs in this church, but without any inscriptions. It has a very fine organ, which at evening prayer accompanied with other instruments is delightful.'

Among the less well-remembered celebrities at the end of the sixteenth and beginning of the seventeenth century was Marocco. This Marocco, a bay gelding shod with silver, was no ordinary horse. His master, a Cheapside vintner named Bankes, had taught him to perform tricks, and in 1595 a piece called *Maroccus Extaticus* was printed. One of the woodcuts shows the horse begging like a dog, with a stick in his mouth. On the ground are two very large dice, so presumably he could count. In 1600 Marocco entered Old St Paul's and its history when he climbed to the top of the tower. Many of the writers of the day mentioned his performance; among them Dekker, who gives a great deal of satirical advice to the well-conducted gallant in his *Gull's Hornbook*. Among the right things to do, he writes, is to climb the tower of Old St Paul's: 'from whence you may descend, to talk about the horse that went up'. Ben Jonson and even Dr Donne—at that time still very much a man of the world, mentioned Marocco, while in the early *Love's Labour's Lost*, Shakespeare makes the page Moth say of the Duke's three-year educational course: '. . . how easy it is to put three years to the word three, and study three years in two words, the dancing horse will tell you.' But between them, Bankes and Marocco made a fatal mistake. They went to Rome, and there both were burnt as wizards.

As Elizabeth's reign ran to its close that spoilt darling of the Court, the Earl of Essex, marred the scene with his idiotic little rebellion: more the action of a thwarted child than a grown man. After his execution in February 1601 a sermon was preached at Paul's Cross, setting out his treason and irresponsible behaviour in the plainest possible terms, for even then he was still something of a popular hero with the man in the street.

Then at Richmond, as the foxes barked in the night, Queen Elizabeth died in 1603, after reigning for forty-four years. Two years before, she told Parliament: 'Though God hath raised me high, yet this I count the glory of my crown, that I have reigned with your loves.' In the next forty years that love turned sour, curdled, and saw what looked like the end for ever of the monarchy in England when Civil War brought down both Crown and Church in a common ruin. Old St Paul's itself was to suffer the humiliation of having a cavalry barracks and a 'preaching house' under its long roof, and brawling soldiers in the churchyard.

9

The first event of James I's reign which concerns Old St Paul's came in 1606, when the revolting ritual of hanging, drawing, and quartering four of the Gunpowder plotters—Bates, Digby, Grant, and Winter—took place outside the west front. They were not the only ones to suffer in the cathedral precincts: it was also the spot chosen for the execution of Father Garnet, charged with withholding from the authorities knowledge of the plot.

A happier event that same year was the visit to the cathedral by James's brother-in-law, Christian IV of Denmark. His was a genuine love of and interest in architecture, and after visiting the Exchange in the City, in the afternoon he 'went by coach unto Paul's Church and into the Quire, and other chapels therein. And then the king, and the Lord Chamberlain, with some others, ascended the top of the steeple, and when he had surveyed the City, he held his foot still whilst Edward Soper, keeper of the Steeple, with his knife cut the length and bredth thereof, in the lead. And for a lasting rememberance thereof, the said Soper within a few days after, made the king's character in gilded copper, and fixed it in the middle of the print of the King's foot, which was no sooner done, but some—minds of this iron age, thinking all gold that glistered, with violent instruments attempted to steal it' (Stow).

As the reign wore on, so the abuses in the cathedral grew worse. But then one of the customs permitted by the authorities themselves was hardly conducive to good order. By immemorial right the choir boys were allowed to claim money from anyone who entered wearing their spurs. In the *Gull's Hornbook* Dekker warns his readers: 'Be sure your silver spurs dog your heels, and then boys will swarm about you like so many white butterflies.'

By now the nave was familiarly known as Paul's Walk, and the aisles on either side the North and South Alley. The south aisle also went by the name of Duke Humphrey's Walk, from the tomb erroneously supposed to be his (p. 104). This spot was the meeting place of those whose full-time employment was the avoidance of employment, and the term 'to dine with Duke Humphrey' was the term used to describe those who spent their dinner hour kicking their heels near the tomb, for the good reason they had not the money to get a meal.

Dekker had something to say on the subject in the chapter headed: 'How a Gallant should behave himself in Paul's Walk.' The reader, he says, must use care: 'Be circumspect and wary what pillar you come in at, and take heed in any case as you love your reputation of your honour, that you avoid the serving man's log (a seat near Duke Humphrey's) and approach not within five fathom of that pillar; but bend your course directly in the middle line, that the whole body of the church may appear to be yours.'

Dekker also mentions the Crypt, St Faith's, in his play *The Shoemaker's Holiday*. Another who had something to say on the subject was Bishop Earle: he wrote: 'Paul's Walk is the land's epitome, or you may call it the lesser aisle of Great Britain. . . . The noise in it is like that of bees, a strange humming or buzz mixed, of walking, tongues and feet; it is a kind of still roar or loud whisper. . . . The visitants are all men without exceptions; but the principal inhabitants and possessors are stale knights and captains out of service, men of long rapiers and breeches, which after all turn merchants and here traffic for news.' One such character was Bardolph in *Henry IV, Part Two*:

FALSTAFF: Where's Bardolph?
PAGE: He's gone to Smithfield to buy your worship a horse.
FALSTAFF: I bought him in Paul's.

Yet another playwright who found a use for Old St Paul's in his writings was Ben Jonson: he set Scene 1 of Act III of *Every man out of his Humour* in the nave of the cathedral; while even the lawyers found their way there to conduct business. There, in the great Norman nave 'each Lawyer and Sergeant at his pillar hear his client's cause, and took notes on his knee'. Nor were all the abuses confined to the inside of the cathedral. Outside, the door into the north aisle, called the Si Quis Door, was perpetually covered with notices of situations vacant, things lost and found, etc: In fact, it was used much as the window of a paper shop and tobacconist's might be used today! Now small shops and houses, like parasites, occupied the spaces between the great buttresses of the New Work; even the chapter house was not immune from this wanton desecration. It had become a builder's store. Beneath the cathedral the vaults were let out to private individuals, and under the nave one Fynche, a carpenter, had set up his business, while under the choir and chancel a printer named Cawood plied his trade. Even the little parish church of St Gregory, nestling along the south side of the nave, did not altogether escape. There the choristers, who were also boy actors, gave performances to anyone with 4d. to spare for admission.

All through the centuries the polluted atmosphere around Old St Paul's had been a source of trouble: so much so that James I 'was moved with such compassion to this decayed fabric, that for prevention of its near approaching ruin, by the corroding quality of the coal smoke, especially in moist weather, whereunto it had long been subject' and on 26th March 1620 he attended a service when the Bishop preached a sermon referring to the cathedral's condition. In November of the same year a Commission was appointed to set about raising funds and carrying out repairs. Among those on the Commission were the Archbishop of Canterbury, the Lord Mayor of London, the Duke of Buckingham, Francis Bacon and 'Inigo Jones Esquire, Surveyor of his Majesty's Works'.

Inigo Jones was a Londoner, born in 1573. By all accounts his father—a cloth worker at the time of his death—had come down in the world, and in his youth Inigo is supposed to have worked as a joiner in Paul's Churchyard. The third Earl of Pembroke (who erected the great monument to his father in the cathedral) discovered his talents and sent him to Italy. From there he went to Denmark, where he was employed by Christian IV, then engaged on embellishing his capital with some of its most charming buildings. The year 1613 saw him once again in Italy where the Palladian city of Vicenza with its wonderful theatre cast its spell over him. On his return to England he was once again working for the King (p. 208) and in 1632 began in earnest the huge task of restoring Old St Paul's. First he added a portico to the west front that was magnificent, but quite out of keeping. A hundred and twenty feet wide and sixty-six feet high, it had an entablature supported by fourteen huge Corinthian columns, while ten statues were to be placed along the top. Of these only two—James I and Charles I—were ever set up. On either side were two (rather clumsily designed) towers capped with wooden lanterns, a hundred and forty feet high.

As soon as this was completed Inigo Jones continued by

translating the whole of the exterior of the nave into the Classic idiom of the day. All the stonework was refaced with Portland stone set in regular courses: the simple Norman buttresses were converted into pilasters, while the tracery was removed from the round-headed windows and all signs of the old style hidden beneath a wealth of classical mouldings and carved swags. Even St Gregory's parish church was pulled down, and this later led to trouble for Inigo Jones during the years of friction between Charles I and Parliament.

By the time the Civil War broke out in 1642 all except the New Work, the aisles on the east side of the transepts and the central tower had been transformed. Now the transept fronts, with their scrolls and obelisks, resembled the west front, though without projecting porticoes. The arbiters of taste of the day pronounced themselves well satisfied with the result: in their eyes Old St Paul's had been made to look civilized, instead of being the uncouth relic of a barbarous age. While to an antiquarian it would seem the Norman part had suffered a fate worse than death; Inigo Jones was only doing what William of Wykeham did at Winchester nearly two centuries earlier when he reclothed the Norman nave in the Perpendicular of his day. And yet, had the portico survived in some other context than as the prefix to a medieval cathedral, surely it would be considered the equal of Inigo Jones's masterpiece of proportion, the Banqueting House.

Among those who contributed to the cost of the restoration was Sir Paul Pindar, who gave £10,000. As secretary to the Ambassador at Constantinople he had been there when Elizabeth I sent a mechanical organ as a present to the Grand Signor, Mehmet III. The Sultan was enchanted with the outsize toy, which resulted in English traders receiving preferential treatment at the expense of the French. Among the work carried out as a result of Pindar's generosity were repairs to the south transept and the stone screen across the entrance to the choir; the latter being embellished with black marble columns and statues of Saxon kings.

All had not been easy for the Commission: especially when it was up against such a member as the Duke of Buckingham.

For some time before the actual work started, roughly shaped blocks of stone had been arriving at the cathedral; and for an equal time the Duke of Buckingham had been quietly appropriating them for his own town house then abuilding. William Laud, Bishop of London, and John Donne, were the two men most responsibile for giving teeth to the Commission; but the Bishop moved on and up, to Canterbury; and in 1631 John Donne died. That, coupled with the uncertain times, meant the pace of the work of restoration was slowed: though it did not come to a stop.

John Donne became Dean of Old St Paul's in 1625, the year of Charles I's accession. As a young man he accompanied the Earl of Essex on his beard-singeing expedition to Cadiz, and on his return he became secretary to Sir Thomas Egerton, Lord Keeper of the Great Seal. Ahead lay difficult years: About 1600 he in secret married his employer's niece, only to lose his job when the secret came to light. The Countess of Bedford befriended him, and in 1607 James I gave him the Deanery of Gloucester, and eighteen years later he moved to Old St Paul's. In later years his fame grew both as a writer and a preacher, but curiously enough much of his poetry, metaphysical in character—by which he is best remembered today, was written when he was still young with a circle of friends who were worldly, in the best sense of the word.

Then, when he knew he was dying (1631), he ordered himself to be painted in a shroud. In that way he could be sure all was to his satisfaction. Later the likeness was used by Nicholas Stone for his memorial. At a cost of £120 he carved the Dean, enveloped in his shroud with only the face showing, as though emerging from an urn. It was to be the last important monument to be placed in the old cathedral. Strangely enough it was the only piece of sculpture to come intact through the holocaust of 1666, and today it stands in Wren's building, within a few feet of its old position in the south choir aisle of the medieval cathedral.

If John Donne received the last memorial to be set up in Old St Paul's, one of the last great men to be buried there was Sir Anthony Van Dyck, who in 1641 was laid in an unmarked grave. The next year the Civil War began its course.

But before then an amusing interlude came in 1630, resulting in a very aggrieved father writing to Charles I to complain about his daughter—evidently one of those young women who simply have to be different—after she had been married on the top of the cathedral tower. Wrote Sir Thomas Gardiner to the King:

'My youngest daughter without my consent or knowledge, shee mounted upp to the Topp of Powles, the nearer to Heaven, for to Shewe God there howe wise she was in her Actions, and there she was married unto Sir Henry Mainewaringe, and yet she was not there taken up into heaven, but came down again upon Earth, here further to trouble me, although the great care and charge I had in breeding her upp did not deserve such disbedience.' Sir Thomas, it would seem, was as much plagued with bad spelling as with a difficult daughter. What he expected the King to do is not quite clear.

At the cathedral the first to suffer when the inevitable clash came between King and Parliament was Paul's Cross. After being the rallying place of the Londoner for centuries, as well as 'for many ages the most solemn place in all this nation for the greatest divines and most eminent scholars to preach at, [it] was pulled down to the ground', and for long only a tall elm marked the spot.

Next it was the turn of the clergy. All bishops, deans, and chapters were abolished, and at Old St Paul's 'all money, goods, and materials bought or given into any place, for reparing or furnishing of this church, or appertaining' was confiscated. For a short while the deanery became a prison for Royalists brought from Chichester. Later the house was granted to the public lecturer, Dr Cornelius Burgess, whose salary of £400 a year came out of the cathedral revenues, while plate was sold 'for the best advantage, and employed towards the providing of necessaries for the Train of Artillery'.

Much of the cathedral, both inside and out, was shrouded in scaffolding left in place when the work of restoration stopped at the outbreak of war. Now, in 1645, this too was appropriated, dismantled and sold for what it would fetch. The sum raised was £1,746 15s. 8d., which Parliament used to pay for the arrears of pay in a regiment commanded by Colonel Jephson. As a result of removing the scaffolding, the vaulting in the south transept collapsed, and the cathedral's ruin was brought a stage nearer. Now saw-pits were dug in the pavements regardless of the graves beneath, and in the choir the stalls were destroyed. Even the vestments and altar frontals were burnt, to extract the gold and silver thread, though several of the latter were sold and found their way to Spain, and to the cathedral at Valencia.

The demolition of St Gregory's at the time of Inigo Jones's restoration now came home to roost. As a result of a complaint from the churchless parishioners he was summoned before Parliament, fined £500 for his act and ordered to rebuild it. More than anything, it was an opportunity for attacking the King through one of his servants.

First Archbishop Laud was beheaded, 1645, and then the King himself, attended by Juxon, Bishop of London, was executed outside the Banqueting House at Whitehall (p. 216). In that same month of January 1649 a Parliamentarian soldier broke his neck in Old St Paul's, through attempting to ride a horse up the steps into the choir. An Act of God, many must have thought, if not daring to say so out loud.

At this time when the attitude of many was summed up by Lord Brooke when he declared 'he hoped one of them (his friends) should live to see no one stone standing left upon another in that building', William Dugdale began his *History of St Paul's:* a book of infinite value. Born in 1605 Dugdale studied at Oxford where he devoted his time to antiquities, and in 1639 was appointed Rouge-Croix Pursuivant at the College of Heralds. 'The said Mr Dugdale therefore receiving encouragement from Sir Christopher Hatton, then a member of that House of Commons, who timely foresaw the near approaching storm, in summer of anno 1641, taking with him Mr William Sedgwick, a skilful arms painter, repaired first to the Abbey Church of Westminster and St Paul's, and there made exact drafts of all the monuments in each of them, copied the epitaphs according to the very letter; as also of all arms in the windows, or cut in stone.' They then went through the Midlands visiting

Ely, Norwich, Peterborough among other places before going north, recording and drawing 'any tombs or monuments . . . to the end that the memory of them, in case of that ruin then imminent, might be preserved for future and better times'.

After taking part in the Civil War as a Royalist, Dugdale returned to his work as an antiquarian, and set about his *History of St Paul's*. Much of the material came from the Scriveners Hall, the Masters of which allowed 'many manuscript books, original charters, old rolls, and other ancient writings in bags and hampers, all relating to that great cathedral, and freely lent to him to be carried to his own lodging, which amounted to no less than ten porters burdens'. The book was published in 1658, and two years later saw the Restoration, when Dugdale became Norroy King of Arms. He was knighted at his creation as Garter King of Arms in 1677, and in 1685 he died.

Dugdale's written description is of great value, but without the illustrations it would be only half the story. These were engraved in 1657 from the drawings of Sedgwick by Wenceslaus Hollar. Originally Hollar intended to follow in his father's footsteps and become a lawyer in his native city of Prague, but soon he turned to art; becoming an engraver. While travelling to broaden his outlook he met the English Ambassador in Cologne, who in 1635 brought him to England. Within a few years he became drawing master to Prince Charles (afterwards Charles II), and like Dugdale fought for the Royalists during the Civil War. In 1657 he etched over forty of the drawings of Old St Paul's for the book, taking the greatest care over the smallest details. He died in 1677, aged seventy. His plates covered nearly every aspect of the English scene, from the trial of Lord Strafford, to the ruins of London after the Great Fire. According to the historian and antiquarian Aubrey 'he was a very friendly good-natured man as could be, but shiftless as to the world, and died not rich'. . . . and died not rich—in his last hours he begged the bailiffs not to take the bed on which he lay. Had the etchings of Old St Paul's been his only work, they would be memorial enough.

The worst of Dugdale's fears were well grounded. In 1649

the cathedral had been divided in two by a wall across the entrance to the choir. The eastern half was used as a preaching house, and the west as a cavalry barracks. At one time eight hundred horse were stabled in the nave. Nearly everywhere it was the same story; six thousand shut up in Worcester cathedral after the Battle of Worcester; at Durham the Scottish prisoners used the choir stalls as firewood, while Exeter was treated like Old St Paul's in that it too was divided by a wall. There an independent preacher held forth in the nave, and in the choir a Presbyterian.

At Old St Paul's matters became out of hand—even by the average Cromwellian major's standards they were bad—for a notice was issued on 27th May 1651: 'For as much as the inhabitants of Paul's Church Yard are much disturbed by the Soldiers, and others, calling out to passengers, and examining them, though they go peaceably and civilly along, and by playing at ninepins at unseasonable hours; these are therefore to command all soldiers and others whom it may concern, that hereafter there shall be no examining and calling out to persons that go peaceably on their way, unless they do approach the Guards, and likewise to forbare playing at ninepins and other sports, from the hour of nine of the clock in the evening till six in the morning.'

Just how foul the great nave must have been at this time can be gathered from an extract from the unlicensed *Mercurius Democritus*, published in December 1652. 'The poor people are so distressed for want of Coals, that they have burnt up all the dry Horse-dung in Paul's, giving for the same 4d and 6d the bushel, which make the Woodmongers so mad, that they hoist up the price of Coals, and like Crafty Merchants, keep their ships at Gravesend, and so come dropping up the river one by one, as they see the City necessitated.' Horse dung from the cathedral at 4d. and 6d. a bushel: surely after that no further degradation was possible.

Outside Old St Paul's the statues of the two Stuart kings were pitched off the portico, and shops built between the columns; so by the time Dugdale's book appeared even his worst fears must surely have been surpassed. But in 1660

Charles II really was king in his own palace at Whitehall, and steps were taken to make good some of the damage of the preceding years.

10

The cathedral was in a deplorable state. The central tower was noticeably out of the vertical, Paul's Cross had been demolished, the vaults of the south transept and the chapter house had collapsed, in 1647 the Bishop's Palace had been demolished, and shops cluttered the portico. Inside, the choir stalls had vanished, along with the bishop's throne, the organ loft, and the screens; while many of the tombs must have been mutilated to a lesser or greater degree. In short, in 1660 St Paul's must have been a sight to make anyone who cared for it want to weep.

In 1663 a Commission was set up on Charles II's instructions to decide what was to—or could—be done, and John Barwick was transferred to London from the deanery at Durham, where he had done yeoman service in restoring that cathedral to something of its former glory. The Commission was a lengthy document which included the names of the Lord Mayor, both the Archbishops, Lord Clarendon, what seemed like half the Upper House, both spiritual and temporal; numerous knights, and further down the long list—William Dugdale.

A subscription book was started, headed by Charles, who gave £1,000, and £2,000 from the Archbishop of Canterbury. A number of the subscribers attached strings to their contributions. 'If I live and hold the place I now have', scrawled Lord Clarendon after his promise of £50 a year. Having come up the political ladder the hard way he had few illusions, and was running no risks. 'As long as the work continues', added Lord Anglesea after his promise of £20 per annum.

The removal of the shops in the portico was the first step, and for the next three years work went on, even through the Plague of 1665. In August, September, and October of that year £153 was spent on repairs. In all, from the time of the setting up of the Commission in 1663 until the end of August 1666 the sum of £3,586 5s. 1¼d. was spent. With very minor results, it must be admitted.

Among those named in the Commission who were actively concerned with getting the work done were Sir John Denham; poet, courtier, Surveyor-General, and architect—in that order; John Webb, a disciple of Inigo Jones; Roger Pratt, a designer of fashionable houses; Hugh May, who combined architecture with the office of Paymaster to the Royal Works, and Dr Wren.

The interior, they all agreed, should be brought into line with Inigo Jones's reclothed exterior; and John Webb added the central tower would have to be rebuilt in its entirety, while Roger Pratt suggested they should merely patch up the cathedral and leave it at that. Having expressed his opinion, he quietly ordered the removal of the rubble from the south transept where it still lay after the collapse of the vaulting, to be carted off for use in the fine new house he was building for Lord Clarendon in Piccadilly.

During the spring of 1666 Dr Wren, as he then was, was asked to draw up a report on Old St Paul's. At this date he had only recently returned from France where the new buildings made a great impression on him; above all the cupolas of several Paris churches: notably Sts Louis et Paul and the Val-de-Grâce. The report he gave was not encouraging. At that time he was even more out of sympathy with the medieval builders than in later years, and he did not mince his words: 'They made great Pillars without any graceful manner; and thick walls without judgement. The work was both ill design'd and ill built from the beginning: ill design'd because the Architect gave no Butment enough to counterpoise the Roof from spreading the walls, for the eye alone will discover to any man that those Pillars, as vast as they are, even eleven Foot in diameter, are bent outwards at least six inches from their first position.' Like some other members of the Commission, Wren want to reface the interior walls in a 'good Roman manner'. Always at the back of his mind was the idea of a large central space. His uncle was Bishop of Ely, so long before he saw the churches in Paris the great central octagon of Ely Cathedral was familiar. 'I cannot propose a better remedy than by cutting off the inner corners of the cross,' he wrote, 'to reduce this middle part into a spacious Dome or Rotondo, with a Cupola or hemispherical roof, and on the cupola, a lantern with a spiring top, to rise proportionably.' And so it was, even before there was any question of replacing the whole cathedral, that the idea of a large central space for St Paul's was born in Wren's mind: the idea that was to be the core of all his subsequent designs for the building.

A strong supporter of this revolutionary idea was John Evelyn; he too had been to France and seen some of the buildings that so impressed Wren, and on 17th August 1666 he was one of the seven who visited the cathedral. Two were for preserving the old tower, but Evelyn backed Wren's proposal sufficiently strongly for it to be agreed that plans which included a cupola should be drawn up for inspection by the Commission.

At the age of thirty-five Wren could indeed count himself fortunate that he had been entrusted with the restoration of Old St Paul's. At that time his reputation rested more on his abilities as an astronomer than as an architect. He wasted no time in drawing up his plans, which provided for the remodelling of the interior of the Norman nave and transepts in Renaissance style, replacing the central tower with a large dome—not unlike the present one—but retaining the Early English choir in its original form. Had there been no fire, and had this idea been carried out, London would have been able to boast the greatest architectural curiosity in Europe, if nothing more.

However, this was not to be. 'This fatal night (2nd September), about ten, began the deplorable fire, near Fish Street, in London', wrote Evelyn in his *Diary*. But it was a fifteen-year-old schoolboy named William Taswell who left the most vivid account of the burning of London and its cathedral.

'On Sunday, between ten and eleven forenoon, as I was standing upon the steps which lead up to the pulpit in Westminster Abbey, I perceived some people below me running to and fro in a seeming disquietude and consternation; immediately almost a report reached my ears that London was in a conflagration; without any ceremony I took leave of the preacher, and having ascended Parliament Steps, near the Thames, I soon perceived four boats crowded with objects of distress. They had escaped from the fire scarce under any covering except that of a blanket.

'... just after sunset at Night (Tuesday, 4th September), I went to the royal bridge (landing stage) in New Palace Yard at Westminster to take a fuller view of the fire. The people who lived contiguous to St Paul's church raised their expectations greatly concerning the absolute security of that place upon account of the immense thickness of its walls and its situation; built in a large piece of ground, on every side remote from houses. Upon this account they filled it will all sorts of goods, and besides, in the church of St Faith's, under that of St Paul's, they deposited libraries of books because it was entirely arched all over; and with great caution and prudence every the least avenue through which the smallest spark might penitrate was stopped up. But this precaution availed them little. As I stood upon the bridge among others, I could not but observe the gradual approach of the fire towards that venerable fabric. About eight o'clock it broke out on the top of St Paul's Church, already scorched by the violent heat of the air, and lightning too, and before nine blazed so conspicious as to enable me to read very clearly a sixteen mo edition of Terence which I carried in my pocket.'

What Taswell saw was the five hundred and seventy-nine-year-old cathedral catching fire in at least three places: the scaffolding around the tower, the ready-made bonfire in St Faith's, and the wooden ceiling of Inigo Jones's Portico.

He continued: 'On Thursday, soon after sunrising, I endeavoured to reach St Paul's. The ground so hot as almost to scorch my shoes, and the air so intensely warm that unless I had stopped some time upon Fleet Bridge to rest myself, I must have fainted under the extreme languor of my spirits. After giving myself a little time to breathe, I made the best of my way to St Paul's.

'And now let any person judge of the violent emotion I was in when I perceived the metal belonging to the bells melting, the ruinous condition of its walls; whole heaps of stone of a large circumference tumbling down with a great noise just upon my feet, ready to crush me to death. I prepared myself for returning back again, having first loaded my pockets with several pieces of bell metal.

'I forgot to mention that near the east walls of St Paul's a human body presented itself to me, parched up as it were with the flames, whole as to skin, meagre as to flesh, yellow as to colour. This was an old woman who fled here for safety, imagining the flames would not reach her there. Her clothes were burnt, and every limb reduced to coal.

'In my way back I saw several engines which were bringing up to its assistance all on fire, and those concerned with them escaping with great eagerness from the flames, which spread instantaneous almost like wild fire; and at last, accoutred with my sword and helmet, which I picked up among many others in the ruins, I traversed this torrid zone back again.

'The papers half burnt, were carried with the wind to Eton. The Oxonians observed the rings of the sun tinged with an unusual kind of redness. A black darkness seemed to cover the whole hemisphere; and the bewailings of the people were great.'

From end to end the vast cathedral, at one time the largest in medieval Europe, was gutted; the vaulting all collapsed, and at the east end the falling masonry had smashed through the pavement, opening St Faith's to the sky. Today St Faith's lives on, combined with the little parish church of St Augustine (though only the tower remains since the Blitz), a few yards east of the present cathedral.

Yet the great tower that for centuries had been a source of anxiety still stood as though unwilling to admit defeat. Some of the lines from Shakespeare's Dirge in *Cymbeline* take on an unexpected and poignant appropriateness:

> Fear no more the heat o' the sun,
> Nor the furious winter's rages;
> Thou thy worldly task hast done,
> Home art gone, and ta'en thy wages. . . .
>
> Fear no more the lightning-flash,
> Nor the all-dreaded thunder-stone;
> Fear not slander, censure rash;
> Thou hast finished joy and moan.

Attempts were made even now to patch up part of the west end of the nave for services, but after some of the arcade collapsed the inevitable was at last recognised; that the time had come for the old cathedral, with a longer history than Westminster Abbey, to be erased in its entirety.

Twenty years later Old St Paul's existed only in the memories of those who had known and loved it, and in the illustrations of Wenceslaus Hollar and a few others.

Old Whitehall Palace

(The Court)

1

In many cases the English palace, like the English cathedral, only grew to greatness with the passing of several centuries. Building, pulling down and altering all went into the creation of St James's, Hampton Court and the vanished Placentia (at Greenwich), Westminster, and Whitehall. Only after one great owner had followed another and left his distinctive imprint did the palaces acquire their true character and identity. A character derived from an aggregation of parts rather than one grandiose whole, as at Versailles.

Above all, this is true of Old Whitehall Palace which grew, haphazard, to become a palace with over a thousand apartments beneath its complex of roofs.

Of the early history of Whitehall it is the occupiers rather than the building itself that are known to us. In the Middle Ages Westminster was little more than a huddle of mean houses about the walls of the Abbey, built by Edward the Confessor and again by Henry III, and the royal palace with its hall built by William Rufus. To the east, plainly visible across open fields and the sweep of the Thames, was the City with its numerous spires, all dominated by the recently completed Old St Paul's.

In 1223 the powerful Hubert de Burgh bought land from the Abbey which was situated along the road linking the royal suburb with London itself. Here, between the road and the river, he built himself a mansion. That he served three kings as diverse as Richard I, John, and Henry III says less for his integrity than for his ambition. During Richard's reign he matured both as a statesman and a soldier. Under John he flourished, and before many years had passed he became castilan of Falaise, with the unfortunate Prince Arthur in his care. Shakespeare was not so far from the truth in *King John*: the messenger who came with the order for the boy's murder was ejected from the castle. But later Arthur was taken from de Burgh's care, to die in unexplained circumstances at Rouen. However, this did not stop de Burgh from accepting preferment at John's hands.

By 1215 he was Lord Chief Justice, and supporting the King at Runnymede against the Barons. In the time of Henry III he fell from favour when his enemy, Peter des Roches, succeeded in displacing him. But by the time of his death in 1243 he had reached a comparatively peaceful old age, and was reconciled to his king. This then was the man who built the mansion destined to grow into Old Whitehall Palace.

After his death at Banstead, according to the chronicler Matthew Paris, de Burgh's body was brought to London and the Black Friars' church: 'to be interred in the house of the brothers of the Preachers, on whom in his lifetime he had bestowed many gifts, and among other things his noble palace at Westminster, and which afterwards the Archbishop of York purchased'.

The transfer of the house by the river had been made during his lifetime, and the actual purchase by the Archbishop was effected before 1243. The new owner was Walter de Grey, a man whose career in the Church and in politics was furthered at great personal cost.

In 1205 he bought the office of Chancellor for £5,000, and like de Burgh he supported John at Runnymede. The King nominated de Grey as Archbishop of York, while the barons preferred Stephen Langton. By way of explanation the canons declared they chose Langton because de Grey was illiterate; but nothing daunted, de Grey made the journey to Rome where on the Pope's orders the decision was reversed. At this the canons justified their enforced change of opinion by stating that although de Grey was admittedly illiterate, he at least was virtuous in his private life. Evidently there were degrees of virtue. To encourage the Pope to declare in his favour had cost de Grey no less than £10,000.

During forty years as Archbishop of York he had a most

successful political career, and perhaps his best memorial is the south transept of York Minster, for which he was responsible. In London he acquired de Burgh's house from the Black Friars for use as a private residence, and in 1245 he transferred it to the See of York, for use by his successors. Now it was called York Place, a name it retained for nearly three hundred years.

All through the Middle Ages, and well into Renaissance times, the palaces of the clergy frequently rivalled those of their secular rivals, if not of the King himself, and in 1360 Edward III stayed at York Place, and even summoned a Parliament to meet there.

A man who did much rebuilding and enlarging—though exactly what cannot be determined now—was Thomas Rotherham, Archbishop of York from 1480 until plague cut short his life in 1500. In 1463 he became a D.D. at Oxford, having previously taken the same degree at Cambridge. After his patroness Elizabeth Woodville became wife to Edward IV his career really prospered. In 1474 he became Chancellor of England, and Archbishop of York six years later. But partial eclipse came in Richard III's reign when he suggested Queen Elizabeth, together with her younger son and daughter, should seek sanctuary at Westminster Abbey. As a guarantee of good faith he surrendered his Great Seal to her. In Act II, Scene 4 of Shakespeare's *Richard III* he declares:

> 'For my part, I'll resign unto your grace
> The seal I keep; and so betide to me
> As well I tender you and all of yours!
> Come, I'll convey you to the sanctuary.'

His action had its consequences when he was arrested at that meeting in the White Tower, which ended in the execution as traitor of Lord Hastings. Rotherham was more fortunate in that after a short spell in prison he was freed.

The dynasty changes, and now the Tudors rule over England. In 1494 the Archbishop was present when Henry VII's younger son, a good-looking boy of three, was created Duke of York. Little could he have dreamed that thirty-five years later the

York Place he had enlarged and enriched would belong to the youth, then Henry VIII, whose path no man crossed with impunity. But all that lay in the future.

2

'Then had he two great crosses of silver, whereof one of them was for his Archbishopric, and the other for his Legacy, born always before him whithersoever he went or rode, by two of the most tallest and comeliest priests that he could get within all this realm.'

Such a description could only fit Cardinal Wolsey, who occupied York Place after receiving the See of York, in addition to the three he already held. Now in 1514, the palace was at the beginning of its greatest period of magnificence. For fourteen years it was the setting for a way of life that not even the King himself could outshine.

With Wolsey everything had to be of the finest. Even the yeomen who formed part of his household were the tallest and most stalwart he could find in the whole country. During these years Thomas Cavendish, whose brother William was to found the fortunes of the Devonshire family, was his gentleman usher, and in later years he wrote a biography of his master. Incidentally, Shakespeare found *The Life of Cardinal Wolsey* invaluable when he came to write *Henry VIII.*

This huge household of some five hundred was ruled over by a steward, a treasurer, and a comptroller—immediately recognizable by the white wands always in their hands. Catering for so many was no small task, and there were two kitchens. One served the majority of the household, and the other the Cardinal himself and his immediate circle. Of these Cavendish wrote: 'He had in the hall-kitchen two clerks of his kitchen, a clerk comptroller, a surveyor of the dresser, a clerk of his spicery. Also there in his hall-kitchen he had two master cooks, and twelve other labourers, and children as they called them (turn-spits and scullions); a yeoman of his scullery, and two others in his silver scullery; two yeomen of his pastry, and two grooms.' That in itself would seem sufficient, but as many and more were employed in the private kitchen.

'Now in his private kitchen he had a Master Cook who went daily in damask satin, or velvet, with a chain of gold about his neck; and two grooms, with six labourers and children to serve in that place; in the Larder there, a yeoman and a groom; in the Scaldinghouse, a yeoman and two grooms; in the Scullery there, two persons; in the Buttery, two yeomen and two grooms, and two other pages; and in the Ewery likewise: in the Cellar, three yeomen, two grooms, and two pages; besides a gentleman for the month.'

Five men were employed in the laundry, three in the bake-house, two in the wood yard, while a yeoman was in charge of the barge. In the stables there was a master of the horse, a clerk of the stable, a yeoman of the stable, a saddler, a farrier, a yeoman of the chariot, a sumpter man, a yeoman of the stirrup, a muleteer, and sixteen grooms in charge of sixty-four geldings. These were only some of those who made up the temporal side of Wolsey's household.

'And for as much as he was Chancellor of England, it was necessary for him to have divers officers of the Chancery to attend daily upon him. That is to say: first, he had the Clerk of the Crown, a Riding Clerk, a Clerk of the Hanaper, a Chafer of Wax. Then he had a Clerk of the Check, as well to check his Chaplains, as his Yeomen of the Chamber; he had also four Footmen, which were apparelled in rich running coats, whensoever he rode any journey. Then he had a Herald at Arms, and a Sergeant at Arms; a Physician and Apothecary; four Minstrels; a Keeper of his Tents, an Armourer; and Instructor of his Wards; two Yeomen in his Wardrobe; and a Keeper of his Chamber in the Court. He had daily in his house the Surveyor of York, a Clerk of the Green Cloth; and an Auditor. All this number of persons were daily attendant upon him in his house, down-lying and up-rising.'

To wait upon him Wolsey had a high chamberlain, a Vice-chamberlain, twelve gentleman ushers, six gentleman ushers to wait in his privy chamber, forty gentleman cup-bearers, carvers, sewers and gentleman daily-waiters, six yeomen ushers, eight grooms of the chamber, two secretaries, two clerks, and four counsellors: all in daily attendance.

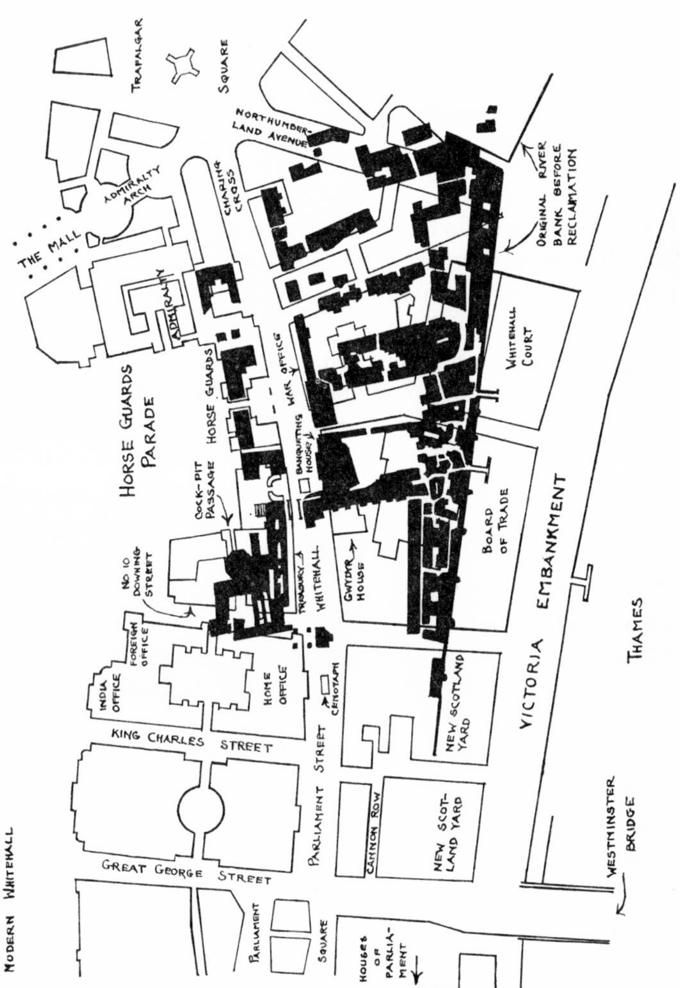

OLD WHITEHALL PALACE IN RELATION TO MODERN WHITEHALL

It is surprising to find that in the midst of so much worldly magnificence, religion was not totally obscured. 'First, he had there a Dean, who was always a great clerk and a divine; a Sub-Dean; a Repeater of the Choir; a Gospeller, a Pisteller; and twelve singing priests: of Scholars, he had first, a Master of the children; twelve singing children; sixteen singing men; with a servant to attend on the said children. But to speak of the furniture of his chapel passeth my capacity to declare the number of the costly ornaments and rich jewels, that were occupied in the same continually. For I have seen there, in a procession, worn forty-four copes of one suit, very rich, besides the sumptuous crosses, candlesticks, and other necessary ornaments to the comely furniture of the same.'

The Cardinal's daily life was played out on the same lavish scale. In the mornings he would hear Mass as soon as he rose, then put on his robes, and appear in the galleries of the palace. This is how the world best remembers him: 'All in red, in the habit of a Cardinal; which was either of fine scarlet, or else of crimson satin, taffety, damask, or caffa, the best that he could get for money: and upon his head a round pillion, with a noble of black velvet set to the same in the inner side; he had also a tippet of fine sables about his neck; holding in his hand a very fair orange, whereof the meat or substance within was taken out, and filled up again with the part of a sponge, wherein was vinegar, and other confections against pestilent airs; the which he most commonly smelt unto, passing among the press, or else when he was pestered with many suitors. There was also borne before him first, the great seal of England, and then his Cardinal's hat, by a nobleman or some worthy gentleman, right solemnly, bareheaded.'

Then to the cries of 'On, my lords and masters, on before; make way for my Lord's Grace,' he made his way to the great door. 'And when he came to the hall door, there was attendant for him his mule, trapped all together in crimson velvet, and gilt stirrups. When he was mounted, with his cross bearers, and pillar bearers, also upon great horses trapped with fine scarlet. Then marched he forward, with his train and furniture in manner I have declared, having about him four footmen, with gilt pollaxes in their hands; and thus he went until he came to Westminster Hall door.' Here he made his way to the Court of Chancery, 'sitting there till eleven o'clock, hearing suitors, and determining of divers matters. And from thence, he would divers times go into the Star Chamber, as occasion did serve; where he spared neither high nor low, but judged every estate according to their merits and deserts.'

Like many others Wolsey, as has already been remarked, would not shoot Old London Bridge, and each Sunday when he left Whitehall to spend the day at Court with Henry VIII at Greenwich, it meant travelling by water. He would take his barge, manned by tall yeomen, as far as the Vintry where he landed. While he was preceded along Thames Street by his two silver crosses and two silver pillars, his cardinal's hat and the Great Seal, the yeomen piloted the barge under Old London Bridge and waited for him to rejoin it at Billingsgate. From there he continued his journey without further interruption to Greenwich.

When it was Wolsey's turn to play the host at York Place, he did so on a lavish scale. 'The banquets were set forth, with masks and mummeries, in so gorgeous a sort and costly manner, that it was a heaven to behold.' So wrote Cavendish as he looked back across some thirty years to his days as gentleman usher. Frequently these social occasions had the air of elaborate masques or charades, in which both guest and host played their part. For all that it was an archbishop's house it lacked nothing likely to appeal to Henry VIII. 'There wanted no dames, or damsels, meet or apt to dance with the maskers, or to garnish the place for a time, with other goodly disports. Then there were all kind of music and harmony set forth, with excellent voices both of men and children.'

What seemed a rather dull banquet might be in progress, with Wolsey presiding at one end of the Hall, beneath a Cloth of Estate which hung over his chair, when suddenly the cannon mounted by the water gate would boom out. Wolsey would pretend to be as surprised and as curious as his guests to know what was afoot, and would ask his lord chamberlain and his comptroller to investigate. After looking from the riverside windows they reported an ambassador or some foreign prince had just landed at the stairs.

'I shall desire you, because ye can speak French, to take the pains to go down into the hall to encounter and receive them, according to their estates, and to conduct them into this chamber, where they shall see us, and all these noble personages sitting merrily at our banquet, desiring them to sit down with us, and to take part in our fare and pastime.'

A few minutes later the newcomers were ushered into the hall, surrounded by twenty blazing torches and preceded by a large number of drums and fifes. Acting as their interpreter the lord chamberlain explained: 'Sir, forasmuch as they be strangers, and can speak no English, they have desired me to declare unto your Grace thus; they, having understanding of this your triumphant banquet, where was assembled such a number of fair dames, could do no less, under the supportation of your good grace, but to repair hither to view as well their incomparable beauty, as for to accompany them at mumchance, and then after to dance with them, and so to have of them acquaintance. And, sir, they furthermore require of your Grace licence to accomplish the cause of their repair.'

Graciously Wolsey played his part, and agreed. The masked strangers moved among the seated guests, playing dice for gold coins which they carried in a large cup. After this excellent opportunity to assess the charms of the Cardinal's female guests the newcomers went up to the great man himself, poured out the gold—about two hundred crowns—on to the table and invited him to dice for it. At one throw he won all, 'whereat was great joy made'.

Then Wolsey addressed his lord chamberlain, for it must be remembered his guests spoke no English, and asked him to find out whether there was one among them worthy to occupy his own seat of honour. The lord chamberlain translated the question, and after a moment's discussion he informed his master: 'Sir, they confess that among them there is such a noble personage, whom, if your Grace can appoint him from the other, he is contented to disclose himself, and to accept your place most worthily.'

For a moment Wolsey stared at each in turn, and then made a mistake. 'Me seemeth the gentleman with the black beard should be even he,' he said, getting up and offering his seat beneath the Cloth of Estate. Another of the guests burst out laughing and pulling off his mask revealed that he, and not the other man, was the King. In good humour Henry pulled off his friend's mask, who now stood revealed as Sir Edward Neville. Everyone laughed, and the festivities began. But first the King went to a room ready prepared, where he changed into fresh clothes, and then returned to the hall to occupy the seat vacated by Wolsey.

While he was absent the half-eaten feast was removed 'and the tables spread again with new and sweet perfumed cloths. Then in came a new banquet before the king's majesty, and to all the rest through the tables, wherein, I suppose, were served two hundred dishes or above, of wonderously costly meats and devices, subtly devised. Thus passed they forth the whole night with banqueting, dancing, and other triumphant devices, to the great comfort of the king, and pleasant regard of the nobility there assembled.'

Cavendish described in some detail the masks and clothes worn by Henry and the dozen or so courtiers who made up the royal party. 'All in garments like shepherds, made of fine cloth of gold and fine crimson satin paned, and caps of the same, with visors of good proportion of visonomy; their hairs, and beards, either of fine gold wire, or else of silver, and some being of black silk.'

But already in the midst of the pomp and magnificence fate was spinning the web in which the Cardinal would eventually be caught. It all began when young Lord Percy, a member of the household at York Place, unwisely confided to Wolsey that he loved and intended to marry one of Katharine of Aragon's ladies-in-waiting. Her name, he said, was Anne Boleyn. Wolsey knew full well that Henry had marked down the girl for himself, though she herself was still unaware of the fact. Off he went to whisper in the royal ear, and when he returned to his palace it was with the injunction to blight this unwelcome romance, and break off the pre-contract of marriage.

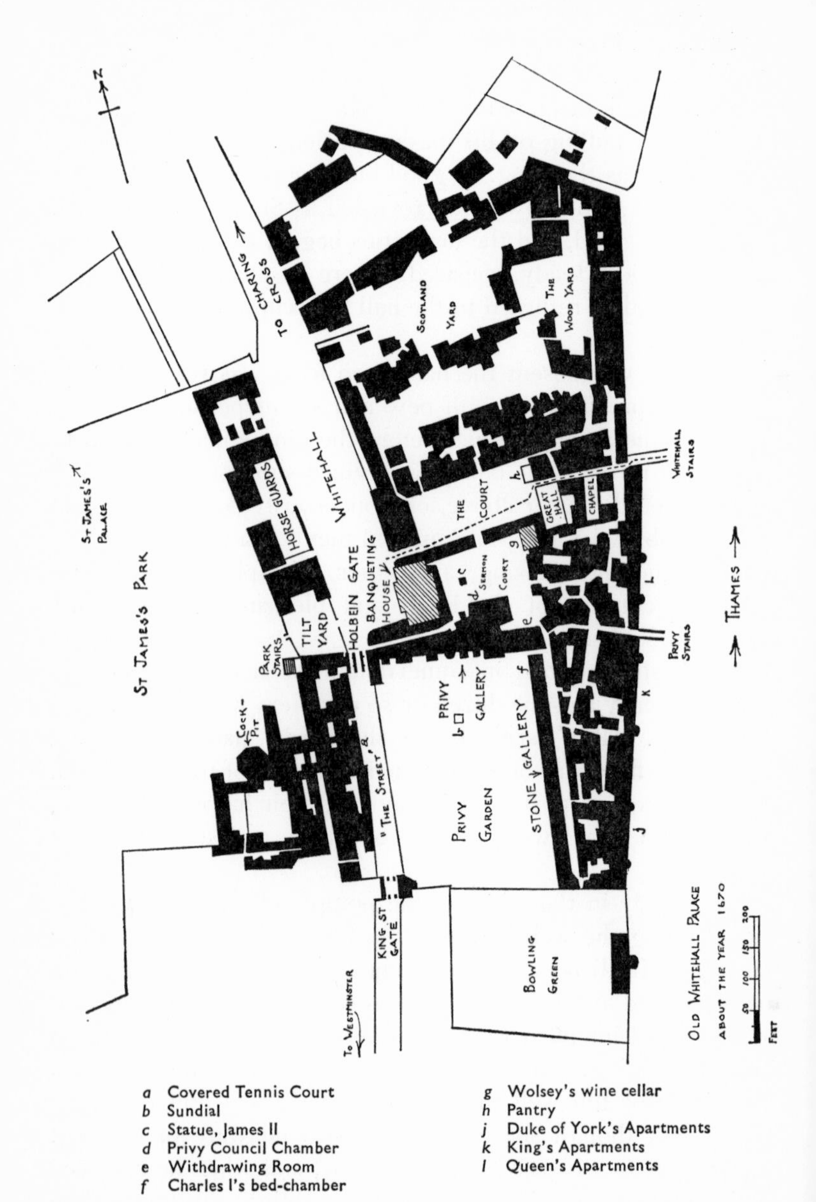

a Covered Tennis Court
b Sundial
c Statue, James II
d Privy Council Chamber
e Withdrawing Room
f Charles I's bed-chamber
g Wolsey's wine cellar
h Pantry
j Duke of York's Apartments
k King's Apartments
l Queen's Apartments

Crabwise he went about his work, not telling Lord Percy the full facts of the case. He called the young man to him in the Long Gallery, and in front of a number of his household rated him thus: 'I marvel not a little of thy peevish folly, that thou wouldst tangle and ensnare thyself with a foolish girl yonder in the Court, I mean Anne Boleyn. Dost thou not consider the estate that God hath called thee unto in this world? For after the death of thy noble father, thou art most like to inherit and possess one of the most worthiest earldoms of this realm.'

Wolsey went on to tell Percy he should first have asked permission of the King as well as of his father. 'Ye have not only offended your natural father, but also your most gracious sovereign lord, and matched yourself with one, such as neither the king, nor yet your father will be agreeable with the matter. And hereof I put you out of doubt, that I will send for your father, and at his coming, he shall either break this unadvised contract, or else disinherit thee for ever.'

'Sir,' said Lord Percy; by now in tears, 'I knew nothing of the king's pleasure therein, for whose displeasure I am very sorry. I considered that I was of good years, and thought myself sufficient to provide me of a convenient wife, whereas my fancy served me best, not doubting but that my lord my father would have been right well persuaded.' He went on to ask how he could with honour break the contract, if that was what he must do. Wolsey assured him it was easily accomplished, adding 'I will send for your father out of the north parts, and he and we shall take such order for the avoiding of this hasty folly as shall be by the king thought most expedient.'

With the final warning that unless he wished to incur the King's anger he must avoid Anne Boleyn's company altogether, Wolsey swept out of the Long Gallery, leaving the discomforted and tearful Lord Percy alone under the curious gaze of a number of the household.

If the interview with Wolsey was unpleasant, what followed with his father—a most dutiful courtier—was far worse. Immediately upon his arrival in London the Earl of Northumberland went to York Place to discover why he had been sent for in this peremptory manner. The Earl and the Cardinal talked together in the Long Gallery, and before they parted the Cardinal sent for wine, and they drank together. Then a number of the household were ordered to wait upon the Earl as he left the palace. Among them was George Cavendish.

The Earl of Northumberland, however, was in no hurry to leave. After seating himself at one end of the gallery on a bench usually occupied by Wolsey's servants (where they would be out of earshot but not out of call of their master), he asked for his son to be sent to him.

The storm broke without warning.

'Sir,' thundered the Earl, 'thou hast always been a proud, presumptious, disdainful, and a very unthrift waster, and even so hast thou now declared thyself—having no manner of regard to me thy natural father, nor in especial unto thy soverign lord, to whom all honest and loyal subjects bear faithful and humble allegiance. But that his Grace of his mere wisdom doth consider the lightness of thy head, and wilful qualities of thy person, his displeasure and indignation were sufficient to cast me and all my posterity into utter subversion and dissolution: but he being my especial and singular good lord and favourable prince, and my Lord Cardinal my good lord hath and doth clearly excuse me in thy lewd fact, and doth rather lament thy lightness than malign the same.'

On and on he went, determined to terrorize his son so that never again would he wish to trespass on royal property.

'For of thy natural inclination thou art disposed to be wasteful prodigal, and to consume all that thy progenitors have with great travail gathered together and kept with honour. For I do not purpose, I assure thee, to make thee mine heir; for, praises be to God, I have more choice of boys who, I trust, will prove themselves much better, and use them more like unto nobility, among whom I will choose and take the best and most likeliest to succeed me.'

For Lord Percy the scene must have been doubly embarrassing because now a number of Wolsey's servants were listening to every word. At last his father came to the sting in the tail of his tirade. Turning to the onlookers he said with bittersweetness: 'Now, masters and good gentlemen, it may be your chance hereafter, when I am dead, to see the proof of these things that I have spoken to my son prove as true as I have spoken them. Yet in the mean season I desire you all to be his friends, wherein ye shall show yourselves and to tell him his fault when he doth amiss, wherein ye shall show yourselves to be much his friends.' Then he left them, going through the palace to where his barge was waiting at the river steps.

The pre-contract was broken off, and in due course Lord Percy found himself married to a daughter of the Earl of Shrewsbury. As for Anne Boleyn, for a few months she was sent home to her father, 'whereat she smoked'.

It was a bad day's work for Wolsey when he became the prime instigator in breaking off the contract of marriage between the young couple. Anne Boleyn might have to wait, but when her revenge came, it was complete. And yet, within six years of Wolsey's downfall brought about by the question of Henry's divorce so he could marry Anne, she herself was disgraced and dead. There is something almost Grecian in the symmetry of the tragedy.

What was once only gossip behind closed doors soon became public property when the man in the street openly talked and speculated about the King's estrangement from Katharine of Aragon. At length Henry himself broached the subject to Wolsey, and inquired about obtaining a divorce. The Cardinal prevaricated and suggested eminent lawyers and bishops should be consulted for their opinion. Perhaps he half hoped Anne Boleyn was only a passing whim on the King's part: if so he was deluding himself and underestimating Henry's capacity for having his own way.

In due course the bishops and many of the university professors assembled at York Place, talked interminably, and eventually departed. Their only concrete suggestion was that Henry should canvass the universities of Europe to discover whether foreign savants were of the opinion that he had a case or not. The actual grounds on which he was basing his claim was that he should never have espoused Katharine of Aragon, who first of all had married Prince Arthur, his elder brother. For her part Katharine of Aragon stoutly denied this short-lived marriage to a sickly youth had ever been consummated.

The idea was agreed upon, and while the royal linen was washed at Louvain, Paris, Orlèans, Padua, Bologna, and elsewhere, Wolsey reigned on at York Place. When the answers came back, with the university seals attached, many were favourable. 'There were inestimable sums of money given to the famous clerks to choke them, and in such especial to such as had the governance and custody of their Universitie's seals.'

For Wolsey the beginning of the end came when he was summoned to the King, and spent more than an hour with him in private conversation. On the way back to York Place he had the Bishop of Carlisle for company in his barge. The day was hot, and as the Bishop mopped his face he remarked:

'Sir, it is a very hot day.'

'Yea,' answered Wolsey with feeling: 'if ye had been well chafed as I have been within this hour, ye would say it were very hot.'

Back at the palace Wolsey went to his room to snatch some sleep, but within two hours Anne Boleyn's father, now the Earl of Wiltshire, was at his bedside with a royal command. The Cardinal was to go without delay to Katharine of Aragon, and persuade her not to oppose the divorce. He sat up in bed and roundly accused the Earl and other lords of the council of making trouble.

'Ye and other my lords of the council, which be near unto the king, are not a little to blame, and misadvised to put any such fantasies into his head.'

Thomas Boleyn, Earl of Wiltshire, knelt by the bed, tears in his eyes, but said nothing. Then, when he had left, Wolsey got up, dressed again and set out on his mission. He failed, and the case dragged on. Cardinal Campeggio came from Rome, achieved nothing, and returned. All the while Anne Boleyn missed no opportunity to blacken Wolsey's name. By now the King was more than half inclined to listen to anything detrimental about his one-time friend.

Perhaps Wolsey did not notice the significance behind a casual conversation with the Duke of Norfolk. Once during dinner he remarked he would be well satisfied if the King would allow him to go to Winchester, one of his four benefices.

'Nay,' said the Duke, 'to your benefice of York, where considereth your greatest honour and charge.'

'Even as it shall please the King,' replied the complacent Wolsey, unaware what lay behind the remark. Casually he changed the subject.

In the autumn of that year, 1529, Wolsey was in residence at York Place, ready for the beginning of the Michaelmas Term at Westminster. The first day he went, riding on a white mule and preceded by the two silver crosses, exactly as he had done for so many years past. But it was to be the last time. The next day York Place was visited by the Dukes of Norfolk and Suffolk, who ordered him to surrender the Great Seal, and retire to his house at Esher. Wolsey refused: there followed an argument, but the Dukes returned empty-handed to Windsor.

Back they came the next day with the order in writing from the King. This time there was no argument. The Great Seal changed hands, and Wolsey was no longer master in York Place. After the messengers had gone he called all the officers of the household to him, and ordered an inventory to be taken at once. For the last time he walked through the magnificent galleries and rooms, looking at the palace he so unwisely had made fit for a king.

The walls of the main gallery were hung with cloth of gold and cloth of silver, and 'There also hung the richest suits of copes of his own provision, which he caused to be made for his colleges of Oxford and Ipswich, that ever I saw in England. Then had he two chambers adjoining to the gallery, the one called the gilt chamber, and the other called, most commonly, the council chamber, wherein were set in each two broad and long tables, upon tressels, whereupon was set such a number of plate of all sorts, as were almost incredible. In the gilt chamber was set out upon the tables nothing but all gilt plate; and a cupboard standing under a window, was garnished wholly with plate of clean gold, whereof some were set with pearl and rich stones. And in the council chamber was set all white plate and parcel gilt; and under the tables in both the chambers, were set baskets with the old plate, which was not esteemed but for broken plate and old, not worthy to be occupied, and books containing the value of and weight of every parcel laid by them ready to be seen.'

After the inventory had been taken, nothing remained to be done, except to prepare to take his barge for the last time. As Wolsey left, Sir William Gascoigne his treasurer said:

'Sir, I am sorry for your grace, for I understand ye shall go straightway to the Tower.'

'Is this the good comfort and council that ye can give your master in adversity?' snapped Wolsey, who was probably thinking along the same lines. 'It hath always been your natural inclination to be very light of credit, and much more lighter in reporting of false news. Therefore go your ways, and give good attendance unto your charge, that nothing be embezzled.'

The news of his fall had spread far and fast. As he entered his barge to go to Putney, and from there travel by mule to another of his residences at Esher, he was watched by the occupants of more than a thousand small craft, tacking to and fro on the Thames, all hoping to see the great man escorted to the Tower.

And so Cardinal Wolsey departed from York Place. Only a few days later, on 2nd November 1529, its new owner moved in, even before the transfer had been completed. In actual fact the palace belonged to the See of York, and had been occupied by Wolsey in his capacity as Archbishop, and not as his own personal property. But then the distinctions of mine and thine were never clearly defined in Henry's brain, whether it concerned people or property.

3

When Henry VIII took over York Place it consisted of the Great Hall, the chapel standing between it and the river, and the apartments in which the great man lived together with his enormous retinue. What these apartments were like no one can say for certain. In all probability they resembled those at Wolsey's other great residence, Hampton Court. Handsome, and yet almost intimate in character.

At that time, 1530, even the name was changed at the whim

of the new owner. From York Place it became Whitehall. Perhaps because of some part kept whitewashed, as was the case with the White Tower. Another theory traces the origin to the Court of Requests, where the Lords met in the Palace of Westminster, which was also called the White Hall.

In *Henry VIII* Shakespeare makes the 3rd Gentleman in Act IV, Scene 1, say of Anne Boleyn's coronation:

> So she parted, [from the Abbey]
> And with the same full state pac'd back again
> To York Place, where the feast is held.

1st GENTLEMAN:
> Sir,
> You must no more call it York Place, that's past:
> For since the Cardinal fell, that title's lost:
> 'Tis now the king's, and call'd Whitehall.

3rd GENTLEMAN:
> I know it;
> But 'tis so lately alter'd that the old name
> Is fresh about me.

The second alteration made by Henry was to build the Privy Stairs, a few yards to the west of those used by the public, and now called Whitehall Stairs. In a sense the Thames was the High Street of London during the Middle Ages and for several of the succeeding centuries, and not even a monarch as absolute as Henry VIII cared to deprive his subjects of access to the river at this point.

That was only the beginning. In 1532 he made extensive purchases from the Abbot of Westminster, acquiring land on either side of the palace. That is, to the south, and to the north beyond Scotland Yard which Wolsey had purchased shortly before his fall. This was a most extensive acquisition, and also included what is now Green Park and St James's Park, stretching as far as where Buckingham Palace now stands.

Magnificent though York Place had been, it was not sufficient for Henry. First two gateways were erected, in 1532, across the roadway, linking up the two main parts of the palace. The one at the southern end came to be called the King's Street Gate, while the northern was the Holbein Gate. The latter was so named from a mistaken idea the painter had been responsible for its design. In fact he did not carry out any work at Whitehall until some four years after its completion. In reality, it was as much a bridge as a gate, enabling one to get from one part of the palace to the other on the opposite side of the road with ease and privacy.

Although these two gates were built at the same time, the Holbein was Tudor Gothic in design and details, while the King's Street Gate was Renaissance; being adorned with pilasters and free-standing busts and having its large turrets capped with cupolas. The main archway through which the traffic passed was flat-topped, while the two smaller ones for pedestrians were round-headed. Above were large windows: these certainly were Gothic in feeling.

Perhaps the most striking detail of the Holbein Gate, also with four turrets, battlements, and windows in the two upper stories, were tiles in two colours; giving an effect not unlike the flint and stonework of so many East Anglian churches. The main fronts were decorated with portrait medallions of the Roman emperors; four on each side. Until the erection of Inigo Jones's Banqueting House in the next century the Holbein Gate must have been the most notable feature of the palace.

The buildings erected by Henry on the other side of the road were given over to sport. About halfway between the two gates arose one of the covered tennis courts. A long building, Late Perpendicular in style, with five traceried windows, buttresses and crocketed pinnacles, it looked more like a chapel than anything else. Behind was another building with an ecclesiastical air quite at variance with its purpose—the cockpit. Eight-sided, with battlements and a pointed roof it must have resembled a cathedral chapter house, such as Southwell or York, rather than a setting for murderous fights between cocks, which in later centuries were armed with additional spurs of razor-sharp steel.

Close by were three more tennis courts. One enclosed, but the others open to the weather. They were referred to as the

Little Close Tennis Court; to distinguish it from its big neighbour; and the Great and Little Open Tennis Courts.

It was not without reason that Henry was famous throughout Europe for his sporting abilities. There was even a tilt-yard for jousting, as well as bowling greens for the less energetic.

But already the King was past his prime as an athlete. Slowly but surely his huge frame was turning to coarseness, and his good looks were waning.

In addition to the Holbein Gate the two parts of the palace were further united by what was called the Privy Gallery, which reached to those apartments overlooking the river. This gallery had been removed wholesale from Wolsey's mansion at Esher, even before the Cardinal went into banishment in the North. Wrote Cavendish in his book: 'The taking away thereof before my lord's face was to him a corrosive, which was invented by his enemies only to torment him.' Corrosive was the most apt of expressions to describe the feelings of such a man as Wolsey: compounded of greatness, meanness and above all, limitless ambition.

The Stone Gallery, to which the Privy Gallery was joined, fronted the river and was used from time to time for important banquets. Immediately above was the Long Gallery, with its ceiling painted by Holbein.

The general plan of the palace at this time is most difficult to describe both briefly and lucidly. Facing the river is the Stone Gallery with the Privy Stairs in front reaching down into the water. To the right is Wolsey's Great Hall, easily recognized by its tall roof with a lantern halfway along its length. In front is the chapel, but this hardly shows, while to the right again are the Whitehall Stairs with a passageway leading to the main road. On the far side of this is Scotland Yard, as yet not built upon by the King. Behind the Stone Gallery is the Orchard, almost square, with the road running along its further side; separating it from the Privy Garden is the Privy Gallery, at right angles to the Stone Gallery, which connects with the Holbein Gate over the road. The righthand side of the Privy Garden (still looking at the Palace from the river) is bounded by the lane from Whitehall Stairs. This lane has a gateway over it where it meets the road. Across the public highway, spanned at the south end by the King's Street Gate which adjoins the top left corner of the Orchard, and at the north by the Holbein Gate, are the cockpit, tennis courts, tilt-yard, etc.

Perhaps the most extraordinary feature of the palace was the way in which it was cut in three portions by public thoroughfares. In Paris a road runs under the very long arms of the Louvre, making the Place de la Carouselle into a square in the usually accepted sense. That is perhaps the nearest existing parallel to the situation at Whitehall.

Henry VIII was indeed fortunate: when his own palaces at Westminster and in the Tower had become dilapidated and out of date, two magnificent new ones, at Hampton Court and Whitehall, fell into his lap. About 1530 the new Chancellor, Thomas Cromwell of the little eyes, cautiously suggested that Henry should be less enthusiastic in his additions to Hampton Court. Now at Whitehall he must have rubbed his hands together most anxiously, and wondered whether he dared broach the subject again.

Although a king and not a cardinal was now the owner at Whitehall, life was no less magnificent. Like Wolsey the King had a vast retinue, and in the Royal Ordinances of the Tudor Household we can glimpse a little of how it was ordered. Good behaviour evidently did not always come naturally to these courtiers and servants.

'All such as have their lodgings within the court shall give straight charge to the ministers and keepers of their chambers, that they do not cast, leave, or lay any manner of dishes, platters, saucers, or broken meat, either in the said galleries, or at their chamber doors, or in the court, or other place.'

As might be expected where a large number of career-conscious courtiers were gathered together; all were ready to clamber to favour over their rivals by way of tale-bearing and spiteful gossip.

'Item, it is ordered that such persons as be appointed of the privy chamber, shall be loving together, and of good unity and accord.'

Since the King's private life took the course it did, there

was good reason for the Item concerning his bedchamber. ' . . . keeping secret all such things as shall be done or said in the same, without disclosing any part thereof to any person not being for the time present in the same chamber; and that the King being absent, without they be commanded to go to his Grace, they shall not only give their continual and diligent attendance in the said chamber, but also leave harkening and enquiring where the King is, or goeth, be it early or late; without grudging, mumbling, or talking of the King's pastime; late or early going to bed; be anything done by his grace, as they will avoid his displeasure; and it is also ordered, that in case any of the said privy chamber shall hear any of his fellows, or other person, of what estate or degree soever he be, speak or use any evil or unfitting language of the King, he shall with diligence disclose and show the same, with the specialities thereof, unto his Highness, or to some of his Privy Council, such as he thinketh meet, to show and declare unto his Grace.'

Even after the King had finally returned to his bedchamber, and gone to sleep, there were those who were to remain wakeful and watchful. In the outer chamber were squires and pages on duty should their royal master require anything. Their conduct was also dealt with in the pages of the Royal Ordinances:

' . . . that no man presume or be suffered to come within the said chamber after the King be served for All-night, but only the esquires for the body and pages, except such as be of the King's privy chamber, who in their passing and repassing through the said chamber shall so use themselves, as they do not disturb the said esquires of their rest and sleep; nor also that there be no manner of playing at dice or cards, used within the same chamber, after the King be served with All-night, except it be by the King's commandment or licence.'

In the morning there was an elaborate ritual laid down which had to be observed concerning bedmaking.

'A groom or page with a torch to stand at the bed's foot; they of the Wardrobe opening the King's stuff of the bed upon a fair sheet between the groom and the bed's foot; two yeomen of the Chamber on each side to make the bed and a gentleman usher to direct them; a yeoman with a dagger to search the straw of the bed, and then to cast the bed of down upon that; and one to tumble over it for the search thereof, & etc: lastly making a cross and kissing it. The two yeomen next the foot making the fires. And so many of them to stick up Angels about the bed and let down the curtains of the said bed.

Item. A Squire for the body or gentleman usher ought to set the King's sword at the bed's head; also to charge a Groom or Page with a light to keep the said bed till the King be disposed to go into it.

Item. A Groom or Page to take a torch while the bed making to fetch a loaf of bread, a pot with ale, a pot with wine for them that make the bed, and every man drinketh.'

Even the dogs that thronged all palaces throughout the ages were regulated here. 'The King's Highness also straightly forbiddeth and inhibiteth, that no person, whatsoever he be, presume to keep any greyhounds, mastiffs, hounds, or other dogs, in the court, other than such few small spaniels for ladies or others.'

Here in the Great Hall it was now the six-foot-two-inch figure of a king, and not a reddish-faced cardinal, before whom all fell back, bowing and deferential, as he took his place at a banquet for some foreign ambassador—or in the day-to-day pomp and ritual of life at Court.

Among those who rubbed shoulders with the great ones of the realm were two servants far more privileged than they. Will Somers and Jane the Fool were the King's Court Jesters, dressed like anyone else of no particular consequence. Yet they could go further with their tongues, under the guise of wit, than any of the gilded courtiers who secretly looked down on them.

Wherever Will Somers went his monkey—perched on his shoulders—went with him. Henry was no mean musician, and often he would sing in a good if high-pitched voice, while Will Somers accompanied him on the harp. Jane the Fool actually formed part of the household of Princess Mary (Mary Tudor), though no doubt she was persona grata wherever she went. Her task must have been difficult at times: to cheer up the strange, brooding half-Spanish girl who not unnaturally resented the disgrace of her mother's protracted divorce.

It was during these early years as a royal palace that Whitehall was the setting for Henry VIII's second marriage, to Anne Boleyn.

By 1532 Anne was seen as the King's constant companion—she had been his acknowledged mistress for years—with her own suite of rooms at Greenwich. Then, on 25th January 1533 she and Henry were married in private in Whitehall Palace. Who actually performed the ceremony is uncertain. Dr Roland Lee, the King's chaplain, is one of the names put forward, while George Brown, an Augustinian friar, is another. The latter seems a likely candidate, for it was he who broke the news of the marriage to the outside world by publicly praying for Queen Anne in April that year. In a letter Archbishop Cranmer wrote: 'She was married much about St Paul's Day last, as the condition thereof doth well appear by reason she is now somewhat big with child.'

That child was destined to become Elizabeth I.

'Madame Anne is not one of the handsomest women in the world', wrote the Venetian Ambassador. 'She is of middling stature, swarthy complexion, long neck, wide mouth, bosom not much raised, and in fact has nothing but the king's great appetite and her eyes, which are black and beautiful.' Now she was England's queen.

Although the marriage took place in January, it was not until May that she was crowned. From the time of Richard II the sovereign and his queen had spent a few days in feasting and pageantry at the Tower before going in a magnificent procession through the City to Westminster Palace and the Abbey. Anne Boleyn was no exception: these were the great days for her: all too soon the power and the glory would disappear when Henry's eyes wandered elsewhere after her failure to produce a male heir.

On 21st May 1533, Anne passed under the newly built Holbein and King's Street Gates as her procession made its way from Old Whitehall Palace to Westminster. She rode in a litter—'sitting in her hair' was how Thomas Cromwell described it. The next day the royal couple returned to Whitehall after the actual coronation, and the round of feasting and dancing began. Soon after, however, the whole household moved away to Hampton Court, to Greenwich and to Windsor, and Whitehall saw them only infrequently.

Life at first must have been placid enough on these occasions when the Court was actually in residence. Although Henry was slowly but surely passing his prime, his love of sport was as strong as ever. Often he must have appeared on the tennis courts as Guistinian, the Venetian Ambassador, described him, 'he is most fond of tennis, at which game it is the prettiest thing in the world to see him play, his fair skin glowing through a shirt of the finest texture.'

Anne, for her part, passed the evenings working at tapestries, or playing cards or backgammon, and Henry like a doting husband paid her gambling debts. But all was not to last. Three years after the glitter of the coronation Anne Boleyn entered Traitor's Gate, charged with incest and adultery.

On 19th May 1536 a cannon on the top of the White Tower boomed out over the City. The few servants still in the deserted Whitehall Palace must have heard it, as did their master who was out hunting, and to all it was the signal that Anne Boleyn was dead.

Ten days later Henry and Jane Seymour were married.

It was at Hampton Court that the last Tudor king, Edward VI, was born. But the price was high, no less than the death of Jane Seymour herself. And it was at Greenwich that the Rabelaisian farce of the marriage to Anne of Cleves ran its eight-day course, while Hampton Court again was the setting for Catharine Howard's downfall, ending with her execution in the Tower.

Towards the close of Henry VIII's reign Old Whitehall Palace comes to the fore once again. Now he is an ageing tyrant: gross, savage, and yet at times almost pathetic. After five marriages, four of them disastrous, he had married not for love, but for happiness. Catharine Parr was no indiscreet girl hardly out of her teens. At thirty-two she was already twice a widow, and now she had the most dangerous husband in Europe.

Now the King's jousting and tennis-playing days were behind him, and because of an ulcer on his right leg he supported himself on a stick. Kindly and practical Catharine Parr could have been sister to Princess Mary, so alike were they in age, while Princess Elizabeth was small for her ten years; with a large head and eyes that already seemed to have left childhood behind. Youngest was Prince Edward; at six he was astonishingly precocious, and far from strong.

Henry, it seemed, was mellowing. Then the old savagery flared up again over the question of who should guide the country after his death. Perhaps the greatest man in England, after the King, was the Duke of Norfolk, in whose veins flowed royal blood. On 12th December 1546 he was arrested, together with 'Henry, Earl of Surrey, his son and heir, upon certain surmises of treason, were committed to the Tower of London, the one by water, the other by land, that the one knew not of the other's apprehension'. Both were charged with conspiring to displace Lord Hertford, Prince Edward's uncle, as the future Protector of England during the boy's minority. Surrey, a gifted poet, was beheaded on Tower Hill on 19th January 1547, and according to instructions his father should make the same journey ten days later.

But meanwhile Henry had come, a very sick man, to Whitehall from his beloved Hampton Court. Everyone except himself realized the truth. He was dying.

In 1540 a horoscope had been cast on the instructions of Lord Hungerford to discover when Henry would die. This form of curiosity ranked as treason, and it was as a traitor that the inquisitive peer died. Now no one in the Palace dared tell Henry he had only a short while left in which to settle the country's affairs. Only when it was obvious that a few hours remained to him did Sir Anthony Denny break it to his master that his life was nearly spent. Henry sent for Archbishop Cranmer, and quite confident that God would forgive his sins, even should they have been greater than they were, he put his hands into that of the churchman, and died.

That was on 28th January. The next day should have seen the execution of the Duke of Norfolk, but thanks to this one death, another was avoided. However, the Duke remained in prison for six and a half years, until the death of Edward VI.

Now all was quiet in Whitehall Palace as the lengthy preparations for the funeral were set in motion. First the King was embalmed. 'Then was the Corpse had into the midst of his privy Chamber and set upon trestles with a rich pall of Cloth of gold and a Cross thereon, with all manner of lights thereto requisite, having divine service about him with Masses, obsequies and prayers, and continually watch being made by his Chapelrys Ordinary and Gentlemen of his Privy Chamber to the number of thirty persons.'

For the five days he lay there, while twenty-four hours out of the twenty-four his chaplains recited prayers, and the preparations went steadily on. Between nine and ten in the morning on 3rd February the mourners, all wearing hoods, went to the chapel where the coffin now lay. After Mass they all moved to the Presence Chamber for a 'sumptuous dinner'. Another ten days pass, then on Sunday 13th February the coffin was taken from the chapel and placed on the hearse, described as a chariot, and covered with a pall of cloth of gold. Upon this was set 'a goodly image like to the King's person in all points, wonderfully richly apparelled with velvet, gold and precious stones of all sorts, holding in ye right hand a Sceptre of gold, in the left hand the ball of the world with a Cross (the Orb): upon the head a crown imperial, of inestimable value, a collar of the Garter about the neck and a garter of gold about the leg'. The wax figure was similar to those in the Chapel of the Pyx in Westminster Abbey which have been restored to something approaching their original condition. Would that the effigy of Henry VIII had also survived.

Next morning the procession was ready to move off. Four miles long it stretched far beyond Westminster before it had even started. Gentlemen of the Household, peers of the Realm, the Commons, members of the Court and quite humble servants all had their part; while in the midst lay the glittering, staring figure of the King, secured to the chariot with ribbons of silk.

Surely not even Wolsey, the former occupier of the Palace, could have been more magnificent in death had he not been supplanted by the man whose funeral cortège was now setting out for Windsor.

4

The advent of Edward VI as king brought little change either to him or to Whitehall. A crown meant no escape from his tutors, and after the excitement and strain of the actual coronation he returned to Windsor and the routine of the school room. Around him jostled and intrigued his two uncles, Edward and Thomas. Eventually both went to the block, leaving a clear field for John Dudley—soon to become Duke of Northumberland—to manipulate the strings attached to the boy-king.

Mercifully Edward was not all New Learning and precocity. He would be seen on the tennis courts where once it had been his father. At least it is to Northumberland's credit that he encouraged the boy in riding, archery, and tennis. Without Northumberland's assistance Edward learned to swear, and scandalized his tutors, who forthwith beat the boy who had instructed him in the manly art.

In his way Northumberland was as ambitious as that earlier kingmaker, Warwick. Late at night he would slip through the deserted galleries of Whitehall Palace to the King's apartments. There he would waken the boy, and repeat whatever it was he wished Edward to do or agree to at the meetings of the Council. Then he would be off again; the seed planted in Edward's mind, half-drugged with sleep. Ideas that Northumberland dare not formulate openly in the Council Chamber in the light of common day.

From the window of the Council Chamber Edward would listen to sermons expounded by divines in the open-air pulpit of Sermon Court. Adjoining was the Great Court, which during this reign acquired an unofficial name, Whalebone Court. This derived from the skeleton of a whale, one of the two brought up from Woolwich in October 1552 (p. 47). It was still there in the time of James I.

During Edward VI's brief reign his half-sister Mary was seldom seen at Court; and for company he had his fellow Protestant, Elizabeth. But the elder of Henry's daughters was not to remain in self-exile for long. By the summer of 1553 Edward was seriously ill. Always delicate, tuberculosis had at last gained a fatal hold. When Mary came to Whitehall to pay her customary visit after Christmas—1552—she found many of the Court blatantly anxious to have her favour. For three days Edward was too ill to see her. But still he lived, and in March, as he could not even go the few hundred yards to Westminster, Parliament came to him for the opening. Then, as the chestnuts and the may came into blossom Edward left Whitehall for the last time, to go to Greenwich. Perhaps the change of air would do him good, thought his baffled physicians. But on 6th July, in his sixteenth year, he died.

At once the scheming Northumberland went to work to make not Mary Tudor, but his own daughter-in-law, Lady Jane Grey, queen. But the days which followed, some of the most dramatic in the country's history, do not concern Old Whitehall Palace. It remained deserted until Mary came to London as the rightful queen, and the ambitious Northumberland, together with the unfortunate relatives dragged down with him in his bid for power, were lodged in the Tower of London.

Once again priests in vestments chanted in Latin in the Chapel Royal, and incense filled the air. But as yet there was no extreme religious reaction. Life in the Palace went on much as it had gone in Henry VIII's reign. That is, until the question arose of Mary Tudor's marriage to Philip of Spain. 'England for the English!' was in essence the cry of the hot-headed Wyatt as he and his followers marched from Kent to London. His aim was not to depose Mary Tudor—nothing so drastic—but simply to shake her out of an alliance that would make half-Protestant England little more than a vassal of the richest and most extreme Catholic country in Europe.

His rebellion was badly planned. Indeed it was bound to fail from the moment he set out from Maidstone market place. After finding the drawbridge of Old London Bridge destroyed in his path (p. 48), he wasted three precious days before marching to Kingston, patching up the partly demolished bridge there, and returning to London along the north bank.

The news travelled quickly, and that night in February 1554 saw Whitehall Palace preparing to withstand an assault. Henry Machyn, an undertaker by profession and diarist by inclination, quoted an account of the scene as recorded by Edward Underhill, one of Mary's household.

'. . . so being all armed we came up into the chamber of presence with our pole axes in our hands, wherewith the ladies were very fearful, some lamenting, crying, wringing their hands, said "Alas, there is some great mischief towards; we shall be destroyed tonight". What a sight is this to see the Queen's chamber full of armed men, the like was never heard of.'

By early next morning, Ash Wednesday, Wyatt and his followers, muddy and chilled to the bone in the pelting rain, approached London. By that time a scratch army of citizens was waiting outside St James's Palace, while across the way Mary Tudor was still in Whitehall Palace, refusing to take refuge in the Tower.

Wyatt pushed on to what is now Trafalgar Square, so cutting off the two palaces from the City. But already the rebellion was breaking up before his eyes. He and a few followers made their way towards the Strand and Fleet Street, while the others turned towards Whitehall Palace itself.

Five hundred men under the command of Sir Richard Southwell waited on the river-side of Scotland Yard, while Sir John Gage—the elderly Lord Chancellor—and his men guarded the Palace Gate and the way to the Privy Stairs. At the sight of the handful of rebels advancing towards him, Sir John literally fell over himself in his haste to get inside the Palace gate again. Watching the scene from the Holbein Gate was Mary Tudor, the calmest individual in Whitehall that day. Unbellicose though the Lord Chancellor's retreat may have been, it stopped Wyatt's men from finding an easy way into the Palace. Now all they could do was loose off a few arrows over the roofs into the courtyard. One pierced the nose of a Lincoln's Inn lawyer.

Although the danger may never have been particularly serious, inside the Palace all was turmoil. Soldiers and servants ran about aimlessly, while women screamed for no other reason than that the panic was contagious. Some shouted, 'Treason!' others, 'All is lost!' and 'Away, away a barge,' and ran to the Queen who was still in the gallery of the Holbein Gate. 'Fall to prayer', she said, 'and I warrant you we shall hear better news anon, for my Lord [Pembroke] will not deceive me, I know well . . . if he would, God will not, whom my chief trust is, who will not deceive me. . . .' She was referring to Lord Pembroke, a faithful follower. But at the back of her mind was the thought of the defection of another peer, the Duke of Norfolk (p. 48).

But when these overwrought soldiers and women stopped talking and listened, it was quiet. Outside the gates the rebels had melted away. On Ludgate Hill Wyatt had sunk down on a seat outside the Belle Sauvage Tavern, and the rebellion was over.

Before long Mary Tudor saw him—she was still at a window of the Holbein Gate—as he was led into the Palace for questioning. From there he was taken by barge to the Tower, where he could make no further trouble. Although the fighting was over, the bloodshed was only just beginning. Not only was Lady Jane Grey executed, but Princess Elizabeth was in deadly peril.

In London examples were made of the rebels. The ringleaders suffered on Tower Hill while their soldiers were hanged on gallows set up throughout the City. But on 22nd February there was an amnesty for those awaiting their turn to die. The prisoners, some four hundred of them, were tied two and two, halters about their necks, and taken from the City to Whitehall. There Mary Tudor was again at the window in the Holbein Gate, and as they knelt in the muddy street she pardoned them all. After that they continued their march to Westminster Hall where their bonds were cut and the halters thrown away amid cheers and the throwing up of caps. Without doubt they could hardly believe their luck; and Mary Tudor was assured that whoever might be involved in any future trouble, these men would not be among them.

They were lucky. For weeks Princess Elizabeth's life hung in the balance. Like Lady Jane Grey she too was a potential source of danger to Mary Tudor's throne. During the rebellion Elizabeth was at Ashridge in Hertfordshire, despite orders to come to London, where she declared she was too ill to travel. Only after two of the Queen's doctors visited her, and found her fit to make the journey, did she come most unwillingly to Whitehall.

'Proud, haughty and defiant', Elizabeth rode into the Palace in a litter, to be lodged in rooms far from those of her half-sister the Queen. Although Wyatt, when on the scaffold, cleared her of complicity in the plot, she was frequently examined by the Council. On 17th March the Marquis of Winchester and the Earl of Sussex came to tell her the shattering news she was to go to the Tower. Her own mother, Anne Boleyn, had been beheaded there, as had the sixteen-year-old Jane Grey. What could she expect? Desperately Elizabeth played for time, hoping her half-sister would change her mind. Beneath the Palace walls the tide was starting to rise, and it gave her an idea. If she could spin out the time for an hour or two, then it would be too late to shoot Old London Bridge that day.

If she was not allowed to see her sister, asked Elizabeth, could she write a letter? The two peers were at first doubtful, but at last they agreed.

Elizabeth wrote as slowly as she dared. It was not so much what she put in the letter as the time it took.

'I have heard in my time of many cast away for want of coming to the presence of their prince, and in late days I heard my Lord Somerset say that if his brother had been suffered to speak with him, he had never suffered. As for the traitor Wyatt, he might peradventure write me a letter, but on my faith I never received any from him; and as for the copy of my letter sent to the French King, I pray God confound me eternally if ever I sent him word, message, token, or letter by any means, and to this my truth I will stand to my death.'

One and a half pages had been covered, the tide had risen, Old London Bridge was unpassable, and so she made an end to the letter. Already Elizabeth was well versed in the ways of intrigue, and drew a thick line diagonally across the blank space. No one was going to interpolate a forgery apparently admitting to her guilt. Then at the very bottom she wrote:

'I humbly crave but one word of answer from yourself. Your Highness' most faithful subject that hath been from the beginning and will be to my end. Elizabeth'

That night she slept at Whitehall, but her half-sister was implacable, and the night following was spent in the very different surroundings of the Bell Tower in the Tower of London. There she remained while Reynard, the sinister Spanish Ambassador, whispered in Mary Tudor's ear that Elizabeth should be executed without delay. To her credit the Queen would not listen, and slowly the danger passed.

By May in that year of 1554 Elizabeth's portrait was restored to its place beside her half-sister's at Whitehall, and that same month she left the Tower, to go to Woodstock.

For Mary Tudor the last years at Whitehall, Windsor, and Greenwich were years of increasing bitterness. Philip, who never returned her genuine love, went back and forth to the Continent, leaving her to endure alone the agonies and humiliations of the false pregnancies that heralded the disease which eventually killed her, while in the country the survival of Protestantism was ensured in those flames meant to see its extinction.

During those years Mary Tudor's court, wherever it happened to be, must have been far from happy. But in November 1558 that strange woman, so kind and thoughtful in small matters in her private life, and so cruelly narrow in public affairs, died in St James's Palace, just across the Park from Whitehall —and Elizabeth was Queen.

5

Although Mary Tudor died on 17th November, it was several weeks before Elizabeth moved from Somerset House to Whitehall. Then on 12th February 1559 'the Queen went by Barge, from Whitehall to the Tower, the Lord Mayor and Citizens attended her Highness with Music and many triumphal shows upon the water'.

Elizabeth had little reason to love the fortress, both for her own and her mother's sake, and after only two days her procession passed beneath Whitehall's two gateways as she rode in a chariot, a two-wheeled vehicle with low sides, and seated on a throne beneath an awning held up by four posts.

On 25th January the young Queen received the Speaker and the Members of the Commons in the great gallery overlooking the tilt-yard (roughly where the Horse Guards now stands), and without doubt she knew the reason for their coming: 'to move her Grace to marriage.'

Like Sir Winston Churchill, Elizabeth I possessed the gift of filling her speeches with happily turned phrases, and her reply to her first Parliament before it assembled at Westminster was no exception.

'I happily chose this kind of life, in the which I yet live, which I assure you for mine own part hath hitherto best contented myself, and I trust hath been most acceptable unto God.' After telling the Commons she would never make an unwise marriage, Elizabeth continued: ' . . . and therefore put that clean out of your heads, for I assure you—what credit my assurance may have with you I cannot tell—but what credit it shall, I will never in that matter conclude anything that shall be prejudicial to the Realm. And in the end this shall be for me sufficient, that a marble stone shall declare, that a Queen having reigned such a time, lived, and died a Virgin. And here I end, and take your coming unto me in good part, and give unto you all my hearty thanks, more yet for your zeal and good meaning, than for your petition.'

Later that same day the Queen and her Commons rode out together. In his *Chronicles*, Holinshed wrote of 'the Queen's Majesty riding to her Parliament from her Palace of Whitehall unto the Abbey Church of Westminster, with the Lords Spiritual and Temporal attending her, likewise in their Parliament robes'.

If Henry VIII had loved Hampton Court the best of his palaces, perhaps it was Greenwich that meant most to his daughter Elizabeth. But since Whitehall was now the principal royal residence in the capital, it was to see her on many official and also on less formal occasions during her reign of forty-five years. In 1560 Henry Machyn wrote in his *Diary*: 'The 11 day of April the Queen's grace kept her Maundy in her hall at court in that afternoon, and her grace gave unto twenty women so many gowns, and one woman had her best gown, and there her grace did wash their feet, and with a new white cup her grace drank unto every woman, and they had the cup and so her grace did likewise unto all, and every woman had in money. . . . The same afternoon she gave unto poor men, women, and children, both whole and lame in St James's Park 2d apiece, a thousand people and upwards.'

In later years the custom of giving clothes to the recipients of the Royal Maundy was discontinued, and a sum of money substituted in its place. Incidentally the word Maundy comes from the Latin *mandatum*, a command—the command of Christ to the disciples to wash the feet of each other.

Although it was in 1559 that Parliament first broached the question of the Queen's marriage, thirty years later it was still a subject for speculation. At one time or another half the rulers of Europe made overtures to the Virgin Queen, from Philip II of Spain (after an assurance from the Pope that marriage to his sister-in-law would not be opposed in Rome), to Ivan the Terrible; a maniac in religion, politics, and sex. But in 1580 it really looked as though Elizabeth might marry the Duc d'Alençon: Catharine dei Medici's well-seasoned youngest son.

A union between England and France was considered preferable to one between England and Spain, so Elizabeth—now forty-eight years old—apparently prepared to become a bride.

Among the preparations for the forthcoming marriage was a new Banqueting House, erected at Whitehall for the reception of the French ambassadors. Like a building put up in 1572, this Banqueting House was also a temporary affair of canvas, wood, and glass. The canvas walls were painted on the outside to look like stone, while inside the roof, also of canvas, clouds, gold stars, and the sun shooting forth its rays were painted. The posts supporting this roof were forty feet high, and for additional decoration there were festoons of artificial fruits and vegetables. Pomegranates, oranges, pumpkins, grapes, and peas. Along each side of the interior were ten rows of stands, banked up against the walls, for those who were permitted to watch the guests eating.

Three hundred and seventy-five workmen were engaged on this rush job, completed in twenty-four days, at a cost of £1,744 19s. 2d. Stow records there were two casualties: workmen who broke their legs by falling off the scaffolding.

At this stage in the negotiations for marriage the Duc

d'Alençon did not appear in person. Instead his eldest brother the Dauphin and the leading French nobles landed at Dover and came in a glittering cavalcade to London. While the ambassadors were entertained in the Banqueting House at Whitehall 'with all kind of Princely pleasures and pastimes', there was muttering among the people, who opposed the alliance. They called d'Alençon not the Duke, but simply Monsieur, and in that one word somehow conveyed all their disapproval.

Not only were there banquets, but jousts and tournaments of different kinds were held in the tilt-yard, where the flower of England pitted itself against the flower of France. Among the English contestants in the lists were the Earls of Arundel and Leicester, and Sir Philip Sidney.

On one occasion the gallery overlooking the tilt-yard became the 'Fortress of Perfect Beauty'. After two cannon had been fired, one filled with scented water and the other with scented powder, the siege by Desire began. Flowers 'and such fancies' were the ammunition used by the attackers, who were also allowed to use 'pretty scaling ladders'. But of course Desire was repulsed, and the Fortress of Perfect Beauty remained unbreached. Who was the unattainable prize within the fortress? Elizabeth. But the parallel, whether conscious or unconscious, went unnoticed by the French.

For six months these entertainments continued, until it dawned upon the ambassadors that perhaps the Queen was not quite as anxious for the marriage to take place as she protested. In letters home they advised d'Alençon to come over and try his luck in person.

He came, and Elizabeth greeted him most kindly, though perhaps treating him more like a brother or a son than a prospective husband. Came the inevitable end to the story. In the gallery of the palace at Greenwich she refused his proposal of marriage, quite definitely, and for the last time. Not long afterwards 'the Duke with great jollity entered into arms against the forces of the Spanish king'. So Elizabeth achieved her object without having to commit herself to matrimony and her country to a definite alliance.

As the reign wore on the theatre began to play an increasingly important part in the life of the Court. In 1579 the *History of the Knight in the Burning Rock* was performed in the Great Hall at Whitehall, and four years later a company of players in the Royal Service was formed by Sir Francis Walsingham. They ranked as Grooms of the Chamber and were allowed their own livery. 'Among these twelve players were two rare men, viz Thomas Wilson for a quick delicate refined extemporal wit, and Richard Tarleton for a wonderous plentiful extemporal wit. He was the wonder of his time.' When Howes prepared the 1631 edition of Stow's *Annals* he added in the margin: 'Tarleton so beloved that men use his picture for their signs.'

Two Germans who wrote travel books about their visits to England were Lupold von Wedel and Paul Hentzner. The former wrote his account *A Journey through England* in 1584, and the latter *A Journey into England* in 1598. Each could count himself fortunate in what they saw, and among the spectacles witnessed by von Wedel was a tournament at Whitehall.

'The combatants had their servants clad in different colours; they, however, did not enter the barrier, but arranged themselves on both sides. Some of the servants were disguised like savages or like Irishmen (!), with the hair hanging down to the middle like women; others had horse manes on their heads; some came driving in a carriage, the horses being equipped like elephants; some carriages were drawn by men, others appeared to move by themselves. When a gentleman with his servant approached the barrier on horseback or in a carriage, he stopped at the foot of the staircase leading to the Queen's room, while one of his servants in pompous attire of a special pattern mounted the steps and addressed the Queen in well composed verses or with a ludicrous speech, making her and her ladies laugh. When the speech was ended, he in the name of his lord offered to the Queen a costly present, which she accepted, and permission given to take part in the tournament. In fact, however, they made sure of the permission before preparing for the combat. Now always two by two rode against each other, breaking lances across the beam. The fête lasted until five o'clock in the afternoon, when milord Leicester, the royal Master of the Horse, gave the sign to stop.'

Although it was at Greenwich that Paul Hentzner actually saw Elizabeth pass by on her way to the chapel one Sunday in the summer of 1598, the ceremonial would have been the same when in residence at Whitehall.

'First went gentlemen, Barons, Earls, Knights of the Garter, all richly dressed and bareheaded; next came the Chancellor, bearing the seals in a red silk purse, between two, one of which carried the royal sceptre, the other the sword of state, in a red scabbard, studded with golden Fleurs-de-Lys, the point upwards. Next came the Queen, in the fifty-sixth year of her age, as we were told, very majestic, her face oblong, fair, but wrinkled, her eyes small, yet black and pleasant. Her nose a little hooked, her lips narrow and her teeth black (a defect the English seem subject to, from their too great use of sugar). She had in her ears two pearls with very rich drops, she wore false hair, and that red. Upon her head she had a small crown. . . . She was guarded on each side by the Gentlemen Pensioners, fifty in number, with gilt battle-axes.'

Hentzner had been misinformed by one of Elizabeth's gallant subjects on the question of her age. Ten years had been lopped off the sixty-six that had gone by since her birth at Greenwich.

As the Court was not in residence at Whitehall when he visited London, Hentzner was allowed to see the principal apartments. Ten things in particular he thought particularly worthy of enumeration.

'(1) The royal library, well stored with Greek, Latin, Italian and French books: among the rest, a little one in French, upon parchment, in the handwriting of the present reigning queen Elizabeth, thus inscribed:

To the most high, puissant, and redoubted prince, Henry VIII of the name, king of England, France and Ireland, Defender of the Faith: Elizabeth, his most humble daughter, health and obedience.

All these books are bound in velvet of different colours, though chiefly red, with clasps of gold and silver; some of them have pearls, and precious stones, set in their bindings.

(2) Two little cabinets of exquisite work, in which the queen keeps her paper, and which she uses for writing boxes.

(3) The queen's bed, ingeniously composed of woods of different colours, with quilts of silk, velvet, gold and embroidery.

(4) A little chest ornamented all over with pearls, in which the queen keeps her bracelets, ear-rings, and other things of extraordinary value.

(5) Christ's Passion, in painted glass.

(6) Portraits: among which are, queen Elizabeth; at sixteen years old; Henry, Richard, Edward, Kings of England. Rosamund; Lucrece, a Grecian bride, in her nuptual habit; the genealogy of the kings of England; a picture of Edward VI representing at first sight something quite deformed, till looking through a small hole in the cover, which is put over it, you see it in its true proportions; Charles V Emperor; Charles Emanuel of Savoy, and Catharine of Spain, his wife; Ferdinand duke of Florence, with his daughters; one of Philip King of Spain, when he came into England and married Mary; Henry VII. Henry VIII and his mother: besides many more illustrious men and women; and a picture of the siege of Malta.

(7) A small hermitage, half hid in a rock, finely carved in wood.

(8) Variety of emblems, on paper, cut in the shape of shields, with mottoes, used by the nobility at tilts and tournaments, hung up here for a memorial. (" . . . and our brused arms, hung up for monuments. . . ." *Richard III*).

(9) A piece of clockwork, an Ethiop riding upon a Rhinoceros, with four attendants, all who make their obeisance, when it strikes the hour; these are all put into motion by winding up the machine.

'In a garden joining to this palace, there is a jet d'eau, with a sun dial, which while strangers are looking at, a quantity of water, forced by a wheel, which the gardener turns at a distance, through a number of little pipes, plentifully sprinkles those that are standing round.'

Four more years remained to Elizabeth from the time of Hentzner's visit: then after her death on 24th March 1603 at Richmond, she came by water to Whitehall for the last time.

A month went by, and on 28th April the great funeral procession set out for Westminster. All the members of her household, no matter how humble, seemed to have been represented.

'First came the Knights Marshall's men to clear the route, then fifteen poor men and two hundred and sixty poor women of Westminster; more servants, porters, trumpets, a horse covered with a cloth bearing the Royal Arms, messengers of the chamber, children and men employed in the scullery, the woodyard, the larder, the scalding house etc: wheat porters, wine porters, the bell-ringer, the maker of spice bags, brewers, candle makers, children and gentlemen of the Chapel, clerks of different kinds, the Master Cook, musicians, apothecaries and surgeons, Gentlemen Ushers, Secretaries of Latin and French, the Master of the Jewel House, Judges, Ambassadors, Peers, Bishops, and the Archbishop of Canterbury. The Somerset, Richmond, York, Chester, Norroy and Clarenceux Heralds. Four horses drew the chariot containing the purple velvet covered coffin with the wax effigy of the queen lying upon it, all sheltered beneath a canopy supported by six knights. Gentlemen Pensioners, their gilt axes carried head downwards. The Master of the Horse, Garter King of Arms, the Chief Mourner (Marchioness of Northampton), Countesses, Viscountesses, earl's daughters, baronesses, maids of honour and finally the Captain of the Guard and the Guard itself (and many others, too numerous to mention).'

The effigy of Elizabeth I still exists, on display in the Chapel of the Pyx in Westminster Abbey, though it was much restored in 1760.

As the cortège made its short journey to the Abbey the feelings of the onlookers were summed up by the continuator of Stow's *Annals* as he brought to a close his account of her reign.

'The 28 day of April, being her funeral day, at which time the City of Westminster was surcharged with multitudes of all sorts of people in their streets, houses, windows, leads, and gutters, that came to see her obsequies, and when they beheld her statue or picture lying upon the coffin set forth in Royal Robes, having a Crown upon the head thereof, and a ball and sceptre in either hand: there was such a general sighing, groaning and weeping, as the like hath not been seen or known in the memory of man, neither doeth any history mention any people, time, or state, to make the like lamentation for the death of their sovereign.'

6

The first year of the new reign saw James VI of Scotland and I of England at Whitehall on only a few occasions. Plague was rampant, and not unnaturally the Court chose to stay at Windsor. During coronation week alone (July 1603), no less than eight hundred and fifty-seven people died in and around London, and at the beginning of August a proclamation was issued forbidding anyone to come near the Court and requiring those who could do so, to disperse to their own homes until the danger was passed.

Even before James reached London on his journey south he had bestowed over two hundred and fifty knighthoods, and on one of the few occasions he went to Whitehall that summer, there were three hundred more happy recipients waiting to receive the accolade in the Palace garden.

For the present then, the King was settling into the new life at Windsor; while his subjects watched, weighed, and found him wanting. Even the most charitable were forced to admit there was singularly little to recommend the man. '. . . middle stature, more corpulent through his clothes than his body, yet fat enough; his eyes large, ever rolling after any stranger that came in his presence. His beard was thin, his tongue too large for his mouth, which ever made him speak full in the mouth, and made him drink very uncomely. His skin was as soft as taffeta sarsanet, which felt so because he never washed his hands, only rubbed his fingers ends slightly with the wet end of a napkin.' As if that was not enough, nature had seen fit to provide him with legs so weak he could not walk in a straight line, and always he had to support himself on another man's shoulders.

As for his handsome wife, Anne of Denmark—she was known to drink. In the circumstances that was understandable if reprehensible. But none the less, it all added up to an inauspicious beginning to the reign.

The only hope, Englishmen felt, lay in the King's eldest son. Although Prince Henry was only ten, he already showed all the qualities that his unfortunate father so obviously lacked. Intelligent, tall, good-looking, and athletic, it would be hard to imagine a more striking contrast. Until his premature death in Old Whitehall Palace at the age of nineteen he quite overshadowed his younger brother Charles, who as the ill-fated king was to die outside its very walls.

The first event of interest in the new reign, so far as it concerns Whitehall, was the creation of Prince Charles as Duke of York, and as a Knight of the Bath, on 6th January 1604. To some extent he shared his father's disability of weak legs, though when he grew to manhood he was possessed of an abundance of the Stuart charm for which men would willingly give their lives; and which his son, Charles II, inherited in all too full measure.

After the ceremonies a banquet was held in the 'Great Chamber'—either the Great Hall or the wooden Banqueting House—where the four-year-old prince sat alone at a table with his two esquires; the Earls of Oxford and of Essex. Essex was the twelve-year-old son of the famous Robert Devereux, Earl of Essex.

At Whitehall the most spectacular events of this reign were the masques which resulted from the collaboration of Inigo Jones and Ben Jonson. The former was responsible for the scenery, and the latter for the verses: between them they produced a form of entertainment that was the precursor of the opera-ballets produced at Versailles half a century later for Louis XIV.

Elizabeth I's temporary Banqueting House, now twenty-three years old, was the setting for the first of the Stuart masques. Called *Blacknesse*, it was written for the Queen and eleven of her ladies, and performed on Twelfth Night 1605, in connection with the festivities for Prince Charles.

At this date Inigo Jones had just returned from working in Denmark for Christian IV (the Queen's brother), and now was designing not buildings, but scenery that was a little less expensive. That no costs were spared, either in the costumes or the settings, can be gathered from the account. In those days £3,000 was an enormous sum, and that was what *Blacknesse* totalled. Among the effects provided by Inigo Jones, 'there was', wrote the slightly disapproving Sir Ralph Winwood, 'a great engine at the lower end of the room, which had motion, and in it were the images of sea horses, with other terrible fishes, which were ridden by Moors. The indecorum was that there was all fish and no water. At the further end was a great shell, in the form of a shallop, wherein were four seats. In the lowest sat the Queen with one Lady Bedford; in the rest were placed my ladies Suffolk, Derby, Rich, Effingham, Anne Herbert, Susan Herbert, Elizabeth Howard, Walsingham, and Bevil. Their appearance was rich, but too light and courtezan like for such great ones.'

For Ben Jonson and Inigo Jones the masque *Blacknesse* must have been something in the nature of a dress rehearsal (albeit a most expensive one) for *Hymenaei*, produced exactly a year later to celebrate the marriage between the Earl of Essex and Frances Howard; and for *Barriers*, produced on the following night. The words of *Hymenaei* were dull and such plot as there was filled with allegorical references to marriages in the ancient world. At the climax players representing Perverse Affections attempted to interrupt the stage marriage, but were overcome by a white-haired figure in a blue robe spangled with stars who represented Reason. The audience itself nearly rivalled the players in the magnificence of their clothes, though most of the jewels that glittered and flashed so expensively in the half-light were hired for the occasion from merchants in the City.

After the masques, with all their erotic undertones, were over the newly married couple took leave of each other, and went their separate ways. Essex returned to his studies, and thirteen-year-old Frances Howard returned to her mother. Four years were to go by before they met again, and the interval proved fatal to the marriage.

While everyone agreed Frances Howard was 'a most sweet and delicate lady', it was a regrettable fact she shared the same

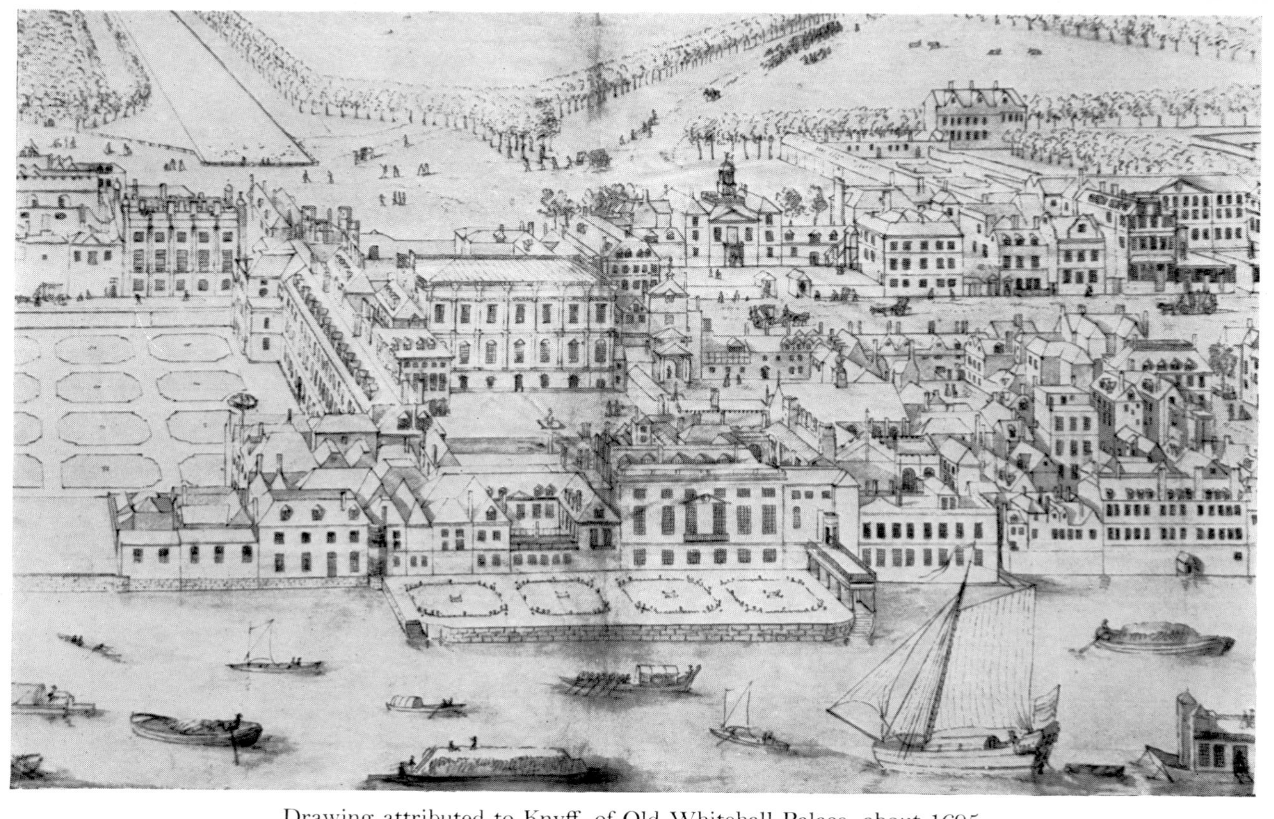

Drawing attributed to Knyff, of Old Whitehall Palace, about 1695.

Banqueting House and Holbein Gate, Whitehall, by Silvestri.

moral outlook as her more celebrated relative of the preceding century: Catharine Howard. So when the time came for Essex to make her his wife in more than name, she was already mistress to Prince Henry, and in love with the King's favourite, Robert Carr. Out of this emotional and moral tangle grew a drama that Webster might have been proud to claim as his own invention. But that lay in the future.

Evidently James did not consider the wooden Banqueting House a fine enough setting for the masques, and the next year, 1606, it was demolished and replaced by a brick and stone building a hundred and twenty feet long by fifty-three feet broad. Inside Doric and Ionic columns, all of wood, supported the ceiling which was elaborately carved and gilded with festoons and such decorations.

The new Banqueting House could not have been completed in time for Christian IV's visit to his sister and brother-in-law in 1606, but most of his time in England was spent with the Court at Greenwich, and he only came to Whitehall for three days to see the sights of London: Westminster Abbey, Old St Paul's, Gresham's Exchange, and the Tower.

When the Banqueting House was opened, in January 1608, it was with a masque entitled *Beautie*. 'The apparatus and the cunning of the stage machinery was a miracle, the abundance and beauty of the lights immence, and the music and dancing most sumptuous', was how the Venetian Ambassador described the occasion.

From then on masques were performed with ever-increasing frequency. 'A most glorious Masque', lasting almost until dawn was held on 12th June 1610, when Prince Henry was created Prince of Wales. On an average each of these lavish productions cost in the region of £1,000. The exact cost of *Oberon the Fairy Prince*, another Ben Jonson–Inigo Jones collaboration, performed in January 1611, was £1,092 6s. 10d.

Although the Banqueting House at this time was chiefly memorable for the masques performed there, the banquets were nothing if not lavish. Velasco, the Constable of Castile, attended one which may be taken as typical, held on 19th August 1604.

'The Audience Chamber was elegantly furnished, having a buffet of several stages, filled with various pieces of ancient and modern gilt plate of excellent workmanship. A railing was placed on each side of the room in order to prevent the crowd from approaching too near the table. At the right hand upon entering was another buffet, containing rich vessels of gold, agate, and other precious stones. The table might be about five yards in length, and more than one yard broad. They took their seats in the following manner: their Majesties sat at the head of the table, at a distance from each other, under the canopy of state, the Queen being on the right hand, on chairs of brocade with a high cushion of the same, and on the side of the King the Prince was seated in a like manner.'

After the banquet the diners flocked to the windows on the south side of the hall to watch the brutal sports of the day.

'Herewith the ball ended, and all then took their places upon a square, where a platform was raised, and a vast crowd had assembled to see the King's bears fight with greyhounds. This afforded great amusement. Presently a bull, tied to the end of a rope, was fiercely baited by dogs. After this certain tumblers came who danced upon a rope, and performed various tricks of agility and skill on horseback. With this ended the entertainment and the day.'

By December 1612 Frances Howard, Countess of Essex, was once again a familiar figure at Whitehall. While rumour had it she was Prince Henry's mistress, she most certainly was completely infatuated with Robert Carr, James's young Scots favourite. Whatever the cost she was determined to be rid of her husband, and if nothing came to light about her past indiscretions, a divorce should be possible on the grounds of non-consummation. But Frances Howard was afraid, and with good reason, of Robert Carr's friend and adviser, Sir Thomas Overbury. If he chose to talk he could ruin her prospects of future happiness and greatness. At all costs he must be removed, if only until she was free to marry Carr.

First of all she set about breaking the friendship between Carr and Overbury. But this was not the immediate success she had hoped, and so her ambitious relatives took a hand. Their interest lay in the fact that if Frances Howard was married to the King's favourite, through her they could forward their own ends. Even in a Court filled with climbing families, the Howards were outstanding. Consequently they advised James to be rid of Overbury, who they declared was overbearing and objectionable. For his part James was jealous of the influence Overbury wielded over Carr, and agreed.

Through a pliant tool, the Archbishop of Canterbury, Overbury was invited to lead a mission to Russia: far enough off even to satisfy Frances Howard. He declined the offer with thanks, and later refused the choice of becoming Ambassador at the Hague or in Paris. Suitably embellished, his replies were repeated to James. That same evening, in April 1613, Overbury was summoned to appear before the King and the Privy Council. Almost before he realized it, he found himself ordered to the Tower for 'contumatious disobedience'. He was hurried from the Council Chamber between two Yeomen of the Guard to the river stairs, where the Council's barge was ready waiting to take him to the fortress via Traitor's Gate. With his head in his hands Carr sat in the barge as it headed downstream.

Robert Carr, Viscount Rochester, as he now was, was sufficiently double-faced to tell his one-time friend he was doing all he could to secure his speedy release. In reality he and the Howards were putting pressure on James to replace the Lieutenant of the Tower, Sir William Waad, by a man less likely to be curious about his new charge. They succeeded, but even now Frances was not satisfied. Overbury would remain a menace, whether in prison or out of it, and she was prepared to use murder to be rid of him for good and all.

For this she enlisted the help of Mrs Turner. At Whitehall Mrs Turner's position was that of dressmaker: she had introduced the enormous yellow starched ruffs into England, in addition to designing many of the costumes used in the masques. That was only one side to her activities. For some of those at Court she procured abortions, for others she simply procured.

In the Tower Overbury was allowed a personal servant to look after him, and the man was none other than Mrs Turner's own servant. By now the Earl of Essex was only too glad to be rid of his troublesome wife, and preparations for the divorce were set in motion. Meanwhile the unfortunate Overbury was the recipient of many pies, tarts, and jellies made by Mrs Turner in the kitchen of Frances Howard's apartments at Whitehall. Nearly all contained a poison of one kind or another. They were slow working, but on 15th September he was dead, killed by sublimate of mercury. A week or so later Abbot, the Archbishop of Canterbury, and the divorce commission ended the first marriage.

Curiously enough James was not possessively jealous at the prospect of Carr's forthcoming wedding. Anything the young man wanted, he must have; he gave preferment to the clerical members of the divorce commission and knighthoods to the secular, and the actual marriage took place in the Chapel Royal at Whitehall. Thomas Campion, the poet-priest, helped officiate. If possible Frances Howard's second marriage was even more spectacular than her first.

By now Robert Carr had been created Earl of Somerset, so his rank was now equal to that of his future wife, while John Donne sent verses extolling her beauty.

> Blest payre of Swans, Oh may you interbring
> Daily new joys and never sing.
> Live on till all grounds of wisdom faile,
> Till honour, yea, till wisdome grow so stale
> That, great new heights to try,
> It must serve your ambition, to die.

At that time it was the custom for a virgin bride to wear her hair hanging free. Frances Howard went to the altar with her hair about her shoulders, and no doubt looked Dr Campion in the eye.

The presents were magnificent. £10,000 worth of jewellery from the King, an expensive piece of plate from each of the City Companies, four beautiful black horses, and many other items. An amusing episode concerned Lord Nottingham's present of a solid gold ewer and basin. He was not as generous as might appear. In the first place the pieces cost him nothing, being a present to him from the Spanish Ambassador, and it soon came to light (when Frances Howard's relatives had the presents valued) that in this case all that glistered was not all gold. Both the ewer and the basin contained a great deal of base metal. They complained.

The next night, 27th December, saw the performance of *Challenge at Tilt*, and on the night following that *The Irish Masque*. Sir Francis Bacon was a man who always kept his eyes open for the main chance—his main chance, and on Twelfth Night he paid for an entertainment at Whitehall called *The Masque of Flowers*. It cost £2,000, but because of the crush of people the performance was quite ruined. A few days later, at additional expense, he had the masque repeated. James was delighted, and in due course Bacon became Attorney-General.

While all these lavish festivities were taking place at Whitehall, perhaps Frances Howard—now the Countess of Somerset—thought of Sir Thomas Overbury, hastily buried on the day of his death in a coffin paid for by her puppet the Lieutenant of the Tower. But perhaps she did not. After all, she had achieved her ambition.

For nearly two years the Somersets paraded in all their glory; then from a totally unexpected quarter the whole astonishing story was broken open. After Overbury's death the assistant who worked for the apothecary who supplied the poisons went abroad. In Holland he fell ill in the summer of 1616, thought he was dying, and made a confession. It reached the ears of the English Ambassador, who brought the story to England and started inquiries. Sir Jervis Elwes, the Lieutenant of the Tower, lost his nerve, and made a statement. Mrs Turner and several others were arrested, and in due course Robert Carr, received the following letter:

'After our very loving commendations to your Lordship: these are by force of his Majesty's letters under his gracious signature to us directed (we having had the consultation of certain examinations and testimonies concerning your Lordship and thereupon having occasion to examine you) in his Majesty's name to will and require you to keep your chamber near the Cockpit at Whitehall, without suffering the access of any to you other than your own necessary servants, until his Majesty's pleasure be further known; and hereof requiring you not to fail—we bid your Lordship farewell from Yorkhouse this 17 of October 1615.

Your very loving friends,
T. Ellesmere (Lord Chancellor)
E. Zouche (Lord Harrington)
Edw: Coke' (Lord Chief Justice)

A similar letter was sent to Lady Somerset, ordering her to stay in a house she owned at Blackfriars.

That same night in his apartments near the Cockpit, Carr and a friend went through all letters that might prove incriminating, burning some and putting false dates on others.

First Mrs Turner and her servant who had been assigned to Overbury in the Tower were tried and hanged. Evidently Lord Chief Justice Coke objected to the fashion of starched ruffs which she had introduced into England. He ordered when she went to Tyburn on 14th November: 'she should be hanged in that dress, that the same might end in shame and detestation'. Not unnaturally Mrs Turner and the fashion died together.

Before long Carr was moved from Whitehall to the Tower, and a few months later, after the birth of a daughter, his wife followed him there. It was perhaps the most astonishing scandal seen in London. Sir Jervis Elwes was hanged on his own gallows on Tower Hill, outside the fortress where he had so recently been Lieutenant. But it was not until the following May that the Earl and Countess were brought to trial in Westminster Hall. Frances Howard was charged first, on 24th May, and pleaded guilty. She was sentenced to death, and returned to the Tower. The next day it was Carr's turn. He pleaded not guilty, and the trial dragged on well into the evening. At all costs the Court wished to keep the King's name out of the affair—as the man who ordered Overbury to the Tower, James was in a sense responsible for the tragedy which followed—and in Westminster Hall a man stood on either side of the accused, ready to stifle him with a cloak should he attempt to attack his royal master.

That day James remained in his private apartments at Whitehall: 'he did retire himself from all company and forbare both dinner and supper until he had heard what answer the said Earl had made.' Like his wife, Robert Carr was found guilty, sentenced to death and taken back to the Tower.

In due course the inevitable happened. James stepped in to use his royal prerogative to pardon the couple, and in 1621 they were released from a not too uncomfortable life of semi-captivity in the Tower. By then they hated the sight of each other. What must have been the worst punishment of all—they were forbidden to come near Whitehall and the Court. As for James's part in the sequel to the story: he soon found a new favourite. Now it was George Villiers, Duke of Buckingham, who ruled where once it had been Robert Carr.

While the Overbury murder had been running its course, life on the surface had continued normally at Whitehall, punctuated at regular intervals by masques, and less regularly by weddings.

As producer of the masques, Inigo Jones and Ben Jonson had parted company by 1612. The reason for the split was trivial enough to cause a lasting breach between two creative artists. Neither could agree whose name should go first on the title-page of a book about to be published. Out of spite Ben Jonson started lampooning Inigo Jones, and introduced him into his play *The Tale of a Tub* under the name Vitruvius Hoop. Vitruvius was that dogmatic architect of Ancient Rome who laid down the laws regarding the proportions of the orders of architecture. In the end Ben Jonson was advised to stop his far from good-natured attacks. The King, he was told, was not amused.

The break did not mean the end of the masques: when Fredrick, Count Palatine of the Rhine, came to London to marry Princess Elizabeth, Inigo Jones collaborated with Chapman to produce entertainment for the occasion. One was given in the Great Hall built by Wolsey: during this reign it was the setting for a number of performances of Shakespeare's plays. Among those performed was *Othello*, *The Merry Wives of Windsor*, *Measure for Measure*, *The Comedy of Errors*, *Love's Labour's Lost*, *Henry V*, and *The Merchant of Venice.* All these were given in the year 1604–5.

The marriage took place in the Chapel Royal, and it seemed as though James could not make the money fly quickly enough.

The dresses and jewels worn by Elizabeth's attendants cost £3,914, the fittings for the bridal chamber £3,023, while the fireworks let off in the evening came to £7,600. In all there was a bill for £93,278. When he came to the English throne James I claimed that soon he would make the English as beggarly as their Scottish neighbours. Many more such weddings and the prophecy would undoubtedly have been fulfilled.

Cunningham described some of the devices used during the masque in considerable detail. 'It is described as having for scenery an artificial rock, nearly as high as the roof. The rock was honeycombed with caves, and there were two winding stairs. The rock turned a golden colour, and "was run quite through with veins of gold'. On one side was a silver edifice labelled in Latin "The Temple of Honour". There were various allusive devices, and after Plutus, the God of Riches, had made a speech, the rock split in pieces with a great crack, and Capriccio stepped out to make his speech, while the broken rock vanished. Next appeared a cloud, then a gold mine in which twelve maskers were triumphantly seated. Over the gold mine was an evening sky, and the red sun was seen to set. There were white cliffs in the background, and from them rose a bank of clouds which hid everything.'

In the years to come Fredrick was to inherit the crown of Bohemia, but it was an empty honour as the Royal couple never even entered their capital, Prague. History best remembers Elizabeth as the Winter Queen: the withdrawn unsmiling mother of Prince Rupert, whose life was largely that of an itinerant exile around the courts of Europe.

That particular masque cost £1,000, but the next year no less than £9,000 was squandered on fireworks and tournaments on the river. It is not without its humour that in the same year the Queen requested one Sir John Spilman 'to repair to Whitehall to receive directions concerning a loan to be raised for her by pawning certain jewels'.

Lack of funds never checked James's love of lavish display, and in 1616 the creation of Charles as Prince of Wales in succession to his brother, Prince Henry, who had died a year or so before, wanted nothing to make the occasion splendid.

During the remaining years of James I's reign the most notable event was the burning of the Banqueting House, and the erection of the present structure: with one exception the only building still standing today. That one exception is Wolsey's brick-built wine cellar, now buried below modern office buildings. The fire happened on 12th January 1619, and within a short while the wooden interior was an inferno. Gerard Herbert described the scene in a letter written a few days after the disaster: 'The fire arising by the neglect and heedlessness of two men that were appointed to sweep the room, and having candles, firing some oily clothes of the devices of the masque (which the king had commanded should all remain to be again at Shrove-tide), that fire inflaming suddenly about and to the roof, which the two men, not able to quench, and fearing to be known that they did it, shut the doors, parting away without speaking thereof, till at last, perceived by others, when too late and irrecoverable. The two, since confessing the truth, are put in prison.' Stow's continuator goes on: '. . . and besides the banqueting house, there were divers lodgings burned, and the writings in the office of the Privy signet, which was under the banqueting house.' From an historical point of view the loss of the Signet and Privy Seal Offices was serious: they contained numerous documents signed by the sovereigns from Henry VIII to James I.

For Inigo Jones this was his great opportunity to prove himself as an architect, and not merely as a designer of insubstantial pageants. Three months after the fire he presented his designs for the new building to the King. On 27th June 1619 he received £37 for making a model of the Banqueting House, and also one for a new Star Chamber at Westminster. While the actual building operations were in progress he received 8s. 4d. a day, and his master mason (Nicholas Stone), 4s. 10d. The other masons were paid at the rate of 1s. to 2s. 6d. a day, according to their skill, as were the carpenters, while the rate for the bricklayers ranged from 1s. 2d. to 2s. 2d. according to skill.

In his youth Inigo Jones is supposed to have worked in Paul's Churchyard, where his talents were first discovered by the third Earl of Pembroke, who thereupon sent him to study in Italy. From Italy he moved to Denmark and found employment working for Christian IV. From 1605 until 1613 Jones was once again in England, where most of his creative activity was channelled into designing the settings for the masques at Whitehall. But in 1613 he was once again in Italy, where the buildings designed by Palladio at Vicenza were to set the fashion for many years to come. Now, in 1619, all these experiences and first-hand impressions of contemporary Renaissance architecture in Italy bore fruit in what is still one of the most perfectly proportioned buildings in London.

Outside, the new Banqueting House was faced with Portland stone, while within brick was used. The dimensions are a hundred and ten feet by fifty-five feet. The two main fronts, to the east and the west, are identical and consist of three storeys surmounted by a balustrade. The elevation is divided into seven bays: At ground level are small windows devoid of decoration, while above are the two principal storeys: the lower with Ionic and the upper with Corinthian pilasters. The middle three bays project slightly and have pierced balustrades in front of the lower windows. Additional decoration is provided by carving swags of fruit and masks set between the capitals of the upper storey.

Inside the building consists of a low crypt-like room supporting the main chamber, which rises up through the two upper storeys, to the ceiling, decorated with panels by Rubens, though the latter were not added until Charles I's reign. As on the exterior, the inner walls are decorated with Ionic and Corinthian pilasters. Above the lower order a gallery ran round the east, west, and north sides, but it was not until the nineteenth century that a fourth was added on the south. Since no provision was made for a staircase an annex was built at the north end, on the blank wall overlooking the gateway leading to the river stairs.

It seems that, as is typical with so many great buildings of this and earlier centuries, little or no attention was paid to the realities of life. The distance from the Privy Kitchen to the Banqueting House must have been nearly three hundred feet, most of it across open courtyard.

This Banqueting House, even admired by the French critics of the day—who it must be admitted were by no means free from chauvinism—was all that Inigo Jones was asked to design. When Charles I was on the throne his pupil John Webb produced an astonishingly ambitious plan for rebuilding Whitehall Palace, but because of the lack of funds and the unsettled times, nothing came of them. The main façade would have had an overall length of one thousand and fifty feet, roughly comparable with Peter the Great's enormous Admiralty in Leningrad.

Only three years remained to James I in which to enjoy his Banqueting House before his death in 1625, and the only addition made to the palace in that time was a sundial which he ordered to be set up in the Privy Gardens. Nearly four and a half feet square and three feet high the table-like top had four sundials in the corners, and a larger semi-spherical one in the centre.

With a neat wit John Chamberlain rounded out the King's life when he wrote to a friend: 'The king's funeral sermon is set forth, wherein the Lord Keeper has shown a great deal of wit and learning in comparing King James to King Solomon in all his actions saving his vices.'

7

What did the Palace look like now, in the year 1625? For the greater part the buildings erected by Wolsey still stood, but now they were not only dominated by the roof of the Great Hall, but also by the Banqueting House. Sermons were still preached from the open air pulpit in Sermon Court—once called the Inward Garden—and members of the royal family listened from the windows of the Council Chamber.

Both James and Charles had their private apartments near the angle formed by the Stone Gallery (along the east side of the Privy Garden) and the Privy Gallery (running up to the Holbein Gate). Here the sovereign had his Withdrawing Room, Breakfast Room, Bedchamber, Lesser Withdrawing Room, Stone Chamber, and the Council Chamber. All these rooms were on the first floor, with direct access to the Privy Garden down the Adam and Eve Staircase, so named from a painting of the primal couple which hung at its head.

Throughout the reigns of the first two Stuarts the Palace continued to spread towards what is today Trafalgar Square. Henry VIII had acquired the land beyond the public way to the river at Whitehall Stairs, but little building was done on it during his lifetime. This was the area called Scotland Yard. In Saxon times it was occupied from time to time by those of the Scottish kings who were required to come south once a year to do homage at Westminster. Later, in the Middle Ages, they were still required to come to London, but in less galling circumstances, as barons of the Realm holding the fief of Cumberland and Huntingdonshire. Margaret, the sister of Henry VIII and widow of James IV of Scotland, was the last queen to live there. Then, some nine hundred years after the first Scottish king came to London to do homage to his English overlord, it was one of that nation who lived and ruled in the adjoining Palace.

Architecturally speaking, the buildings put up in Scotland Yard were of no consequence. Nearly all were concerned with the more mundane side of life in Old Whitehall Palace. Here was the Spicery, the Cider House, the Scalding Yard, the Confectionary, the Coal Yard, and the Wood Yard.

Through his many fine portraits, Charles I is a familiar figure, and it comes as something of a shock to discover that in reality he was only five foot two inches tall, weak in the legs, and afflicted with such a stutter that at the opening of his first Parliament he handed his speech to the Speaker to read, rather than risk being unable to complete it himself. Without doubt the stubbornness that was to cost him his head was due to a burning desire to assert himself, despite his physical insignificance.

And now, when he had most need of a strong wife who would give him confidence, he was tormented with a scolding parakeet of a woman. Later Charles and Henrietta Maria came to love each other, but for the present the king was little more than the traditional hen-pecked husband, unable to get a word in edgeways, and not even master in his own house.

In his helplessness he turned to the mischief-making Duke of Buckingham, and used him as a go-between who might be able to tame his shrew. By pointing out to Henrietta Maria 'Queens of England have been beheaded before now' he brought her to some degree of reasonableness. Though offensive, the Queen had laid herself open to censure. Since coming to England she had done nothing to endear herself to her new subjects by marriage. In Whitehall she insulated herself from the rest of the Court with a circle of ladies in waiting, priests, musicians, and servants; all French. As for the outside world: that saw a queen who as a Catholic refused to attend her husband's coronation, and crawled on her knees to Tyburn where a number of Jesuits had been executed not for religious but for treasonable activities resulting from a loyalty divided between a Pope and a Protestant England.

No, she was not making matters easy for herself or for her husband.

Eventually Marshal Bassompière, the French Ambassador, took a hand and tried to smooth out the differences between the royal couple. As a result the Queen's entourage was reduced to a bishop, ten priests, ten musicians, two ladies of the bedchamber, an apothecary, a surgeon, a chamberlain, an esquire, a secretary, and two gentlemen ushers. All the others, including eighteen or nineteen priests, were returned to France. As might be expected this was not achieved without the generation of a great deal of heat by Henrietta Maria. 'The women howled and lamented, as if they had been going to execution; but all in vain, for the Yeomen of the Guard, by that Lord's appointment (Lord Conway, sent to see the expulsions really took place), thrust all their country's folk out of the Queen's lodgings, and locked the doors after them. It is said also that the Queen, when she understood the design, grew very impatient, and broke the glass windows with her fist; but since then her rage is appeased, and the King and she, since they went together to Nonsuch, have been very joined together.' So wrote John Pory in a letter to a friend.

An alteration of some importance was carried out at Whitehall in 1629–32 when Inigo Jones converted the Cockpit into a theatre. Two galleries, supported on Corinthian and Composite columns, were added, and a considerable amount of gilt lavished on the carved decorations: fruit, masks, etc.

Next it was the turn of the Banqueting House to be completed by the addition of a painted ceiling. The scheme had been planned as far back as 1621, but it was not until 1634 that Charles I could look up at the huge painting of his father, surrounded as he never wished to be in life, by young women of ample charms. The ceiling, of wood heavily carved and gilt, was divided into nine panels. In the riot of Baroque figures in the centre panel James I swirls aloft: one foot on a globe, the other on an eagle, and with a massive arm for additional support. The arm belongs to one of the female figures; for Religion, Victory, Zeal, and Honour accompany him on his apotheosis; to say nothing of ten cherubs, some blowing trumpets, and all likely to hinder the royal upward progress. His immediate future is an *embarras de richesse*. Two cherubs offer the crown, another the orb, two of the women offer a wreath, while another is held ready by yet two more cherubs.

Even if the women are not, mercifully, quite as muscular as some of Michelangelo's creations, these massive monuments of womanhood by Rubens are huge-limbed and full-breasted. They might all be figures representing Ceres from one of the masques so beloved by James I. The scale is indeed enormous. The cherubs—or genii, for here the Christian and Pagan elements are intermixed with an abandon reminiscent of religious art in fourth-century Rome—that fill the side panels are nine feet in length. The centre panel at the north end shows Prince Charles: James I points to him as his successor, while in the panel at the south end of the Banqueting House (it balances the design) James points to Peace and Plenty, while Minerva suppresses Rebellion. Within a few years of 1634 her wisdom was put to the test, but she could not suppress the Great Rebellion, and save Charles I.

For this work Peter Paul Rubens received £3,000, and also a knighthood. It was the King's wish that Van Dyck should decorate the walls with a series of paintings dealing with the founding of the Order of the Garter, but lack of funds put a stop to what would have been a magnificent but impossibly expensive scheme. Yet how much more worth while than the thousands scattered about by James I in 1613 at his daughter Elizabeth's wedding. When the final gilding was added in 1635 the Banqueting House stood complete. Fifty years later Azout, a French architect, declared: 'It is the most finished of the modern buildings on this side of the Alps.' From a Frenchman, familiar with the Trianon and Louis XIV's greater achievements, this was praise indeed.

The Triumph of Peace was perhaps the most magnificent masque ever seen at Whitehall. The reasons that brought it into being were political. In 1634 Prynne had published a pamphlet, 'Histriomastix, the Player's Scourge', which was taken as an attack on the Queen and her love for masques and the theatre. For his impudence Archbishop Laud—a religious dictator—ordered the revolting but all too common punishment for pamphleteers. Prynne was branded on the forehead, his ears cut off, and his nose slit. The Court smarted under the pamphlet, and as a gesture of support for the throne the Societies of Law arranged and performed *The Triumph of Peace*, at Whitehall. The cost to them was £2,000: approximately £90,000 at modern rates. Inigo Jones designed the scenery and Shirley wrote the words. As an occasion it was as spectacular as it was ill timed. Already the greater part of the country was in no mood to sympathize with any kind of extravagance at Court.

But the masques continued, and in 1637 Charles I ordered a special Masque House to be built as he feared the flaring, smoking torches might damage Rubens's ceiling in the Banqueting House. Although only built of deal it cost £2,500—roughly £112,000 today. The masque that opened the new building was yet another of Inigo Jones's masterpieces: *Britannia Triumphans*. This time it was Davenant who was responsible for the words.

Perhaps the fire was burning brightest just before it went out: ahead lay the Civil War, disaster, and death. In the early stages of the conflict it was the City 'prentices who were most open in their hostility to the throne. Frequently they demonstrated outside Whitehall Palace, and on 30th December 1641

Thomas Smith wrote: 'The 'Prentices, and our Soldiers have lately had some bickerings, wherein many of the 'Prentices were wounded, and lost their hats and cloaks. This was done yesterday at Whitehall Gate, as the 'Prentices were coming from demanding an answer to their petition, lately exhibited to the Parliament House. These wounds of the 'Prentices have so exasperated them, that it is feared they will be at Whitehall this day to the number of ten thousand; whereupon the soldiers have increased their number, built up a Court of Guard without the Gate, and have called down the military company to their assistance, and what will be the event, God knows.'

During one of these demonstrations Henrietta Maria unintentionally coined a word which in due course passed into the English language. As she looked from a window of the Palace at the young men in the street below, her thoughts were more concerned with them themselves than with the reason for their coming—in this case to protest against the nomination by the King of a most unpopular man as Lieutenant of the Tower. 'See what a fine round head is there,' she exclaimed, and so gave the popular name to the Royalist's opponents. The original Roundhead was Samuel Barnadiston, the son of a Suffolk squire and landowner. Later he repented of his political views, enthusiastically welcomed Charles II at the Restoration, and received a knighthood. He is buried in Kedington parish church in Suffolk, but unfortunately only a tablet commemorates him. It would have been interesting to know exactly what the first Roundhead looked like.

Although relations between the King and Queen were better than during the early years of their marriage, they were at times very strained. Life in the royal household in 1640–2 must have been enough to try the nerves and patience of the most balanced of individuals. Some idea of the conditions under which they lived can be gathered from one small detail. On several occasions Henrietta Maria received visitors to her apartments with the curtains drawn, though it was broad daylight, so they should not see the tattered condition of the furnishings, cushions, carpets, and bed hangings.

'Go, you coward, and pull me these rogues out by the ears,

Wax effigy of Queen Elizabeth I.

Wax effigy of Charles II.

The Rubens Ceiling, the Banqueting House, Old Whitehall Palace, 1634.

or never see my face more,' were her words ringing in Charles's ears as he went from Whitehall to Westminster with the intention of arresting the five Members; among them Hampden and Pym. The 4th January 1642 was in a sense the climax of the quarrel between King and Parliament: after that it would be war.

Although royalty might be able to carry off such high-handed actions in Henrietta Maria's own country—for France the Revolution was still nearly a hundred and fifty years hence—in England tempers were rising rapidly. That day spies slipped out of the Palace ahead of the King, and when he reached the House he found the members gone. Gone too was much of his prestige. Six days later, on 10th January, Whitehall was vacated in favour of Hampton Court, and from there the Court soon moved to the comforting strength of Windsor Castle. Only for a few hours would Whitehall see Charles again, and those would be his last.

As the Civil War dragged on the Palace remained empty: an art gallery unseen and uncared-for. Of all the English kings Charles I was the greatest connoisseur and patron of painting. When the Court left Whitehall it housed some four hundred and sixty canvases, most of them masterpieces. Today the list seems almost incredible: twenty-eight Titians, nine Raphaels, forty-six Julio Romanos, four Guidos, and seven Parmiagianos; as well as others by Holbein (among which could be included the ceiling of the Stone Gallery), Rubens, and Correggio.

The Chapel Royal was despoiled, the stained glass broken, and the fittings either destroyed or dispersed, while the palace itself became a barracks. Two contemporary entries speak for themselves.

'(1) Paid unto Mr John Hunte, in persuance of an order of the Commons House, 14 Jan. 1647 to be issued by the Committee of Whitehall, for providing of bedding and other provisions fitting for accommodating the forces appointed to be quartered in Whitehall and the Mews, by virtue of three several warrants of this Committee, £2,500.

'(2) Paid unto the said Mr Hunte by way of Loan, to be repaid out of the moneys to be raised of the sale of certain hangings which have superstitious and idolatrous pictures in them, at Whitehall, by order of the Commons House, 19 Feb. 1647, for to provide fire, candles, and other necessaries for the said soldiers, by warrant dated 21st Febr. 1647, £100.'

But all this was to be overshadowed by the personal tragedy of Charles I: his execution outside the Banqueting House. In January 1649 Charles was confined in St James's Palace, and each day of the trial—as a traitor to the laws of the country—was taken by barge to Westminster Hall; except on the last when he was carried there in a sedan chair. Bradshaw, 'the bold traitor', passed sentence on the king, with the agreement of the sixty-seven members of the Court. Within a few days, however, a number were already having second thoughts in the matter, and only fifty-nine actually signed the death warrant.

'At the high Court of Justice for trying and Judging of Charles Stuart, king of England January XXIXth Anno Dni 1648.

'Whereas Charles Stuart king of England is and standeth convicted attainted and condemned of High Treason and other high Crimes And sentence upon Saturday last was pronounced against him by this Court to be put to death by the severing of his head from his body Of which sentence execution yet remaineth to be done These are therefore to will and require you to see the said sentence executed In the open Street before Whitehall upon the morrow being the Thirtieth day of this instant month of January between the hours of Ten in the morning and five in the afternoon of the same day with full effect And for so doing this shall be your sufficient warrant And these are to require All Officers and Soldiers and other good people of this nation of England to be assisting unto you in this service Given under our hands and Seals.

'To Colonel Francis Hacker Colonel Hunks and Lieutenant Colonel Phayre and to every of them.'

Then followed the signatures of the Regicides. Bradshaw's name came first, Cromwell's third, and that of his son-in-law Ireton, ninth.

Although Charles I's execution 'In the open street before Whitehall' is one of the most famous events in English history, it is remarkable that it should still be surrounded by a number of minor mysteries; none of which seem any nearer being solved after the lapse of more than three hundred years. They are: through which window did the King step from the Banqueting House on to the scaffold? What was meant by his last remark to Bishop Juxon? Who actually wielded the axe?

Charles spent his last night in St James's Palace, and on the morning of Tuesday, 30th January, was brought across the park. The morning was bitterly cold, and it was his wish to walk briskly lest any of those about him thought he shivered with fear.

In the *Journal of the Earl of Leicester* is the entry: 'with a regiment of foot, part before, and part behind him, with colours flying, drums beating, his private guard of Partizans, with some of his gentlemen before and some behind, bareheaded. Dr Juxon next behind him, and Colonel Tomlinson (who had charge of him) talking with the king bareheaded'.

Then came a pathetic incident that hardly interrupted the sharp walk across the frost-bound park. One of the King's dogs, tied up in St James's Palace, broke free and ran, his chain trailing, after his master. A soldier caught up the broken chain and led the dog away. Later, he exhibited it as being the pet of the late king, but it pined and died within a short while of his master.

When the party reached that part of Whitehall on the west side of the road, it ascended the Park Stairs and entered the Tilt-yard Gallery, from which in happier times Charles had watched tournaments and festivities. Then over the Holbein Gate to where the King was to await the final summons from his old bed-chamber.

Now Sir Philip Warwick takes up the story in his *Memoirs of the Reign of King Charles*.

'It was a very cold day, and they at Whitehall had prepared two or three dishes of meat for him to dine upon: but he refused to eat anything; and the Bishop told me, he resolved to touch nothing after the Sacrament; but the Bishop expostulated with him, and let him know how long he had fasted; and how sharp the weather was; and how some fit of fainting might take him upon the scaffold; which he knew he was troubled at, for the interpretation his murderers would put upon it; which prevail'd with him to eat half a manchet of bread, and drink a glass of wine; and thus prepared, when he was called, he marcht to the scaffold.'

Sir Thomas Herbert takes up the story: 'Colonel Hacker attending still at the Chamber Door, the King took notice of it, and said, "open the door", and bade Hacker go, he would follow. A guard was made all along the Galleries and the Banqueting House; but behind the soldiers, abundance of men and women crowded in, though with some peril to their persons, to behold the saddest sight England ever saw. And as his Majesty pass'd by with a cheerful look, heard them pray for him, the soldiers not rebuking any of them; by their silence and dejected faces seemed afflicted rather than insulting.

The King was led along all the galleries of the Banqueting House, and there was a passage broken through, the wall, by which the King passed upon the scaffold.'

But was the breach made in one of the main windows between the Ionic pilasters, or through a window in the annex added at the north end of the Banqueting House to enclose the staircase? During the Civil War the main windows on to the street had been bricked up for safety; while the smaller was, in all probability, left as it was.

Time was not altogether on the side of the Regicides. Since the warrant had only been signed some time during the previous day—and taking into account the shortness of the days, there was not long in which to have everything ready by ten o'clock. Surely it would have been quicker to knock out the frame of the tall window in the annex which was flush with the front of the Banqueting House, than to break down the temporary brick-work, as well as four feet of carved stonework in the lower part of one of the main windows.

In 1713 Terrason engraved the Banqueting House as it then stood. A few years later the engraving was very closely copied by George Vertue, the official engraver to the Society of Antiquaries (1717–56). However, he made one addition: above the windows of the annex he placed a crown and 'C.R.' and below '1648'. In accordance with the old Julian Calendar the new year did not begin until March, and Charles was beheaded in January. The same reason applies for the dating at the end of the death warrant. Above this small addition Vertue wrote: 'Tis, according to the truest reports, said that out of this window, King Charles went upon the scaffold to be beheaded: the window-frame being taken out purposely to make the passage on to the scaffold, which is equal to the landing place of the hall, within side.'

In Edgar Sheppard's book on Whitehall, published at the beginning of the present century, he uses as further evidence Herbert's words 'a passage broken through the wall'. The wall in question being the one separating the Banqueting House from the annex.

Evidence in favour of a rival theory that the King stepped through the second window from the north end is supported in a letter written about 1880 by Mr Thoms, an engineer. 'On the 1st May, 1831, I arrived in London . . . when we walked to see the Abbey (and my memory is most clear), Hill showed me in the foot pavement a stone, placed lozenge wise. It was a blue stone, most likely slate or blue lias. He told me it marked the site of the scaffold on which Charles I was slaughtered. The stone was under the second or third window of Whitehall next to Charing Cross (i.e. the north end). Of this point I am a little at a loss; but my memory inclines most to the second window as the one it marked from which the scaffold was entered.'

Even so, the position of the stone, supposing it to have been accurately placed, does not invalidate the first theory. The entrance through the annex could have been at the extreme left of the scaffold, most of which was erected in front of the two adjacent windows. In that case it would presumably have ended at the angle formed by the slight projection of the three centre bays of the front.

That leads to the second unsolved problem. What was meant by the last remark of the King: 'Remember.' After stepping forward into the sight of the huge silent crowd that filled the public thoroughfare almost as far as Charing Cross, Charles made a brief speech, ending: ' . . . if I would have given way to an arbitrary way, for to have all laws changed according to the power of the sword, I needed not to have come here, and therefore I tell you . . . and I pray God it be not laid to your charge . . . that I am the Martyr of the people.'

To the end Charles wore his 'George'; the emblem of the Order of the Garter, and as he handed it to Bishop Juxon he said, 'Remember.' A great deal of speculation has surrounded that one word: some conjecturing that it referred to Charles's wish that the Church should receive back alienated property. Others that the King was instructing the Bishop to tell his son to forgive the Regicides, if ever he came to the throne of England as Charles II. But in all probability there was less in the remark than meets the eye. Some time during that last morning Charles may have made the Bishop promise that somehow he would see the 'George' was passed on to Prince Charles, wherever he was. And now as the sands of his life ran out he handed it over with a reminder of that promise.

In fact, in a book published in 1649, *Medulla Historiae Anglicanae*, its author claimed that Charles was heard to say: 'Remember (twas said) to send it to the Prince.' Unfortunately the author did not or could not quote an authority for the statement.

That leaves the third question to deal with: who actually put Charles to death? In the *Journal of the Earl of Leicester* is the entry: 'The executioners were two, and disguised in sailors' clothes with visards and periques unknown; yet some have a conceit that he that gave the stroke was one Colonel Fox, and the other Colonel Joyce, who took the king from Holmby, but it is not believed. This I heard for certain, that Gregory Brandon, the common hangman of London, refused absolutely to do it, and professed that he would rather be shot or otherways killed rather than do it.' The writer meant Richard Brandon, not his father Gregory, who had been dead for years.

A complete contradiction of this statement is contained in the burial register of the parish of St Mary, Whitechapel, where Richard Brandon lived and died.

'1649 June 21st: Richard Brandon, a man out of Rosemary Lane;

'This Richard Brandon is supposed to have cut off the head of Charles the First.'

More support for Brandon's doubtful claim to fame comes from a curious pamphlet printed in that year, called: 'The Confession of Richard Brandon, the Hangman.'

'He likewise confessed that he had thirty pounds for his pains, all paid him in half-crowns within an hour after the blow was given; and that he had an orange stuck full of cloves, and a handkerchief out of the King's pocket, so soon as he was carried off the scaffold, for which orange he was proffered twenty shillings by a gentleman in Whitehall, but refused the same, and afterwards sold it for ten shillings in Rosemary Lane.'

After the Restoration the Royalist Government attempted to discover the man's identity, and William Lilley, an astrologer, told an investigating commission that Cromwell's secretary, Robert Spavin, once said: 'It was Lieutenant Colonel Joyce. I was in the room when he fitted himself for the work . . . stood behind him, when he did it . . . when done went in again with him.' By 1660 Spavin was dead, and the astrologer's statement could not be checked.

Whatever the rights and wrongs of the case, if Charles I had not been such a thorough-going exponent of the divine right of kings, he might have saved the country a great deal of misery. But he was a Stuart, and like Mary his grandmother, and the Duke of Monmouth his grandson, he knew how to die with dignity when the time came.

Now all that remained for the King to do was to put up his long hair beneath an embroidered cap, and lie down at the block, only a few inches high. Andrew Marvell's lines may have become hackneyed with the passing of time and not always a correct quotation; but they contained much truth.

> He nothing common did or mean
> Upon that memorable scene;
> But with his keener eye
> The axe's edge did try;
> Nor called the gods, with vulgar spite,
> To vindicate his helpless right;

But bowed his comely head
Down, as upon a bed.

Followed by only a few friends Charles's body was taken to Windsor, and as the snow fell, carried into St George's Chapel for burial.

Among those at Whitehall that day were Samuel Pepys and Weesop, a Dutch artist. Another ten years was to elapse before Pepys started his *Diary*, but Weesop painted the scene. He left England almost at once: a country which could kill its king was not one in which he cared to live; and judging by inaccuracies in the background, his painting may have been done after a lapse of several months. He omits the uppermost story of the Banqueting House and gives it eight instead of seven bays.

The painting was copied on several occasions, and appeared on top of a broad-sheet, but perhaps the most remarkable of all the reproductions is in Burstwick parish church, in the East Riding of Yorkshire. There it forms the centre of a memorial to Charles I, and is painted on the back of a set of Royal Arms. It was ordered by John Catlyn, Vicar of Burstwick, in 1676, and set up in the church on the anniversary of the execution. A curious feature is that all the details are reversed from those in the Weesop—as though seen in a looking-glass.

After the Restoration several churches were dedicated to King Charles the Martyr. One is at Tunbridge Wells, and another at Shelland, in Suffolk.

8

Although Old Whitehall Palace had a new master in Oliver Cromwell, he at first chose to live in the apartments near the Cockpit Theatre. He may have been out of place in such surroundings, but at least there was the honest freshness of the country about the man. As his reign wore on—and in the light of subsequent events the word is not altogether inappropriate, a distinct liking for the trappings of royalty became more and more noticeable. But for the present he was still the God-fearing farmer from Huntingdonshire. When his portrait was about to be painted he made the famous remark: 'Mr Lely, I desire you would use all your skill to paint my picture truly like me, and not flatter me at all; but remark all these roughnesses, pimples, warts and everything, otherwise I never will pay a farthing for it.'

Whatever many of his subordinates may have been, Cromwell was no out-and-out fanatic permeated by a dismal piety and a ruthless intolerance of any opinions but his own. Much of the legend was not unnaturally put about by the Royalists, and kept alive by those who believed all Royalists were wrong but romantic, and all Roundheads right but revolting. Nor were all Roundheads drawn from social ranks inferior to the Royalists. Nor for that matter were all the battles of the Civil War polite encounters fought out, as it were, in the grounds of large country houses. The truth, as it usually does in such matters, lies several degrees away from the popular conception.

As for Cromwell the man; when he had time to spare for his own amusements they were hunting, hawking, singing, and above all being with his family.

Many of the treasures had gone from Whitehall by now, either scattered or sold, but to his credit Cromwell did not encourage the practice of dispersing the royal collection. He himself bought the Raphael cartoons (now in the Victoria and Albert Museum), and when the Restoration came they were found in the Palace, safely crated up out of harm's way.

Although the King was dead, the Civil War was not yet at an end, and London itself was not free from disturbances. As a result a guard-house was set up in 1649 nearly opposite the Banqueting House. Later it was to be rebuilt and greatly enlarged. It is still there: the Horse Guards.

A man much more typical of the worse aspects of the Commonwealth was the City leatherseller, Praise-God Barebones —he was baptised John, and originally his surname had been Barbon, of Huguenot origin. These extraordinary names were common currency at the time. Perhaps the funniest by modern standards is Mr Kill-Sin Pimple.

Early in 1653 Cromwell dissolved the Long Parliament, by then curtailed to the Rump, which had been sitting since 1641, and with the help of his Council of State set about preparing a new one. On 6th June a communication was delivered to Mr Praise-God Barebones and a hundred and nineteen other men of similar calibre.

'Gen. Oliver Cromwell to Praise-God Barebones Esq. As on the dissolution of the late Parliament, it became necessary that peace and good government should be provided for, I and my council of officers have nominated persons of fidelity to whom this great charge is to be committed; and having assurance of your love to God and interest in this people, I, as the Commander-in-Chief of the Commonwealth, summon you, being one of the persons so nominated, to appear at the Council Chamber, Whitehall, on 4th July, and take upon you the said trust as member for the City of London.'

Nearly a month later, 4th July, the newly nominated (not elected) members assembled in the Council Chamber in Whitehall Palace. They were to govern, Cromwell told them, for fifteen months, and then choose a new Parliament to be their successor. Off they went to Westminster bent on creating heaven on earth, though by the time they had finished even moderate men were beginning to wonder exactly what it was they had come near to achieving. Worst of all were the 'Days of Public Humiliation', which were as frequent as saints days in Central America, but as mortifying as Victor Hugo's conception of the English Sabbath of his time.

Plays of any sort were completely banned; at Whitehall the Cockpit Theatre had been deserted since the outbreak of the Civil War, and even the 'prentices were forbidden to play football.

Having, as they thought, set the man in the street upon the strait and narrow, these holy meddlers next turned their attention to the Army, and to advising Cromwell himself. On the 12th December two Army officers with soldiers descended on Westminster while the House was debating customs dues, dismissed the saints and locked the doors behind them.

A document agreeing to their resignation was drawn up, placed on a table in a room of the Palace, and as soon as the majority had signed, Praise-God Barebones' Parliament had passed into history. That same day, 16th December, Cromwell was installed as Lord Protector of England, with almost unlimited powers. Already he showed signs of his hankering after the rights of royalty.

For the installation he rode to Westminster Hall in one of the State Coaches, while the judges, the Lord Mayor and aldermen of the City lent colour and weight to the procession by their presence. For this occasion the coronation chair was brought across from the Abbey—where such sovereigns as Edward III and Henry VIII had sat robed in purple, holding the orb and sceptre, now sat Oliver Cromwell, robed in purple and holding a sceptre and a sword. Only the crown was missing. The greater part of the regalia had been broken down after the execution of Charles I, but it may be that a specially made crown was placed beside the Bible on a table covered with gold-fringed velvet.

Now men were to uncover their heads as he passed by in St James's Park, and on 23rd February 1654 M. de Bordeaux wrote: 'Towards the foreign ambassadors the Protector deports himself as a King, for the power of King is not greater than his.' On 13th April of the following year Cromwell moved across the road into the main part of the Palace. The *Weekly Intelligencer* reported: 'The Privy Lodgings for his Highness the Lord Protector in Whitehall, are now in readiness as also the lodgings for his Lady Protectoress; and likewise the Privy Kitchen and other Kitchens, butteries and offices, and it is conceived the whole family will be ready settled there before Easter.'

By and large both Cromwell's mother and wife were slower to enter whole-heartedly into the ways of kings. In fact, old Mrs Cromwell never did so. According to the memoirs of Edmund Ludlow: 'By reason of her great age, (she) was not so easily flattered by these temptations, very much mistrusted the issue of affairs, and would often be afraid, when she heard the noise of a musket, that her son was shot, being exceedingly dissatisfied unless she might see him once a day at least.'

James I might have spent over £93,000 on his daughter's marriage to Frederick, Count Palatine of the Rhine, but not even the most ardent Royalist could truthfully call the Lady Protectoress a spendthrift. In the 'Court and Kitchen of Cromwell, 1664', there is an amusing account of her domestic economy. She ordered 'a surveyor to make her some little labyrinths and trap stairs by which she might, at all times unseen, pass too and fro, and come unawares upon her servants and keep them vigilant in their places and honest in the discharge thereof.'

Not that meals were dull or mean. Monday was always kept as the day on which any officer of captain's rank or above could come to Whitehall, and find 'open table'. Nor did foreign ambassadors have cause to complain: 'April 27th 1654. The Lords Ambassadors of the United Provinces at Whitehall, and the Lords of the Council with some Colonels and other gentlemen at two tables in the same room . . . and twenty gentlemen were taken into his Highness's Life guard of foot, who carried up the meat, and many gentlemen attended, and after dinner there was a banquet. The coats of the Guards are grey cloth with black velvet collars, and silver traces and trimmings.'

If Cromwell was seeking the glory of kings, he also found the debit side: the fear of assassination. From across the North Sea word reached him that Charles II was offering a life pension of £500 a year to anyone who would rid England of its Protector. The King was not particular: the assassin could use pistol, sword, or poison. In the circumstances it was not unnatural that Cromwell was anxious for his own safety.

One of these attempts which concerns Whitehall was made in January 1657, when a cashiered soldier, Miles Sindercom, attempted to fire the Palace in the hope of killing Cromwell in the confusion which should follow. In a statement made to the Lieutenant of the Tower, after the affair had run its course, one Colonel Sexby stated he had come over from the Continent and bribed Sindercom with £500 to kill Cromwell. Sindercom and a confederate called Cecil concocted a plan: 'They resolved to fire Whitehall. To this end they cut a hole in one of the doors of the Chapel, and so unbolting it, they, on the eighth of this month, went in and placed the materials for firing, which were discovered about nine o'clock that night, for in one of the seats was found upon the floor a basket filled with a strange composition of combustable stuff, and two lighted matches, aptly placed, which matches had been rubbed over with gunpowder, on purpose to keep them surely burning, and by the length of them, it was conceived they would have given fire to the basket about one o'clock in the morning. The basket being removed, and trial being made of some parts of the ingredients, it appeared to be most active flaming stuff. The next day, the two persons being apprehended, they were found to have screwed pistols, which upon trial appear notable instruments to do execution at a distance more than ordinary; and they had also a strange sort of long bullets, in the nature of slugs, contrived on purpose to rend and tear.'

The law ground into action and Miles Sindercom was sentenced to death; to be hanged, drawn, and quartered as a traitor. In his prison in the Tower he was supposed to have offered his gaoler £700 to allow him to escape. That failed, but on the night before his execution he committed suicide. How he managed this is uncertain, but on her last visit his sister may have slipped him poison.

At about the time of these happenings John Evelyn came to Whitehall, to see for himself how the Palace was faring under the Commonwealth.

11th February 1656. 'I ventured to go to Whitehall, where of many years I had not been, and found it very glorious and well furnished, as far as I could safely go, and was glad to find they had not much defaced that rare piece of Henry VII etc: done on the walls of the King's privy chamber.'

'Insolent fools' was the cutting description used by Lucy Hutchinson about Cromwell's daughters, and on 12th November 1657 one of them, Frances, married Robert Rich in the Palace with festivities of a most unpuritanical nature. '48 violins and 50 trumpets, and much mirth, with frolics, besides mixt dancing (a thing heretofore accounted profane), till five of the clock.' And yet, when Parliament offered Cromwell the crown, he declined it. But even here, at the heart of the Commonwealth, the tide was beginning to turn in favour of the old order and a way of life which many had thought stamped out for ever.

Certainly the end was approaching for both Cromwell and the Interregnum itself. In August 1658 the Protector's other daughter, Elizabeth, died at Hampton Court (today she is the only Cromwell to sleep undisturbed in Westminster Abbey), and before long her father had come to Whitehall for the last time.

When all is said, he was one of England's greatest soldiers and statesmen, and there was a fitting finality to the course of his life. On 3rd September 1650 he won the Battle of Dunbar; on 3rd September 1651 he won the Battle of Worcester—extinguishing the Civil War in England, and on 3rd September 1658 his life slipped away on the winds of a tearing, ravaging storm. 'It is a fearful thing to fall into the hands of the living God,' he murmured as the windows of the palace rattled without ceasing, chimneys and tiles tumbled down and in St James's Park trees were uprooted like weeds.

The trappings of royalty remained with Cromwell to the end. A wax effigy, that symbol of a king's funeral, lay in state with the coffin in Somerset House. It was clad in velvet trimmed with gold lace, over which was placed the 'Royal large Robe of the like Purple Velvet laced, and furr'd with Ermines'. Close by a sword, and 'in the right hand is the sceptre representing Government; in his left hand is held the globe, representing Principality; upon his head, the Cap of Regality of Purple Velvet, furred with ermines. Behind the head is a rich chair of Estate of cloth of gold tissued; upon the Cushion of the Chair stands the Imperial Crown set with stones'.

There was no mistaking the signs: a crown might be placed by his coffin, but soon another would be placed upon the head of Charles II. *THE* Cromwell was dead, and in his place ruled his earnest but uninspired and uninspiring son Richard.

> And Richard yet, where his great parent led,
> Beats on the rugged track: he virtue dead
> Revives, and by his milder beams assures:
> And yet how much of them his grief obscures.
> He, as his father, long was kept from sight
> In private, to be viewed by better light:
> But open'd once, what splendour does he throw!
> A Cromwell in an hour will grow.

A decade before Andrew Marvell had sharpened his pen to write about Charles I: now he was writing about the brief reign of the new Protector. Poor Richard, if history remembers him at all, it is as Tumble-down Dick.

At Whitehall his father went in fear of assassins; his son went in fear of creditors. In May 1659 he willed away his grand eloquent title, 'His Serene Highness the Lord Protector', and in May 1659 he stepped down from public affairs, leaving it to others to guide events along their inevitable course.

The Army called on those members who had composed the Rump to meet in the Painted Chamber at Whitehall. There that particular parliament was re-formed, and on 10th May it decided the Palace itself should be sold, together with Somerset House, 'towards the satisfaction of the great arrears and pay due unto the Army'. But this was never acted upon, and all through that summer England seethed and fermented, while in Scotland General Monck (who had his own quarters at Whitehall), watched and waited. On 3rd February he reached Whitehall, as the crowds looked on, silent, puzzled, and wondering what would happen next.

By March people in the City were openly calling out 'God save King Charles', and breaking the windows of Praise-God Barebones' house in Fetter Lane, and in May Parliament came out in favour of restoring the monarchy. Now it only remained for Charles II to come to Whitehall as its rightful owner.

For the first time in this year of 1660 Whitehall enters the *Diary* of Samuel Pepys. At the outset of his career he and his young wife Elizabeth occupied humble apartments in the Palace itself—possibly those over the Palace Gate—when he first became secretary to his kinsman Edward Montagu, later Lord Sandwich. In the next ten years Pepys would be a frequent visitor to Whitehall; but this, one of the first occasions on which he mentions going there is not very auspicious. '23rd January. In the garden at Whitehall, going through to the Stone Gallery, I fell in a ditch, it being very dark.'

9

'If any of our Court shall be noised to be a profane person, an outrageous rioter, a ribald, a notorious drunkard, swearer, railer, ribald or quarreller, a fugitive from his master, a bankrupt, suspected for a pilferer or a thief, or be otherwise so vicious and unmannerly that he be unfit to live in virtuous and civil company, he shall be convened before his superior officer to be examined, and thereupon admonished or punished as cause shall require.'

Such a code of behaviour suggests Praise-God Barebones as its author, but in fact that item comes from the Household Ordinances issued at the beginning of Charles II's reign. This new king seen for the first time by the Londoners was no disappointment. At six foot two inches he was exactly a foot taller than his father: athletic, a skilled though far from honest diplomat; interested in science, architecture, the theatre, and possessing a charm that could turn away the most justified wrath. The Divine Right of Kings died outside the Banqueting House with his father, yet such was his subtlety that Charles II was able to become an absolute monarch, and yet keep his throne. Lord Russell and Algernon Sidney were among the few who saw where it was the English were being led, and had their lives cut short as a result.

With his Newmarket Races and his dogs Charles seemed very much a product of the country; yet the amount of English blood in his veins was minute. Elizabeth of York, five generations back, was the nearest all-English ancestor. For the remainder he was Scottish on the male side, and Anglo-Welsh, Danish, and Franco-Italian through the female. By his mother he was related to the Medicis of Florence, and from her he also inherited a dark skin and a bold expression.

But the merchants pacing the Exchange, the clergy at Old St Paul's, the shop-keepers on Old London Bridge—all in fact, were satisfied. Gone were the self-righteous, scripture-drunk fanatics, and in their place was a King and his Court.

By degrees the old order was re-established at Whitehall. Where possible, paintings sold during the Commonwealth were recovered, including a number bought by a Dutchman and returned to London after his death by the State of Holland. Among the canvases once again on view was one, probably of no great value, which particularly caught Pepys's fancy. It was a *trompe-l'œil*, and he recorded in his *Diary*: 'I saw most incomparable pictures. Among the rest a book open upon a desk, which durst have sworn was a real book.'

The other great diarist of the period, Evelyn, also went to Whitehall to see the treasures, and in the entry for 1st November 1660 he wrote: 'I went with some of my relations to Court, to show them his Majesty's cabinet and closet of rarities; the miniatures of Peter Oliver after Raphael, Titian, and other masters, which I infinitely esteem; also that large piece of the Duchess of Lennox done in enamel by Pettitot, and a vast number of agates, onyxes and intaglios, especially a medallion of Caesar, as broad as my hand.'

The Chapel Royal was restored and on 8th July 1660 Pepys wrote of it: 'To Whitehall Chapel, where I got in with ease by going before the Lord Chancellor with Mr Kipps. Here I heard very good music the first time that ever I remember to have heard organs and singing-men in surplices in my life.' A whole generation, Pepys among them, had grown to maturity during the Civil War and the Commonwealth, and to them it must have been like seeing everything in colour for the first time.

Later that year he was again in the Chapel Royal. This time he saw the Royal Family at its devotions: a not particularly edifying sight. 'To White Hall chapel, where one Dr Crofts made an indifferent sermon, and after it an anthem, ill-sung, which made the king laugh. Here I also observed, how the Duke of York and Mrs Palmer [the notorious Barbara Villiers] did talk to one another very wantonly through the hangings that parts the King's closet from where the ladies sit.'

Naturally the theatre was not forgotten in this renaissance at Whitehall, and in October 1660 Pepys attended a performance of Fletcher's *The Woman's Prize*. Today it is difficult to realize just how much the King lived among his subjects. Although the theatre was part of the palace, it was open to the paying public, while during the day anyone respectably dressed could enter the Stone Gallery—if he could push his way through the crowd—to see the King pass to and fro.

Among the customs revived at this time none was stranger than touching for King's Evil. The anointing of the coronation ceremony set him apart from, and above other men. One of the supernatural gifts he was supposed to possess was the power to cure scrofula simply by touching the sufferer. Charles II was most lavish in bestowing his gifts, whether natural or supernatural, and during his reign he touched no less than ninety-two thousand, one hundred and seven people of all classes.

Evelyn described the scene on 6th July 1660: 'His Majesty sitting under his state in the Banqueting House, the chirurgeons cause the sick to be brought or led up to the throne, where they kneeling, the King strokes their faces or cheeks with both his hands at once, at which instant a chaplain in his formalities says, "He put his hands upon them and he healed them." This is said to every one in particular. When they have been all touched they come up again in the same order, and the other chaplain kneeling, and having angel gold strung on white ribbon on his arm, delivers them one by one to his Majesty, who puts them about the necks of the touched as they pass, whilst the first chaplain repeats, "that is the true light who come into the world." Then follows an Epistle (as at first a Gospel) with the Liturgy, prayers for the sick, with some alteration, lastly the blessing; and then the Lord Chamberlain and the Comptroller of the Household bring a basin, ewer, and towel, for his Majesty to wash.'

The custom went out with Queen Anne, but not before she had touched a boy from Lichfield; Samuel Johnson.

Although Charles II might be invested with supernatural healing powers, he could not save Prince Henry, his youngest brother, from dying of small-pox on 13th September that year. 'The next day a council was called and consideration had of disposing his body, and both because it was not fit that any dead corpse should remain in his Majesty's house and that his Royal Highness died of small pox it was ordered that his body should be instantly embalmed and carried to Somerset House, and placed in the Privy Chamber there.'

Before the year was out Charles was to lose another of his relatives. On Christmas Eve his sister the Princess of Orange died in the Palace, also of small-pox. Both were buried in Westminster Abbey.

It was not until November, six months after the Restoration, that Henrietta Maria came over from France to join her son. In the years that had gone by since last she was at Whitehall she had aged almost out of recognition. Pepys and his wife saw her at close range in the Presence Chamber. 'The Queen, a very little, plain old woman, and nothing more in her presence in any respect nor garb than any ordinary woman. The Princess Henrietta (a younger daughter) is very pretty, but much below my expectation; and her dressing of herself with her hair frizzed short up to her ears did make her seem much less to me. But my wife standing near her with two or three black patches on, and well dressed did seem to me much handsomer than she.' No doubt much of Pepys's satisfaction at his wife's superior charm lay in the fact that she, like the old Queen, was French.

Another of the customs revived with the return of the monarchy was that concerned with Maundy Thursday. In 1661 Charles was thirty-one years old and so, as Rugge recorded in his journal; 'he was pleased to wash thirty-one poor men's feet in the great hall in Whitehall, and gave every man a purse of white leather, in it thirty-one pence, and a red purse, in it a piece of gold, and a shirt, a suit of clothes, shoes and stockings, a wooden dish, and a basket wherein was four loaves, half a salmon, a whole ling, and herrings red and white. Every man drank claret wine in the Hall, and after service was done by the usual Vicar, that belonged to the King's Chapel, also the sound of the organs, they all departed and said . . . God save the King.'

Soon it was Charles's coronation, and for the last time a king went in procession from the Tower to Westminster on the day preceding. 'The streets all gravelled, and the houses with carpets before them, made a brave show, and the ladies out of the windows. So glorious was the show with gold and silver, that we (Pepys, his wife and friends) were not able to look at it, our eyes at last being so much overcome.'

All concerned were fortunate that coronation day. It remained fine until the late afternoon when the King was on his way back to Whitehall, then a thunderstorm cracked open the sky.

Even in that pre-industrial age all was not sweetness and light around London, let alone in the City (p. 97). Fog from coal fires was a particular nuisance, and in a pamphlet of 1661 Evelyn wrote: 'as I was walking in your Majesty's Palace of Whitehall (where I have sometimes the honour to refresh myself with the sight of your illustrious presence, where is the joy of your people's hearts), a presumptuous smoke issuing from one or two tunnels near Northumberland House and not far from Scotland Yard, did so invade the court that all the rooms, galleries and places about it were filled and infested with it: to such a degree as men could hardly discern one another for the cloud and none could support without manifest inconvenience.'

Periodically a sense of duty towards his country overtook Charles, and on one such occasion he contracted a marriage with the Portuguese princess, Catharine of Braganza. However, such a step did not mean any alteration to his mode of life. Barbara Villiers, who might perhaps be described as headmistress of the Royal Household, still reigned supreme, and by now the complacency of her husband had been rewarded with the title of Viscount Castlemaine. Pepys, in his attitude towards her, was a mixture of disapproval, envy, and worship from afar.

21st May 1662. 'My wife and I to my Lord's lodgings (Lord Sandwich, his patron); where she and I stayed walking in White Hall garden. And in the Privy Garden saw the finest smocks and linen petticoats of my Lady Castlemaine, laced with rich lace at the bottom, that ever I saw; and it did me good to look at them.'

During this period Lady Castlemaine still occupied a house in King's Street (now occupied by the present street of Whitehall), and when bonfires were lit to celebrate the approach to English waters of the future queen there was one notable exception. 'The king was there, but there was no fire at her door, though at all the rest of the doors almost in the street; which was much observed: and that the king and she did send for a pair of scales and weighed one another; and she being with child, was said to be the heaviest.' That piece of interesting information came to Pepys's ears from Lord Sandwich's housekeeper, who knew nearly all the palace gossip. The child soon to be born was the future Duke of Southampton.

From the start the unfortunate Catharine of Braganza was a source of amusement to the cynical and immoral Court, which was as unlike the royal backwater from which she had come as could be imagined. At Lisbon they were a little out of touch with fashion trends, and when the convent-bred girl stepped ashore she was wearing a farthingale; a dress Elizabeth I would have put on to go to Old St Paul's to give thanks for the defeat of the Armada some seventy years previously.

After a speedy marriage at Portsmouth, Charles and his sniggering retinue set off for Hampton Court. There he and his sense of duty—or rather of decency—soon parted company when he attempted to make Lady Castlemaine, newly risen from her childbed, one of the Queen's ladies of the bed-chamber. However, Catharine of Braganza refused to take her into her circle: forewarned either by feminine intuition or else by some kind friend who felt it her duty to inform her of the situation.

Although Pepys climbed to the roof of the Banqueting House to watch Catharine of Braganza's arrival by water from Hampton Court, he had eyes only for his Distant Beloved, who, it must be admitted, was behaving most oddly. 23rd August 1662. 'Anon come the King and Queen in a barge, under a canopy, with a thousand barges and boats, I know, for we could see no water for them, nor discern the King and Queen. And so they landed at Whitehall Bridge (pier) and the great guns on the other side went off. But that which pleased me best was, that my Lady Castlemaine stood over against us upon a piece of White Hall. But methought it was strange to see her Lord (Castlemaine) and her upon the same place walking up and down without taking notice one of another; only at first entry, he put off his hat, and she made him a very civil salute: but took no notice one of the other; but both of them, now and then, would take their child, which the nurse held in her arms, and dandle it.'

One can only hope for Catharine of Braganza's sake that amid the bustle and excitement of landing she did not notice Lady Castlemaine and her cuckold husband holding the King's baby; turn and turn about.

By a cruel irony of fate Lady Castlemaine mothered four of the King's numerous children, while Catharine was barren stock. Thrust into the background as of no use or importance, deprived of nearly all her Portuguese ladies in waiting, despised by the Court, she is one of the most pathetic of English queens. Although Lady Castlemaine might be, to all intents and purposes, Queen of Whitehall, she was only one of that monstrous regiment of beautiful women that surrounded Charles II at all times.

Frances Stuart, later Duchess of Richmond, was so beautiful that Pepys had to admit she even outshone his Distant Beloved. In fact he was sufficiently disloyal to imagine himself sporting with her. In all fairness to Pepys it should be remembered that he did more towards laying the foundations of the modern Navy than anyone else; and in his *Diary*—never meant for other eyes—he merely wrote what many men would think in similar circumstances, but never have the honesty to record.

The world has not yet forgotten Frances Stuart. With her parrot, a companion for more than forty years, she stands among the wax effigies of kings and queens and great statesmen and national figures in the Chapel of the Pyx in Westminster Abbey. Also, she was the original Britannia on the halfpennies.

Another with apartments at Whitehall was Louise de Querouaille, the calculating Frenchwoman who received a life peerage, that of Duchess of Portsmouth, from the King; and was not above combining a little spying on behalf of Louis XIV with her other activities. Noticing a defect in her eyes Nell Gwyn triumphantly nicknamed her 'Squintabella'. Then there were Jane Middleton, Lady Falmouth, the Duchess of Mazarin, and of course Nell Gwyn. But the list could be extended much further, and still all the beautiful occupants of Whitehall would not be accounted for.

Every action, they say, must have an equal and opposite reaction: this was certainly true of the licence which followed on the heels of Praise-God Barebones, the saints and their days of public humiliation. The church preached a few tentative sermons, but there were no thundering admonitions from the site of Paul's Cross, flaying the vices of the Court. On Christmas Day 1662, the Bishop of Worcester offered a mild reproof in the Chapel Royal. Wrote Pepys: 'Methought he made but a poor sermon, but long, and reprehending the common jollity of the Court of the true joy that shall and ought to be on these days, he particularised concerning there excess in plays and gaming. Upon which it was worth observing how far they are come from taking the reprehensions of a bishop seriously, that they all laugh in the chapel when he reflected on their ill actions and courses.'

A few days later it was New Year's Eve, and to his infinite content Pepys and his wife were onlookers at the ball in the Palace. 'By and by, comes the King and Queen, the Duke and Duchess, and all the great ones and after seating themselves, the King takes out the Duchess of York; and the Duke, the Duchess of Buckingham; the Duke of Monmouth, my Lady Castlemaine; and so other lords and ladies: and they danced the Brantle. After that, the King led a lady a single Coranto; and then the rest of the lords, one after another, other ladies: very noble it was, and great pleasure to see. Then to country dances; the king leading the first, which he called for; which was, says he "Cuckolds all awry", the old dance of England (Charles was at least redeemed with a sense of humour). The manner was, when the King dances, all the ladies in the room, and the Queen herself, stand up; and indeed he dances rarely, and much better than the Duke of York. Having stayed here as long as I thought fit, to my infinite content, it being the greatest pleasure I could wish now to see at Court, I went home, leaving them dancing.'

In addition to the spectacle of the Court entertaining itself there were more formal occasions; such as the audience granted to the Russian Ambassador two days before the ball. Now it is Evelyn writing. 'Saw the audience of the Muscovy Ambassador which was with extraordinary state, his retinue being numerous, all clad in vests of several colours, with buskins after ye Eastern manner: their caps of fur: tunics richly embroidered with gold and pearls, made a glorious show. The King being seated under a Canopy in ye Banqueting House, the Secretary of ye Embassy went before ye Ambassador in a grave march, holding up his master's letters of credence in a crimson taffeta scarf before his forehead. The Ambassadors then deliver'd it with a profound reverence to ye King, who gave it to our Secretary of State: it was written in a long and lofty style. Then came in the presents, borne by a hundred and sixty-five of his retinue, consisting of mantles, and other large pieces lined with sable, black fox and ermine; Persian carpets, the ground cloth of gold and velvet; hawks, such as they said never came the like; horses said to be Persian; bows and arrows, and extraordinary etc: These borne by so long a train, rendered it very extraordinary. Wind music played all the while in ye gallery above. This finish'd, ye Ambassador was conveyed by ye Master of ye Ceremonies to York House.'

Although only a figure in the background, the Queen continued to live at Whitehall. Compared with the apartments occupied by Lady Castlemaine or the Duchess of Portsmouth, her own were sparsely furnished. The principal objects were religious pictures and devotional books, a vessel holding holy water at the head of her bed, and a clock incorporating a lamp so she could tell the time in the dark. Her apartments overlooked the river, and much of her time must have been passed gazing at the slow moving scene outside the windows, or amusing herself with her cage birds. They must have had much in common.

How different the Duchess of Portsmouth's apartments were, can be gathered from Evelyn. 'I went with the few who attended him (the King) into the Duchess of Portsmouth's dressing-room within her bed-chamber, where she was in her morning loose garment, her maids combing her hair, newly out of her bed, his Majesty and the gallants standing about her; but that which engaged my curiosity was the rich and splendid furniture of this woman's apartment, now twice or thrice pulled down to satisfy her prodigal and expensive pleasures, whilst her Majesty's does not exceed some gentlemen's ladies in furniture and accommodation.'

Evelyn goes on to describe the new tapestry on the walls, Japanese cabinets, screens, clocks, vases etc: 'besides some of her Majesty's best paintings.'

So much for Louise de Querouaille. Nothing, not even too little fire or too much water could keep the King from Lady Castlemaine. From time to time the Thames spilt over its banks and flooded the low-lying palace. This happened on 13th October 1663, and again on 6th December, when all the ground floor was flooded. 'My Lady Castlemaine, I hear, is in as great favour as ever, and the King supped with her . . . there being a chine of beef to roast . . . and the tide rising into their kitchen that it could not be roasted there, and the cook telling her of it, she answered: 'Zounds! she must set the house on fire but it should be roasted.' Pepys must have found Lord Sandwich's housekeeper a mine of information. In this case Sarah was speaking at first hand: the meat was brought to her husband to roast.

Those years neatly gathered under the heading of the Restoration had their serious side. The King's interest in science was more than passing. A laboratory was built beneath the Privy Gallery where he and his physician, Edmund Dickinson, spent hours carrying out experiments. He took a personal interest in plans drawn up by Wren, and not even Pepys could have regenerated the Navy to the point he did without some degree of royal authority. But it is the elegant Charles, lace at his wrists and throat, surrounded by his women and his dogs, passing through the galleries of Old Whitehall Palace or walking in the park that springs to mind.

There were many Sarahs in the Palace, who naturally retailed what they heard and saw to friends and acquaintances outside, and periodically Charles's popularity sank, as it did when the man in the street heard about his attempt to thrust Lady Castlemaine into the Queen's household. And then, by personal charm and perhaps some gesture that caught the public's fancy, the King would blow away all the resentment and disapproval building up against him. He possessed a gift so lamentably lacking in either of his Stuart predecessors: the common touch.

If one man can epitomize the Restoration, it is not Charles, but that sensational young man, John Wilmot, second Earl of Rochester. His father fought for Charles I, and accompanied the young prince into exile after the Battle of Worcester in 1651. His son, born in 1647, remained behind in England and in due course inherited the title. His career as a classical scholar at Oxford was brilliant. At fourteen he became an M.A., and at eighteen he appeared at Court; already a man of the world capable of holding his own with a tongue as wicked as it was witty.

His first action to set not only Whitehall, but all London buzzing, came in May 1664 when he kidnapped Elizabeth Malet. Perhaps it was her fortune he really loved, for he had none of his own. As she was returning from an evening spent with Frances Stuart at Whitehall her coach was stopped at Whitehall, and she was forced to get into another, which then drove off at top speed. In it was Rochester, protesting that love had driven him to such an extremity. But the plot failed when the coach was overtaken at Uxbridge, and Elizabeth Malet was returned to her distraught grandfather and the Earl spent three weeks in the Tower for 'high misdemeanours'.

Maybe Rochester was mortified at the failure of his scheme, for in July he enlisted in the Navy, and for two years vanished from the scene at Whitehall.

All through the oppressively hot summer of June 1665 the number of houses marked with the sinister red crosses grew alarmingly. On 29th June Pepys recorded: 'By water to White Hall, where the Court full of waggons and people ready to go out of town. This end of the town every day grows very bad of the plague. The Mortality Bill is come to 267, which is about ninety more than the last: and of these but four in the City.'

On 7th July Charles and his Court rode off to the safety of Isleworth, and from there to Hampton Court, Salisbury, and Oxford, where the round of balls and parties was taken up again as though there was no terrible reason behind the migration. But Old Whitehall Palace was not quite deserted: General Monck, now Duke of Albemarle, stayed on in his apartments by the Cockpit; while in the City the Lord Mayor remained amid the tolling of bells, the rumbling of burial carts and the crackling bonfires lit in the streets to ward off the Plague. They were two of the bravest men in London that summer. The opportunity to escape was open to both of them, but they chose to stay among those who were too poor or too dependent on their businesses to leave.

The following February, when the Plague was a thing of the past, the Court returned. Seven months later a new catastrophe threatened. Pepys was the first to bring the news of the Fire, hurrying from viewing the burning City from the White Tower and by Old London Bridge (p. 61). 'I to Whitehall . . . and there up to the King's closet in the Chapel, where people come about me, and I did give them an account dismayed them all, and was carried in to the King. So I was called for, and did tell the King and the Duke of York what I saw; and that, unless his majesty did command houses to be pulled down, nothing could stop the fire. They seemed much troubled, and the King commanded me to go to the Lord Mayor from him, and command him to spare no houses, but to pull down before the fire every way.'

The medieval City was dying, and dying quickly. Before long Charles and his brother James were in the City, personally directing the fire-fighting operations. But still the flames spread westwards, and by Wednesday, 5th September, it was a question of whether Whitehall Palace itself could be saved. On the King's orders Sir John Denham's house, newly built on the site of Scotland Yard, was unroofed to make a fire-break. In the palace itself people were hurrying to and fro, removing everything of value that could be packed on to a cart. Only a little while before no place had been considered safer than the Tower, and the goldsmiths used it as a temporary refuge for their wares, valued at £1,200,000, until it too was threatened by the all-engulfing flames. Then they removed their property westwards, to Whitehall, confident the fire would not spread so far to the west. But now it looked as though nothing could save the Palace. Then, suddenly, the easterly wind died away, and the fire was checked. Later the poet Crouch wrote some lines about the statue of Elizabeth I (then on Ludgate, and now outside St Dunstan in the West):

> 'Methinks the Queen on White-Hall cast her Eye:
> An arrow could not more directly fly.
> But when she saw her Palace safe, her fears
> Vanish, one eye drops smiles, the other tears.'

Among the rumours circulating while the fire raged was one that the French were responsible, and one who lived in the City, Belland, firework maker to the King, fled for safety to Whitehall. There he hid in Lady Killigrew's apartments, but two neighbours trailed his servants when they were taking food from his house in the City, saw where they went in, and followed. There was the makings of an ugly scene, for the trackers were confident they had discovered London's destroyer; but eventually matters were cleared up to everyone's satisfaction, and Belland was allowed to go free. Compared with a number of his fellow countrymen who were caught by the half-crazed mob and brutally beaten, he was more than lucky to escape unharmed.

The Great Fire was in September: in November another and more immediate scare came to Whitehall when the Horse Guards opposite the Banqueting House blazed up. Pepys was dining with friends at Whitehall when it started: 'and so we run up to the garret, and find it so; a horrid great fire; and by and by we saw and heard part of it being blown up with powder. The ladies begun presently to be afraid: one fell into fits. The whole town in alarum. Drums beat and trumpets, and the Horse Guards every where spread, running up and down in the street. By and by comes the news that the fire is slackened; so then we were a little cheered up again, and to supper and pretty merry. After supper, another dance or two, and then news that the fire is as great as ever, which puts us all to our wit's-end; and I mighty anxious to get home . . . [but] by people coming from the fire, understood that the fire was overcome and all well, we merrily parted, and home.'

But at Whitehall the alarms were soon forgotten, and on 29th October Pepys went to the theatre to see '"Love in a Tub";

a silly play.' However, he had the consolation of watching Lady Castlemaine. By now the plays were no longer given in the Cockpit Theatre, but in the Great Hall which had been fitted up with a permanent stage, boxes, and a gallery.

As might be expected, Charles and his Court did their best to rival the splendours and extravagances of Louis XIV. At least on one occasion they must have succeeded: when Louis discovered Whitehall was preening itself in the Persian style, he ordered his footmen to be similarly dressed. Sartorially speaking, his English rival had stolen a march, and all he could do was kill the fashion stone dead by making it ridiculous.

But for all the outward show, the Court of Charles II was in little better financial position than that of James I. In September 1667 the day came when the King had only three neckbands, and no handkerchiefs. Hardly surprising; he owed the linen draper £5,000.

By the second half of the seventeenth century the attitude towards dogs was very different from that laid down in the Ordinances of Henry VIII's Household. Then they were hardly to be seen, still less to be heard; but now all manner of dogs—above all the royal spaniels—were everywhere. In fact a wire screen had to be made to keep them off Charles's bed, but evidently they were compensated when 'Cushions for ye Doggs' were provided.

Among those who kept dogs in the Palace was Prince Rupert, cousin to Charles. During the Civil War the Parliamentarian victors shot his dog, Boy, regarding it as a familiar. Some of that bad luck with animals must have remained with him. At the beginning of October 1667 he was advertising in the *London Gazette* after losing two greyhounds. 'Lost in Dean's Yard, Westminster, on the 26th October last, a young white spaniel, about six months old, with a black head, red eyebrows, and a black spot upon his back. Lost, also about the same time, near Camberwell, a Yorkshire Buckhound, having black spots upon his back, red ears and a wall eye, and P.R. upon his shoulder; both belonging to his Highness Prince Rupert; if anyone can bring them to Prince Rupert's lodgings in the Stone Gallery at Whitehall he shall be well rewarded for his pains.'

The fact that John Wilmot, Earl of Rochester, had returned to Court in 1667, after covering himself with ignominy in the Navy, might be guessed from an unusually censorious entry by Pepys on 27th July. 'He (Mr Fenn) tells me that the King and Court were never in the world so bad as they are now for gaming, swearing, women, and drinking, and the most abominable vices that ever were in the world.'

Certainly war with Holland had given way to peace, but in the City the merchants felt it was made 'only to preserve the King for a time in his lusts and ease, and to sacrifice trade and his kingdoms only to his own pleasures'. There was little reason to respect the monarchy. Lady Castlemaine, about to bear the King yet another child, had quarrelled openly, and all London knew she had sworn that unless the child was owned to by Charles and baptised in the Chapel Royal, she would 'bring it into White Hall gallery, and dash the brains out before the King's face'. And as if that was not enough, Rochester had turned up again.

In a later age Rochester would have become a gossip columnist, kept within the bounds of reason and decency by the laws of libel. But in those days there were no laws of libel, so the young man stopped at nothing. From time to time, however, his pen and his conduct were too much even for the easy-going Charles, and he was banished from Court. In all probability these enforced rest periods in the country helped prolong his existence to thirty-three years, when life capitulated, to the relief of many.

Rochester boasted that for five consecutive years he was never sober, and there is little reason to doubt his word. For all his conquests he was almost effeminate in appearance, with sharp features and soft little hands. On one occasion this had its use—when he carried through his most notorious seduction in the disguise of a female pedlar.

His popularity, such as it was, rested on a dangerous foundation. While everyone wanted to hear about the latest Palace intrigues, they also feared the day when they themselves might be the target for his wit. Had he not chosen to be consistently obscene he might be remembered as a middling poet and playwright. As it is only a small part of his output is printable.

Without a King like Charles such a man as Rochester could not have flourished, and yet the venomous little rake never spared his master. He it was who pinned those famous lines on Charles's bedroom door at Whitehall:

'Here lies our Sovereign lord the King
Whose word no man relies on;
Who never said a Foolish Thing,
And never did a Wise One.'

Rochester must have been robbed of some of his malicious pleasure when Charles good-naturedly capped it: 'It is very true; my sayings are my own; my doings, my ministers'.'

Unable to hurt with wit, Rochester suddenly turned patriot, wishing to save England from such a King as Charles. Now he wrote:

'Then farewell all British sacred Majesty,
Let's pull all British Tyrants down;
Where men are born and still live free,
Here ev'ry Head doth wear a Crown.'

But politics were not really Rochester's métier: he was much more at home dressing up a paid informer as one of the palace sentries, and posting him outside doors where he smelt scandal. In that way the Earl came by much of the material for his verses, and no one could discover his source.

He left his mark on Whitehall Palace when he destroyed a valuable sundial set up in 1669 in the Privy Garden. It was the work of a Jesuit, Father Hall, and consisted of a top-heavy structure of wrought iron, glass bowls, globes, and portraits of the royal family, and survived until 25th June 1675.

'The glories of our blood and state', sang the actor Bowman; but such sentiments were too much for Rochester, in his anti-monarchy mood. More drunk than sober he lurched out into the garden, threw his arms around the sundial and toppled it over, declaring:

'Sceptre and crown
Must tumble down
And so must thou.'

Now it was the turn of the industrious Andrew Marvell to versify. Having recorded the death of Charles I, the accession of Richard Cromwell to the Protectorship; he now sharpened his quill and wrote:

'This place for a dial was too insecure,
Since a guard and a garden could not it defend,
For so near to the Court they will never endure
Any witness to show how their time they misspend.'

There was one occasion when a woman actually bested Rochester. As Lady Castlemaine was descending from her carriage at Whitehall one day he stepped forward and attempted to kiss her. A stunning backhand blow across the face sent him reeling, and as Pepys said of quite a different occasion 'he took a great and dirty fall' in the muddy roadway.

Few alterations were made to the Palace in Charles II's reign, and those carried out were of minor importance. In 1665 the Great Hall was converted into a theatre, and in 1668 the Whitehall Gate—adjoining the Banqueting House—was remodelled, making the approach from the street more handsome by means of a curving passage on either side of the arch. Eight years later the battlements above were removed, and a pyramid-shaped roof substituted. In 1669 a gallery of brick was built in place of the wooden structure dividing the Sermon Court from the Great Court. The Great Court was part of the public right of way leading to Whitehall Stairs. The Palace still remained what it had always been, a haphazard collection of small apartments, in all including some two thousand rooms. Along the river front the apartments were occupied by the royal family. From the south to north as follows: the Duke of York, the King, the Queen, Sir William Killigrew, the Privy Kitchen and the cooks' apartments. Since Lady Castlemaine's kitchen stood immediately behind the King's apartments her rooms must have been near by; while Lady Falmouth was lodged behind Sir William Killigrew's apartments. As a mark of especial favour

Charles granted her all the revenues from the dues paid by shipping and lighters moored in the Pool of London.

Among others who undoubtedly lived in this part of the Palace were the Earl of Rochester and Frances Stuart, now Duchess of Richmond. She was considered rather feather-brained, and yet was she so silly? She assured herself a very special place in Charles's affections by refusing to surrender at the first time of asking to the Stuart charms. This was something new to the King, and far from being offended, it increased his admiration for her. But in the end, vanity was her undoing. A calache, the very latest thing in carriages had just arrived from France, and Castlemaine, Portsmouth, Yarmouth, Falmouth, and the rest were clamouring for the honour of being the first to drive out in it. Charles struck a bargain with Frances Stuart, and it was she who had the honour. It was not without good reason that his disrespectful courtiers called him Old Roley: Roley was a singularly virile stallion in the Royal stables.

The best remembered of Charles's ladies is Nell Gwyn, but the sad fact remains that she left singularly little impression on Old Whitehall Palace. Even the site of her apartments is obscure, but evidently they were frequently used for parties. 'They met either in the lodgings of Louise, Duchess of Portsmouth, or in those of Chiffinch near the back-stairs, or in the apartments of Eleanor Gwynne.' Chiffinch was surely the most discreet gentleman's gentleman ever possessed by king or commoner. Not even the Earl of Rochester could make headway against such a servant.

That part of Whitehall Palace on the west side of the street also had its noble occupants. Until his death in 1670 General Monck, Duke of Albemarle, lived near the Holbein Gate. But the most important resident was James, Duke of Monmouth who lived in the converted tennis court; the most famous of the King's illegitimate children. The young man possessed much of his father's charm, but was feckless and in time of crisis not very brave. In the next reign, that of James II, Whitehall would be the scene of the last chapter but one in his short life.

It must be admitted that with the exception of the Holbein Gate and the adjoining Banqueting House, Whitehall, as the

17

principal residence of the King of England, was not very impressive to the casual observer. A man who came, saw and disapproved, was Cosmo III of Tuscany, one of Charles's Medici relatives.

'All the apartments,' he wrote, 'however, are small, and badly arranged, and without doors; so that every person, whose appearance does not bespeak him to be military, is permitted to go into the King's ante-chamber; on the floor of which stands a clock, which tells not only the hour, but the way of the wind. In the gallery formerly enriched by Cardinal Wolsey with choice paintings, which were taken away and sold by Cromwell, there are now fastened up some vile daubings of battles by sea and land, in the time of Henry VIII.'

Even the library did not escape criticism by that dyed-in-the-wool courtier, Evelyn. By a little judicious tipping, the 'ancient woman' who kept the keys allowed him to spend three or four whole days going through the collection. Afterwards he wrote: 'I went with expectation of finding some curiosities, but though there were a thousand volumes, there were few of importance I had not perused before.'

In short, if the King of France lived in a palace, the King of England lived in an outsize stately home.

With the Restoration came a revival of the masques, but with one exception they did not rival those of James I's time. That exception was *Calistro*, based on the third book of Ovid's *Metamorphoses*. Taking part were two future queens; Mary and Anne, the daughters of James, Duke of York. That was in December 1674. Three years later Mary was married to William of Orange. They were cousins; both directly descended from James I. In 1683 it was the turn of Anne to walk to the altar of the Chapel Royal as bride. For husband she had the unmemorable George of Denmark. Indeed, were it not for her numerous pregnancies, his very existence might have been doubted. In his own words Charles tried him drunk and tried him sober, but could make nothing of him; while Evelyn was moved to write: 'He had the Danish countenance, blond, of few words, spake French but ill, seeme'd somewhat heavy, but reputed to be brave.'

It was Jeremiah Clarke who provided him with his only memorial; 'The Prince of Denmark's March', included in a set of pieces for harpsichord. But even that cannot really keep his memory alive. The march, in an orchestral version, usually goes by the title of 'The Trumpet Voluntary', attributed to Purcell!

Among the distinguished musicians who preceded Henry Purcell as organist at the Chapel Royal were Thomas Tallis, Byrd, John Bull—all in Elizabeth I's reign—Orlando Gibbons (James I), and John Blow (Charles II).

Pepys may have been delighted by the King's twenty-four violins during the coronation service, but by and large their introduction into the Chapel Royal was less successful. 'Instead of ye ancient grave and solemn wind music, accompanying ye organ, was introduc'd a concert of twenty four violins between every pause after ye French fantastical light way, better suiting a tavern or playhouse than a Church.'

As a Roman Catholic, Catharine of Braganza worshipped in her own chapel, which was served by both English and Portuguese priests, and one of Charles II's few creditable actions towards his wife came during the monstrous Popish Plot. While Catholics were being ruined and even executed on the word of Titus Oates—now ensconced in apartments in the Palace—the King stoutly defended her from the hysteria sweeping the country. Ironically enough, the plot was supposed to revolve round his assassination and the setting up of his Catholic brother James as King. In secret Charles was as much a Catholic as his wife or brother.

Such were the rumours and scares that a trustworthy man was posted 'to watch and attend every night under the King's seat in the Hall at the time His Majesty shall be at ye play theatre in Whitehall'.

Although Charing Cross is well beyond the bounds of Whitehall, its historical connections were close to the Palace. The original cross was the last of those set up to mark where Queen Eleanor's funeral cortège stopped on its journey from Nottinghamshire to Westminster Abbey in 1290. That lasted until 1647, when it was destroyed by order of Parliament. Then the site remained empty until le Sueur's beautiful statue of Charles I was set up on a pedestal designed by Wren. The cross that exists today was only erected in 1863, in the forecourt of Charing Cross Station, and so has only its name to connect it with the famous site, several hundred yards away in what is now Trafalgar Square.

Le Sueur's statue had a chequered history: it was cast in 1633, but left lying on a piece of land near St Paul's, Covent Garden, and hidden in that church's crypt in 1642. Thirteen years later Parliament ordered its destruction. 'For the rate of old brass, by the pound rate' was how the order ran. Instead of breaking it up as ordered, the brazier hid it away, and produced a large number of knife handles, candlesticks, thimbles, and nutcrackers; all apparently made from the statue. The deception worked, and only after the Restoration did the statue reappear. In 1675 it was bought from the brazier's widow, and set up on the present site.

Death, when it came to Charles, was unexpected. 'I can never forget', wrote Evelyn, 'the inexpressable luxury and profaneness, gaming and all dissoluteness, and as it were total forgetfulness of God (it being Sunday evening), which this sennight I was witness of the King sitting and toying with his concubines, Portsmouth, Cleveland (Lady Castlemaine was now Duchess of Cleveland), and Mazarine etc: and a French boy singing love songs in that glorious gallery, whilst about twenty of the great Courtiers and other dissolute persons were at Basset, round a large table, a bank of at least £2,000 in gold before them.'

Whether he could have pulled round if left alone is unlikely; but the emetics, purges, Jesuits' Powders and repeated bleedings prescribed by his numerous physicians were enough to bring a fit man to the grave. With a flash of the old charm he apologized to those about him for being a most unconscionable time dying: surely it was they who should have apologized for tormenting him so. Charles died on 6th February 1685, aged fifty-four, and if the story is true his thoughts at the end were with the most humble and likeable of his mistresses. 'Do not let poor Nelly starve,' he said, and was gone.

In his time Charles II had fooled the nation to the top of its bent, but when the news of his death spread beyond the Palace, men wept openly. Perhaps some of their tears were for the future. Despite all attempts to exclude his brother from the succession, for three years James was to be King at Whitehall.

But for the present the Palace was plunged into mourning. 'There come over,' wrote Evelyn, 'divers envoys and great persons to condole the death of the late King, who were receiv'd by the Queen Dowager on a bed of mourning, the whole chamber, ceiling and floor hung with black, and tapers were lighted, so as nothing could be more lugubrious and solemn. The Queen Consort sat under a state of a black footcloth to entertain the Circle (as the Queen us'd to) and that very decently.'

Immediately after his brother's death James was announced at the Palace gate as the new sovereign: 'in the form of his grandfather, King James I, was after ye death of Queen Elizabeth'. But for Whitehall the great days were departing, slowly but surely. James II indulged in a considerable amount of rebuilding, but he preferred to spend most of his time at St James's Palace; while his successor, William of Orange, chose the drier atmosphere of Kensington Palace. He suffered acutely from asthma.

11

At the time of his coronation James II made two innovations. He chose to stay at St James's Palace, instead of passing a day or two at the Tower, and so in consequence there was no great procession through the City. On the actual day he crossed St James's Park and entered his barge at Whitehall Stairs, which took him and his second wife, Mary of Modena, to Westminster and the Abbey.

That evening, when London was bright with bonfires and loud with the ringing of bells, the couple returned to Whitehall. There they went out on to the flat roof of the Queen's Apartments and watched a firework display on the river.

Whatever James might do to upset the political and religious life of the country he continued with such customs as the Royal

Maundy. It appears that the Chapel Royal was used, at least on the first occasion. 'On Maundy Thursday, April 16th 1685, our gracious King James ye 2nd wash'd, wip'd, and kiss'd the feet of fifty-two poor men with wonderful humility. And all the service of the Church of England usual on that occasion was perform'd, his majesty being present all the time.'

But soon more urgent affairs occupied the King's time. In June his nephew, James, Duke of Monmouth, sailed from Holland, bent on saving England from Catholicism, and acquiring a crown for himself. He landed at Brixham, was acclaimed as King Monmouth, to distinguish him from the real King James, and soon the west was in the hollow of his hand. But all that was changed by the Battle of Sedgemoor: the morning after he was found cowering in a ditch; and the wild adventure was over.

Years before Henry VIII's enclosed tennis court had been converted into apartments for him, when he lived at Whitehall like a prince; but now Monmouth was an unkempt prisoner brought before James in one of the great galleries. When all went well he had the appearance of being brave; now he was devoid of either courage or dignity. The stakes he played for were high, and he had lost. On his knees Charles II's favourite son grovelled for his life, his arms pinioned behind him with a silken cord, swearing he would turn Catholic if only James would spare his life. But the King refused to listen, and two days later, 15th July, Monmouth was beheaded on Tower Hill.

Although the reign lasted only three and a half years, in that time James achieved more in the way of alterations than his brother had done in twenty-five. The Privy Gallery—brought from Wolsey's house at Esher and re-erected at Whitehall on Henry VIII's orders—was demolished and replaced by a three-storey building of brick, designed by Wren. As an addition to the palace it must have been worthy of the Banqueting House which it adjoined. Inside was a Council Chamber, Treasury Office, and the Queen's Apartments: the latter with a chimney piece carved by Grinling Gibbons and a ceiling painted by Verrio.

Another of James's additions, viewed with misgivings by his subjects, was a Roman Catholic chapel built in the north-west corner of the Privy Garden, overlooking the street. Here again Grinling Gibbons was called in, and also Verrio, while the organ was the work of Renatus Harris. Harris was a Catholic, which was probably the reason for choosing him in preference to his professional rival 'Father' Smith. However, Smith's work was later represented at Whitehall. In 1699 he provided an organ for the Banqueting House, which by that date had become the Chapel Royal, and in 1890 it was moved to St Peter ad Vincula in the Tower. Unfortunately it was much altered in Victorian times; but then it is the rarest thing today to find an organ as it was left by either Harris or Smith. One by the latter does survive intact in the Chapel at Staunton Harold in Leicestershire, and fortunately for posterity, in 1691 Queen Mary gave the Renatus Harris organ to St James's Piccadilly; so it escaped destruction when Whitehall Palace was burnt seven years later.

'I went to hear the music of the Italians in the New Chapel,' wrote Evelyn in December 1686, 'now first open'd at Whitehall for the Popish service. Nothing can be finer than the magnificent marble work and architecture at the end where are four statues representing St John, St Peter, St Paul, and the Church, in white marble, the work of Mr Gibbons, with all the carving and pillars of exquisite art, and great cost.'

In the 1690s, when the Protestant William and Mary were on the throne, the contents of the chapel were dispersed. Eventually the Grinling Gibbons altarpiece found its way to Burnham parish church, the pulpit to a church somewhere in the south of England, while the fate of the organ has already been mentioned. The frescoes were left in place, but compared with those painted in the Palace itself by Holbein, their destruction by fire was not a major loss.

A much larger commission carried out by Grinling Gibbons was the statue of the King set up at the beginning of 1687. Originally it stood on a tall pedestal in what used to be the Sermon Court behind the Banqueting House. James II is clad in a toga and holds a baton in his right hand. In the course of time the story grew up that he was pointing to the spot where

Charles I was executed. This was nonsense: the scaffold stood against the other side of the Banqueting House in the open street. The gesture looked regal, but apart from that it was empty and quite devoid of significance.

Charles I, Charles II, and James II all enriched London with statues of themselves that are beautiful and first-rate works of art: a quality notable by its absence among nearly all the others. James II spent much of his in exile, moving from place to place, and it seems his statue would emulate him. In 1897 it was moved into the adjoining garden of Gwydyr House; in 1903 it was set up in St James's Park, and from there taken to Trafalgar Square in 1948.

Whilst James II did not choose to emulate his brother's numerous attachments, his wife Mary of Modena did not claim his undivided attention. Himself not handsome he chose a plain woman for his first wife, Anne Hyde, and another, Catharine Sedley, for his mistress. Of the former Charles remarked with more wit than charity that he thought his brother James must have been ordered to marry her as a penance imposed by his Jesuit confessor; while Catharine Sedley remarked philosophically of herself: 'It cannot be my beauty, for he must see that I have none; and it cannot be my wit; for he has not enough to know that I have any.'

As a penance for this *ménage à trois* James scourged himself, but since flagellation is sometimes referred to on the Continent as the English vice, it probably served to increase instead of diminish his attraction.

By now changes had taken place in that part of Whitehall Palace west of the road from Westminster to the City. The Cockpit had been demolished in 1675; and in 1684 Princess Anne and her Danish husband were living in lodgings built on the site, while the adjoining house erected for the Duke of Buckingham in 1673 had to be reconstructed within four years owing to faulty foundations.

But not long remained for James II to enjoy either Whitehall or St James's Palace. As early as 1686 he was watching to see which way the wind was blowing. Nor was that merely a figure of speech. William of Orange was ready to set sail from Holland at a moment's notice to supplant his uncle on the throne: so James ordered a weathercock to be set up on top of the little annex at the north end of the Banqueting House. It was visible from his private apartments, and presumably when the wind was in the east he knew the danger from a Dutch fleet setting sail was at its greatest.

The weathercock is there to this day.

Two years later came the 'Glorious Revolution': the Protestant Wind, as it was called, blew, and on 8th November 1688 William of Orange set foot in England. James stayed where he was in London, but on the 26th of that month, Princess Anne slipped out of her apartments and went to join her husband, already on the side of the rebels. 'The Princess went to bed at the usual time to prevent suspicion,' wrote her friend Mrs Sarah Churchill: 'I came to her soon after; and by the back stairs which went down from her closet, her Royal Highness, my Lady Fitzharding, and I, with one servant, walked to the coach, where we found the Bishop and the Earl of Dorset.'

Earlier that year the Bishop of London was one of the famous seven ordered to the Tower by James: now Fortune's Wheel was turning fast. But the King did not wait for it to come to that extremity. Preparations for the flight were made, and when all was ready in the small hours of 7th December James wakened his wife, and two of the nurses who had charge of their infant son—one day to be the Old Pretender. The three women went down the back-stairs of the royal apartments to where a boat was waiting to carry them across the river to Lambeth. There they were to pick up a coach to take them to Gravesend. Macaulay described what happened when they reached the opposite bank.

'She (the Queen) remained with her child cowering for shelter from the storm under the tower of Lambeth Church, and distracted with terror whenever the ostler approached with his lantern. Two of her women attended her, one who gave suck to the Prince, and one whose office was to rock his cradle; but they could be of little use to their mistress, for both were foreigners, who could hardly speak the English language and who shuddered at the rigour of the English climate. The only consolatory circumstance was that the little boy was well and uttered not a single cry.'

Then Father Orleans, one of the Queen's household, takes up the story. 'The Queen, waiting in the rain under the church wall for a coach, the curiosity of a man who happened to come out of a neighbouring inn with a light gave considerable cause for alarm. He was making towards the spot where she was standing, when Rida, one of her attendants, suddenly rushed forward and jostled him, so that they both fell in the mire. It was a happy diversion, as, the stranger believing it to be the result of accident, they both apologised, and so the matter ended.'

After what seemed an age the coach arrived. The fugitives drove to Gravesend, boarded the ship, and by next afternoon were in Calais.

A few days passed, and then in the night of 11th December James made the same ignominious escape by the back-stairs, and set off down the river. However, at Sheppey he was stopped by plunder-hungry fishermen, who at first did not realize he was the King, and brought him back to London. But for the authorities the most convenient thing would be to let him escape across the Channel, and in the words of Macaulay: 'On the morning of the eighteenth of December, a rainy and stormy morning, the royal barge was early at Whitehall Stairs: and round it were eight or ten boats filled with Dutch soldiers. Several noblemen and gentlemen attended the King to the water-side. It is said, and may well be believed, that many tears were shed. For even the most zealous friend of liberty could scarcely have been unmoved, at the sad and ignominious close of a dynasty which might have been so great.'

12

After a lapse of eleven years Princess Mary was once again in Whitehall Palace, as the wife of the man who had ousted her father from the throne. For her it was something of a home-coming and a happy occasion, as her behaviour showed in the slightly disapproving writings of Mrs Churchill. 'She ran about it, looking into every closet and convenience, and turning up the quilts of the bed, as people do when they come to an inn, and with no sort of concern in her appearance and behaviour, which, though at the time I was extremely caressed by her, I thought very strange and unbecoming; for whatever necessity there was of disposing King James he was still her father, and had so lately been driven from that chamber and that bed; and if she felt no tenderness, I thought she should still have looked grave, or even pensively sad, at so melancholy a reverse of his fortune.'

That was on 13th February 1689: the next day Mary pulled herself together, and sat by the side of William beneath a Canopy of Estate in the Banqueting House, where they were jointly offered the crown: the only husband and wife in English history to have equal status as ruling sovereigns.

'Near the northern door, on the right hand, a large number of Peers had assembled. On the left were the Commons with their Speaker, attended by the mace. The southern door opened: and the Prince and Princess of Orange, side by side, entered, and took their place under the canopy of state.' The Clerk of the House of Lords read the Declaration of Right, by which the new sovereigns were to rule, and William and Mary were invited to accept the crown. 'William in his own name and in that of his wife, answered that the crown was in their estimation the more valuable because it was presented to them as a token of the confidence of the nation. "We thankfully accept," he said, "what you have offered us." The Lords and the Commons then reverendly returned from the Banqueting House and went in procession to the Great Gate of Whitehall, where the Heralds and pursuivants were waiting in their gorgeous tabards. All the space as far as Charing Cross was one sea of heads. The kettle drums struck up: the trumpets pealed, and Garter King at Arms, in a loud voice, proclaimed the prince and princess of Orange King and Queen of England.'

From time to time throughout its existence as a palace, Whitehall was plagued by fire, and on 9th April 1691 the cry went up yet again. At the time William and his heart were in the same place, the Hague, and so the Palace was empty except for a few servants. A maid threw away a candle whilst it was still alight, and at eight in the morning fire broke out in the Duchess of Portsmouth's old apartments. Soon it spread to the Stone Gallery, and that spelt the end for Holbein's frescoes painted on the ceiling of the upper room, the Matted Gallery as it was by then called.

After eight hours the flames were brought under control, gunpowder being used to make fire-breaks; but by then the maze of old buildings fronting on to the river had gone for ever.

Rebuilding started at once, and two years later, a terrace, built out over the river, was complete. Wren was the architect, and at each end were flights of steps down into the water. Two hundred and eighty feet long by seventy feet wide, it was divided into four lawns, with access from the Queen's apartments behind. It alone cost £10,000, but two years later Mary lay dead from small-pox in Kensington Palace. After that the asthmatic King was seldom seen at Whitehall, and no more building was carried out.

Perhaps it was appropriate that a funeral should be the last event of importance connected with Whitehall Palace. All the pageantry of another age came to the fore: to mourn for Mary there were three hundred poor women in mourning gowns and hoods—they went four and four; followed by side-drummers, ushers, members of the Palace staff, children of the Chapel Royal, more drummers, chaplains, trumpeters, aldermen, Sir Christopher Wren (as Surveyor-General of the Works), the Lord Mayor, more trumpeters, the banners of Chester, Wales, Cornwall, Ireland, and Scotland. More trumpeters and drummers, and then the banners of France and England. The Mourning Horse, covered with purple velvet, came next; then the Helmet, the Crest, the Target, the Sword, and Coat of Arms: all the appurtenances of a medieval funeral. The coffin itself was borne on a chariot pulled by eight horses, and behind it came the mourners, led by the Duchess of Somerset, maids of honour, women of the bed-chamber and Yeomen of the Guard.

The great cavalcade moved out of Whitehall, under the King Street Gate and on to Westminster Abbey on a day in March 1695—three years later the Palace itself existed no longer.

Sooner or later the inevitable would have happened in a building containing so many apartments, so many kitchens, and so many open fires. When the end came, on 4th January 1698, the destruction was quick and complete.

A Dutch laundress employed by one Colonel Stanley made a fire of charcoal in an upstairs room, hung linen in front to dry, and went out. Soon people living near by noticed the smoke and flames, but by then the blaze had taken too strong a hold for the inadequate fire fighting apparatus to be of any real use. By midnight all was on fire from the river to the street, with the exception of the Banqueting House. Later, when it was over, William—living in Kensington Palace at the time—declared the accident 'affected him less than it might another, because Whitehall was a palace in which he could not live'. But even so, when the fire was at its height he ordered special efforts to be made to save the Banqueting House. That at least was achieved.

Twelve people, all humble, lost their lives: the Dutch maid who began the fire, two soldiers, a painter, and a waterman among them. The loss of the old buildings was bad enough from an historical point of view, but the destruction of so many of the treasures it contained was a much greater disaster.

Gone were the two chapels; one built by Wolsey at the height of his glory, and the other by James II; the Great Hall, scene of so many banquets, masques, and plays; the Council Chamber; the Queen's lodgings and about a hundred and fifty apartments belonging to various members of the Court.

William came to see for himself how bad was the damage, and talked to Wren of rebuilding; but nothing came of it. Old Whitehall Palace was gone, and with it the direct contact with the memories, and perhaps the ghosts, of Wolsey, Henry VIII, and his queens, Elizabeth I, James I, Charles I, Cromwell, Charles II, James II and all their relations, friends, flatterers, and enemies. Now all were routed, as though they had never been there; ruling, intriguing, loving, marrying, and dying.

Although Old Whitehall Palace ceased to exist that lurid January night, the story was not quite finished. The gardens, and where the fire had raged, were leased out as building plots, and during the eighteenth century many town houses were erected for a number of peers. Among them Montagu House (1733), Pelham House (1755), Pembroke House (1757), Carrington House (1764), and—still standing, Gwydyr House (1772).

As the decades passed, Scotland Yard, which escaped the flames, was completely built over with houses and offices. In 1829 the newly formed Metropolitan Police headquarters were set up there, but by 1891 they had quite outgrown the original premises, and a move was necessary. By then the Embankment had been built, setting the river some three hundred feet further back from its original line against the Palace walls, and New Scotland Yard was built at the southern end of the new roadway, adjoining Westminster Bridge. Originally it had been intended to build an opera house on the site, but since the scheme fell through for lack of funds, Dartmoor convicts set about quarrying granite for the future Police headquarters. A fact that is not without its humour.

The Treasury Office, originally situated in the building put up in James II's reign, was moved to the Cockpit site after the fire, and its successor, adjoining Downing Street, is still there. In the eighteenth century No. 10 Downing Street and its neighbours were Crown property, and George II arranged with Walpole that it should go with the offices of the First Lord of the Treasury, and since that post was also held by the Prime Minister, it became his official residence.

When the present Treasury Offices were built in 1846, Henry VIII's old tennis court, which had been converted into offices, was demolished. In February 1961, during extensive restorations and alterations, portions of the old Tudor structure were rediscovered.

The Horse Guards, nearly opposite the Banqueting House, stood until 1750, when it was replaced by the present handsome building. Whitehall Gate remained until 1765 when another was set up in its place. That in its turn was demolished in 1813, and now only the entrance of Horseguards Avenue marks the site. That leaves the two gateways across the street and the Banqueting House to be accounted for. In 1723 the King Street Gate was demolished, and in 1759 a similar fate befell the

Holbein Gate. Originally there was talk of setting it up again in Windsor Park; but nothing came of the idea, and only the busts of Roman emperors were saved. Two found their way to Hampton Court, where they were placed in niches on the gateways, while two more went to Hanworth House.

Two parallel streets were thrown together in 1900 to make the Parliament Square end of Whitehall, and today Parliament Street is a broad curving street running up to Trafalgar Square, with only the Banqueting House, isolated and almost overshadowed by Government offices, as a memorial to a great palace.

The old Chapel Royal was destroyed in the fire of 1698, but before the year was out Wren had fitted up the Banqueting House as a place of worship, and so it remained until 1890. In the reigns of the first three Georges it was frequently used for the distribution of the Royal Maundy. From 1809 to 1829 the Army used it as a Military Chapel, and twelve eagles and standards, captured from the French during the Peninsular Campaign, were kept there. These trophies were removed to Wellington Barracks when it reverted to its former use as a Chapel Royal.

Curiously enough, the Chapel was never consecrated, and in October 1890 Queen Victoria agreed that as such it should be closed, and become the United Services Museum. The organ went to St Peter ad Vincula in the Tower, and the fittings were removed. By a wise stipulation no alterations could be made to the building itself. In addition to housing relics of bygone battles, models of some of the more famous battle-fields and the personal possessions of great soldiers, it contains a number of mementoes of Charles I. Looking down on the scene is the Rubens ceiling: cleaned in 1686, 1729 (by Cipriani), 1830 (by Soane), and again in 1906. During the Second World War the nine panels were removed to a place of safety, and only replaced in 1951.

Two years before their return an outstanding piece of engineering work—though all but unseen—began when Wolsey's wine cellar was moved, *in toto*, to make way for the foundations of the huge new Government departments about to be built on the site once covered by the oldest part of the Palace. Rollers were placed beneath the brick-built cellar, it weighed eight hundred tons, which was moved sideways for forty-three feet, then lowered eighteen feet nine inches, and still on its rollers, moved back until almost directly below its original position.

Pevensey Bay
April 1960

Principal Dates

OLD LONDON BRIDGE

A.D. 100–400 London Bridge (of wood) first built during Roman occupation.

1014 Broken down by Kings Olaf and Ethelred during campaign against the Danes.

1091 Bridge swept away in a gale.

1136 Bridge burnt, and replaced by a structure of elm.

1176 Stone bridge begun by Peter of Colechurch.

1209 Bridge completed.

1212 or 1213 Many houses burnt. Casualties.

1263 Queen Eleanor's barge pelted by dissatisfied Londoners on the bridge.

1357 King John II of France, a prisoner of war, received at the bridge on his way to the Tower.

1381 Peasants' Revolt.

1384–96 Chapel rebuilt.

1390 Joust held on the bridge.

1415 Henry V's welcome after Agincourt.

1422 Henry V's funeral procession.

1426 Drawbridge Gateway (New Stone Gate) built.

1437 Great Stone Gate collapses.

1445 Reception of Margaret of Anjou.

1450 Cade's Rebellion. Bitter fighting on the bridge.

1471 Attack by Warwick the Kingmaker and Falconbridge.

1501 Reception of Katharine of Aragon.

1535 Heads of Sir Thomas More and Bishop Fisher displayed over the Great Stone Gate.

1553 Chapel converted into a shop and a house.

1554 Wyatt's Rebellion.

1559 Mill-wheels set up beneath two arches at south end.

1577 Nonsuch House replaces the New Stone Gateway.

1580 Water-wheels to pump water into the City set up under arches at the north end.

1633 Fire. Half the houses destroyed.
1641 Mrs Kirke, a Lady of the Bedchamber, drowned.
1647 Fairfax's army crosses during Civil War.
1660 Reception of Charles II.
1666 Great Fire. Houses at north end burnt.
1671 Houses rebuilt along the whole length.
1684 Frost Fair.
1715–16 Frost Fair.
1725 Fire in Southwark. Great Stone Gate burnt and rebuilt.
1740 Frost Fair.
1745 Houses at north end rebuilt by George Dance the Elder.
1749 Westminster Bridge built.
1760 Temporary wooden bridge built alongside Old London Bridge burnt.
1760–2 Houses demolished and bridge widened.
1821 Committee chooses design for new bridge by John Rennie Senior.
1825 New bridge begun upstream of Old London Bridge.
1831–2 New bridge completed.
1831–2 Old London Bridge demolished.
1920 Arch on north bank of old bridge rediscovered on a building site, and demolished.

OLD ST PAUL'S

A.D. 604 St Mellitus ordained first Bishop of London. Cathedral begun.
675 St Erkenwald Bishop of London.
690 King Sebba buried in St Paul's.
961 Cathedral burnt, and rebuilt.
1017 Ethelred the Unready buried.
1087 Saxon cathedral destroyed by fire. The medieval Old St Paul's begun.
1135 The unfinished cathedral damaged by fire.
1148 Choir completed.
1167 Excommunication in the cathedral of Bishop Foliot.
1191 Prince John summons a Council in the cathedral to charge the Bishop of Ely with acts of tyranny.

c. 1200 Early English clerestory and vaulting added to nave and transepts.

1216 Archbishop Langton meets the barons and clergy in the cathedral prior to Magna Carta.
The French Dauphin offered the throne, attends Mass.

1221 Tower and spire completed.

1250 Archbishop Boniface refused admittance by the Dean. The Dean excommunicated.

1256 'New Work' begun.

1275 The offering of a buck and a doe instituted.

1285 Churchyard enclosed.

1315 Upper part of the spire rebuilt.

1327 'New Work' completed.

1332 Cloister and chapter house begun.

1341 Spire struck by lightning.

1360 King John II of France visits the cathedral. Sir John Beauchamp's tomb in nave (later known as Duke Humphrey's).

1374 John of Gaunt commissions tomb.

1387 Sir Simon Burley's tomb.

1399 John of Gaunt buried. Henry Bolingbroke prays for the deposition of Richard II. Richard II lies in state.

1425 Henry VI, aged five, visits the cathedral.

1444 Spire struck by lightning.

1448 Paul's Cross rebuilt.

1471 The murdered Henry VI brought to Old St Paul's.

1483 Sermon preached at Paul's Cross in favour of Richard III.

1501 Marriage of Prince Arthur and Katharine of Aragon.

1509 Dean Colet founds St Paul's School.

1527 Recanted Lutherans see heretical books burnt in the cathedral.

1547 The rood and figures removed.

1548–9 The Commissioners visit the cathedral. Cloisters and chapels on the north side demolished.

1552 Book of Common Prayer first used at Old St Paul's.

1553 Roman Catholic form of worship restored under Mary Tudor.

1554 Philip of Spain visits the cathedral.

1561 Spire struck by lightning, destroyed, and the whole cathedral seriously damaged by fire.
1570 Papal Bull nailed to the door of the Bishop's Palace.
1572 Earl of Pembroke's tomb erected.
1579 Sir Nicholas Bacon buried.
1586 Sir Philip Sidney buried.
1588 Thanksgiving service for the defeat of the Armada.
1592 Sir Christopher Hatton buried.
1600 Tower climbed by the horse Marocco.
1625 John Donne Dean.
1628 William Laud Bishop.
1632 Inigo Jones begins restoration work and additions.
1641 Van Dyck buried. William Dugdale and William Sedgwick visit Old St Paul's to draw and record accounts of the building and its monuments.
1642 Restoration work stopped by the Civil War. Paul's Cross demolished.
1647 Bishop's Palace demolished.
1649 Nave of Old St Paul's converted into a cavalry barracks, and the choir arm into a 'preaching house'.
1663 Commission to advise on restoration. Minor repairs carried out 1663–6.
1666 May. Wren's unfavourable report. August. Commission visits cathedral. September. Old St Paul's ruined in the Great Fire.

OLD WHITEHALL PALACE

1223 Hubert de Burgh buys land for a house between the Thames and the road from Westminster to the City.
1243 Property bought by Walter de Grey.
1245 Transferred to the See of York for use by the Archbishop. Now called York Place.
c. 1480 Enlarged by Archbishop Rotherham.
1515–29 Occupied by Wolsey. Galleries, chapel, hall, built.
1529 Wolsey's fall. Now called Whitehall Palace. Occupied by Henry VIII.

1532 Gateways built. Land purchased on opposite side of the road. Cockpit, tennis courts and tilt-yard added. Privy Gallery (from Wolsey's house at Esher) set up at Whitehall.

1533 25th January. Henry VIII and Anne Boleyn married. 21st May. Anne Boleyn's Coronation.

1547 28th January. Death of Henry VIII. Edward VI at Whitehall.

1554 Attempted siege of the Palace during Wyatt's Rebellion. 18th March. Princess Elizabeth sent from Whitehall to the Tower.

1558 Elizabeth I's accession.

1559 25th January. Elizabeth receives the Commons at Whitehall.

1572 Wooden Banqueting House erected.

1579 *History of the Knight in the Burning Rock* given in the Great Hall.

1598 Palace visited by Paul Hentzner.

1603 28th April. Elizabeth I's funeral.

1605–12 Masques for James I by Inigo Jones and Ben Jonson.

1605 Marriage of Earl of Essex and Frances Howard.

1606–7 Banqueting House rebuilt in brick and stone.

1613 Frances Howard's divorce. Sir Thomas Overbury's murder. Princess Elizabeth and Fredrick, Count Palatine of the Rhine, married.

1619 Banqueting House burnt.

1622 Banqueting House designed by Inigo Jones completed.

1625 Charles I, King.

1635 Ceiling by Rubens completed in the Banqueting House.

1637 Masque House built.

1641 Civil War.

1642 4th January. Charles and the Five Members. 10th January. Court leaves Whitehall Palace.

1649 30th January. Execution of Charles I outside the Banqueting House.
Guard House built opposite the Banqueting House.

1654 13th April. Cromwell and his family move into the royal apartments.

1657 Attempt to assassinate Cromwell.
1658 3rd September. Cromwell dies in the Palace.
1660 The Restoration.
1662 23rd August. Catharine of Braganza arrives at Whitehall.
1665 Great Hall converted into a theatre.
The Plague.
1666 The Great Fire.
1675 The Cockpit demolished.
1677 Princess Mary and William of Orange married.
1683 Princess Anne and George, Prince of Denmark married.
1685 6th February. Charles II dies in the Palace.
13th July. The Duke of Monmouth brought before James II after the failure of his rebellion.
Additions and alterations to the Palace.
Roman Catholic chapel built.
1686 Weathercock erected on the Banqueting House to watch for the 'Protestant Wind'.
1687 Statue of James II set up.
1688 The royal family flee from the Palace.
1689 14th February. William and Mary offered the Crown in the Banqueting House.
1691 9th April. Fire. Stone Gallery among the buildings destroyed.
1693 Rebuilding carried out, and a terrace added.
1695 Queen Mary's funeral.
1698 4th January. Palace destroyed with the exception of the Holbein and King Street Gates and the Banqueting House. Twelve killed. The site leased out as building plots. The Banqueting House converted in the Chapel Royal.
1723 King Street Gate demolished.
1750 The present Horse Guards built.
1759 Holbein Gate demolished.
1829 Metropolitan Police headquarters set up on the site of Scotland Yard.
1846 Treasury Offices built.
1864 Victoria Embankment built.

1868 Home Office built.

1890 Banqueting House becomes the United Services Museum.

1891 Metropolitan Police headquarters moved to New Scotland Yard.

1899 War Office built.

1900 Parliament Street assumes its present form.

Dimensions of Old St Paul's

LENGTH	585 feet.	The overall length including the portico added *c.* 1632 was about 635 feet. St Peter's, Rome, 710 feet. Cluny Abbey, France (demolished early nineteenth century), about 650 feet. Glastonbury Abbey (demolished sixteenth–seventeenth century) 592 feet.
WIDTH	100 feet.	About 10 feet wider than the average in England for a major cathedral.
Internal height		
NAVE	85 feet.	Average for the vaulting of an English cathedral. Winchester 77 feet 6 inches.
CHOIR	93 feet.	
LENGTH ACROSS TRANSEPTS	290 feet.	Old St Paul's was remarkably wide; more than the overall length of Ripon or Southwark.
TOWER AND SPIRE	245 feet. 450 feet.	At Canterbury the Bell Harry Tower is 235 feet high. Until its destruction in Edward VI's reign, the spire of Old St Paul's was surpassed in England only by Lincoln, 524 feet; Salisbury, 404 feet; Ulm, Germany (nineteenth century), 529 feet.
AREA	81,300 square feet	St Peter's, Rome 163,000 square feet. Milan 125,900 square feet. Seville 124,000 square feet. The present St Paul's covers an area of 84,000 square feet.

Bibliography

Annals of St Paul's	Milman
The Three Cathedrals of St Paul's	Longman
History of St Paul's (1658 and 1817)	Dugdale
Old St Paul's Cathedral	Cook
A History of St Paul's Cathedral	Matthews & Atkins
History of England	Trevelyan
History of the Coronation	Tanner
Cathedrals of Great Britain	Ditchfield
Henry Yevele	Harvey
Heritage of the Cathedral	Prentice
Gothic Architecture	West
Canterbury Tales	Chaucer
Plays	Shakespeare
'Prologue' to the *Decameron*	Boccaccio
Chronicles (1578)	Holinshed
Stow's translation of Sir Thomas More's *History*	
Survey of London	Stow
Annals (1631 edition)	Stow
Autobiography and Anecdotes	Taswell
Old and New London	Thornbury
History of his Own Time	Burnet
History of the Great Rebellion	Clarendon
Confession (1649)	Brandon
Diary	Evelyn
Diary	Pepys
Journey into England	Hentzner
Memoirs	Herbert
History	Macaulay
Works	Marvell
Anecdotes of Painting	Walpole
Murder of Sir Thomas Overbury	McElwee
Old Whitehall Palace	Sheppard
The Fire of London	Bell
The Plague of London	Bell
Whitehall through the Centuries	G. S. Dugdale
City Puritain	Lane
Charles II	Bryant

Diary	MACHYN
Elizabeth the Great	JENKINS
Mary Tudor	PRESTCOTT
Memoirs	WARWICK
Old London Bridge	HOME
History of the Tower Bridge	WELCH
Chronicles of London Bridge (1827)	THOMPSON
London Bridge	BESANT
Tudor London	BESANT
Stuart London	BESANT
Encyclopedia of London	KENT
Hampton Court	LINDSAY
The Day they Killed the King	H. ROSS WILLIAMSON
Ordinances of the Royal (Tudor) Household	
Dictionary of National Biography	
London's Riverside	E. DE MARÉ

Index